VAN HALEN

Van Halen onstage at Madison Square Garden, New York City, March 30, 1984. *Ebet Roberts.*

VAN HALEN

THE ERUPTION AND THE AFTERSHOCK

MICHAEL CHRISTOPHER

Backbeat
Books

Published by Backbeat Books
An imprint of Globe Pequot, the trade division of
The Rowman & Littlefield Publishing Group, Inc.
4501 Forbes Blvd., Ste. 200
Lanham, MD 20706
www.rowman.com

Distributed by NATIONAL BOOK NETWORK

Front cover photographs, clockwise from top left:
Ebet Roberts (2), Eddie Malluk, author's collection,
Ebet Roberts (2), author's collection.
Back cover photographs: author's collection.

Book design by Tom Seabrook

Library of Congress Cataloging-in-Publication Data available

Library of Congress Control Number: 2021944610
ISBN 978-1-4930-6209-6 (paperback)
ISBN 978-1-4930-6210-2 (e-book)

♾™ The paper used in this publication meets the minimum
requirements of American National Standard for Information
Sciences—Permanence of Paper for Printed Library Materials,
ANSI/NISO Z39.48-1992

CONTENTS

INTRODUCTION   7

PROLOGUE: THE ERUPTION   10
1   YOUNG AND WILD   13
2   LET'S GET ROCKIN'   25
3   GET THE SHOW ON THE ROAD   31
4   ON FIRE   39
5   BOTTOMS UP   48
6   EVERYBODY WANTS SOME!!   55
7   SO THIS IS LOVE?   65
8   WHERE HAVE ALL THE GOOD TIMES GONE!   75
9   SECRETS   81
10   I'LL WAIT   90
11   JUMP   98
12   HOUSE OF PAIN   104
13   I WANT SOME ACTION   112
14   GET UP   121
15   SUMMER NIGHTS   127
16   BEST OF BOTH WORLDS   133
17   FEELS SO GOOD   140
18   TOP OF THE WORLD   148
19   NOT ENOUGH   157
20   CAN'T GET THIS STUFF NO MORE   165
21   HUMANS BEING   177

22	FIRE IN THE HOLE	187
23	IT'S ABOUT TIME	198
24	BLOOD AND FIRE	208
25	STAY FROSTY	217
	EPILOGUE: THE AFTERSHOCK	228
	ACKNOWLEDGMENTS	231
	SELECTED BIBLIOGRAPHY	234
	INDEX	238
	ABOUT THE AUTHOR	248

INTRODUCTION

To say it was a life-altering experience when my uncle dropped the needle on *Women and Children First* and first played the record for me wouldn't do justice to happenings that tend to transform one's being. It truly was my caveman-discovering-fire moment. The sounds coming out of the speakers were so foreign, so sensational, and so explosive that it left me—probably for the only time—absolutely speechless. From that moment on, I was fully invested in Van Halen, determined to stick with them no matter what.

It was a pact that would soon become more than just saving up to purchase their music, because these guys were going to work their way into the very fabric of any diehard fan in ways that few other artists could. Van Halen didn't put out records, they released time capsules of attitude and bold steps into uncharted sonic territory a young and overly impressionable listener couldn't help but become mesmerized by at each and every turn.

Then, if that weren't enough, along came the music-video revolution, and while acts from all genres were trying to outdo each other with who could spend the most to dazzle the eyes and ears of viewers, Van Halen raised the bar by filming a clip for the song "Jump" at a pittance, showing up everyone else for the cost of a long weekend at some dilapidated hotel in an off-the-beaten-path beach town. They didn't need all the ancillary pomp and circumstance to prove themselves; their own personalities beamed bright enough.

Guitarist Eddie Van Halen's impassioned and effortless playing was topped only by his toothy grin—one of those smiles that made you do the same whenever it flashed. Swaggering frontman David Lee Roth, jumping off drummer Alex Van Halen's riser to do a spread eagle "Air Dave" some fifteen feet in the air and landing on his feet, was unlike anything else on MTV at the time. Let's just say I wasn't as impressed anymore by the furry, spinning guitars of ZZ Top unless they were going to mix in a backflip or two. The singer's physical aerobatics were complemented by verbal gymnastics, and the rock-solid bassist, Michael Anthony, rounded out a foursome who felt like familiar faces rather than untouchables a million miles away with each new video or interview.

My music tastes evolved over the years, but Van Halen were never far off the radar. I made some of my best friends over a shared love for the group. To be a supporter of Van Halen had the potential to get really messy when Dave left and Sammy Hagar came in and it was made to feel like sides had to be chosen. Or you could embrace both factions, which is what we did, although there was always a wonder about *what if Dave came back . . . ?*

As teens evolved into twenties, a conversation opener at a bar with someone would always be some version of, "So . . . Dave or Sammy?" Everyone knew what it was referencing. We tortured—*tortured*—people by incessantly going on and on about the inner workings of group dynamics and making endless references to band members and things the respective frontmen said in the bootleg live recordings we coveted.

A girl I lived with did not at all appreciate a particular late-night, one-sided conversation while she was dead asleep when I decided it would be a good time to bring up potential names for the cat we were getting, each option some variation on a Van Halen song. "So This Is Cat?" "Poundcat?" "Atomic Cat?" "Why Can't This Be Cat?" Ultimately, a play on "Me Wise Magic" was decided upon, and the feline was named "Magick" . . . but only after "Me Wise Cat" was shot down. It was funny—depending on your perspective—but it was also serious; or, as my mother would say to me, "Something's seriously wrong with you." I wasn't just being annoying: I really did want to know what your favorite Van Halen record was and why, and, if you had to name a pet after one of their songs, which would it be?

During college, when I first started writing about music and talking to artists, I ended every single interview by asking the subject the "Dave or Sammy" question. It didn't matter if it was the drummer for the Black Crowes, the singer for Jimmy Eat World, the guitarist for Buckcherry, or an up-and-coming singer/songwriter destined to become a one-hit wonder—they all had an opinion.

More than that, they enjoyed talking about Van Halen and weighing in on the drama. I kept on with that tactic until things became so unwieldy in the VH camp that too many caveats were involved to expect a succinct response.

A core group of my circle never gave up on the ghost of the band, though—not after the botched MTV Video Music Awards reunion with Roth in 1996, nor following the inexplicable move made to bring in Gary Cherone that same year as singer number three. The soap opera was fun to dissect, but if the catalogue of music hadn't been great, it wouldn't have held our attention. And even when the shows weren't the best, like the 2004 tour with Hagar back in the fold, the times we had with Van Halen as the soundtrack were the memories that made it worth it.

When Eddie Van Halen passed away in October 2020, I was preparing for the release of my first book, on synth-pop legends Depeche Mode. It was a devastating time, knowing that I'd never get to see his smile shine from the stage again, and I dealt with the grief of that as a fan and a writer in the only way I knew how, which was expressing my feelings through the written and spoken word. You can only do so many tribute pieces, though, and ultimately the news cycle moved on and the interest wasn't there to keep talking about Van Halen. I didn't *want* to stop talking about it, though, which is where *Van Halen: The Eruption and the Aftershock* stems from. There's still much to say, by myself, the fans, musicians, and so, so many more, as this book illustrates.

And now, ladies and gentlemen, I give you: The Mighty Van Halen.

Michael Christopher
Boston, Massachusetts
May 2021

PROLOGUE
THE ERUPTION

A cold wave was moving across the United States as 1978 dawned, and, from the few-degrees-below-normal chill in Los Angeles to the crippling blizzard bringing the Quad Cities to a standstill in late January—and another that entombed the Northeast a week later—it was shaping up to be a long, frigid winter. A respite from the bleakness came when teens around the country dropped the needle on the newly released eponymous debut LP from a foursome out of Pasadena, California: Van Halen.

The band's namesake brothers were Alex Van Halen on drums and the prodigious guitarist Edward "Eddie" Van Halen. Michael Anthony plugged away on bass but had a much more important role on backing vocals; his high tenor masked any vocal shortcomings of singer David Lee Roth, while giving the band as a whole a more robust and unique element. That was to take nothing away from the frontman, who would glean his onstage cues from the best who came before him, then add a gymnast's flair, with unmatched bravado and banter. It all gelled together in a perfect manifestation of musicianship, personal combustibility, and innovation that immediately grabbed listeners from the first note—or sound, in this case.

Van Halen came out February 10, 1978, and began with what appeared to be the alarm of a locomotive steamrolling down the tracks, rumbling across the tundra, breaking through the ice and snow like the train in Jacques Lob and Jean-Marc Rochette's postapocalyptic 1982 graphic novel *Le Transperceneige* (later translated into English as *Snowpiercer*). "Runnin' with the Devil" needed no

10

interpretation, however, and no matter what the effect sounded like—in actuality, it was an amalgam of car horns lifted out of a Mercedes, a Volkswagen, an Opel, and a Volvo, then sonically decelerated—it might as well have been an air-raid siren. The blare was a signal to the youth and a warning to the old guard that everything was about to change.

Bands who made their bones in the late '60s and '70s were now floundering in their success, bloated by alcohol, their creativity dampened by drugs, and unaware they were increasingly out of touch with an audience that was now outmoding them while looking for something lean, fresh, and vibrant. And if it wasn't apparent from that first burst of pulsating swagger and melodic harmonies that would make Motown swoon, the second track on *Van Halen* would be a crystalline-clear shock to the system.

Forget about the sheer gall, madness, or stupidity—as others perceived it—for a new rock and roll band to slot in at number two on their first full-length what was technically an instrumental but for all intents and purposes a guitar solo, because all of that would fall by the wayside once Eddie Van Halen unleashed his six-string salvo. Following a brief yet none-too-subtle drum, bass, and guitar pilfering of the intro to the Cactus deep cut "Let Me Swim," the guitarist cut loose with a fiery and frenetic assault across 102 seconds that would change the perception of the instrument for eternity.

Both groundbreaking in its speed and a throwback to classical arpeggios—with more than a dash of controlled frenzy added for good measure—"Eruption" was the sonic equivalent of seeing Dorothy Gale step from the sepia-toned confines of Kansas to the Technicolor of Oz. Eddie's two-handed tapping on the track, inspired by the solo he saw Jimmy Page do during "Heartbreaker" at a Led Zeppelin concert some years prior, would become his signature movement. Though he wasn't the first to do it, he was the one who popularized the technique—one that would be imitated for years to come by hundreds of aspirational guitarists, most of whom seemed to fall just short of capturing the feeling Eddie achieved so effortlessly.

There are two amazing foundations of note regarding "Eruption." First, it wasn't even supposed to be on the record; the track that led every kid from coast to coast who saved up enough morning paper-route cash to buy their first guitar was in fact a warmup exercise for a live spot. By happenstance, producer Ted

Templeman overheard Eddie playing it in the studio one day, and, rightfully blown away, insisted it be laid down on tape. And, as iconic and influential as the solo turned out to be, the guitarist not only said almost immediately after the recording that he could improve upon it, but he would also later claim to have bungled the beginning.

"I took one pass at it and they put it on the record—I didn't even play it right," Eddie later told *Guitar World*. "There's a mistake at the top end of it. To this day, whenever I hear it, I always think, 'Man, I could've played it better.'"

While other artists would consciously decide to place a piece of music on an album, going over it again and again to get it just right, in this case it was almost like an offhanded throwaway. A loosening-up drill. The demure assertion from the composer that it could have been done in a superior manner if he'd just had another shot at it. When it came to Van Halen, nothing was ever straightforward—even the creation of a genuine masterpiece. From day one up until the metaphorical train came to a grinding halt some four decades later, there was an endless supply of killer songs, behind-the-scenes drama, and an unequaled impact on the musical landscape.

"Eruption" was just the beginning.

1

YOUNG AND WILD

Netherlands-born jazz musician Jan van Halen—proficient in both saxophone and clarinet—met Eugénie van Beers while he was performing on a six-week radio contract in her home country of Indonesia. They fell in love, married, and spent six years together there, until the Indonesian National Revolution ended in 1949 with the country gaining independence from Dutch rule. The van Halens shortly thereafter decided to relocate to Amsterdam—the capital city of the Netherlands, located in the province of North Holland—where they settled into an apartment at 39 Michelangelo Street. It is there that the Van Halen story begins with the birth of Alexander Arthur van Halen on May 8, 1953.

Less than two years later, on January 26, 1955, Edward Lodewijk van Halen was born at the family's new home, 6 Nico van Suchtelen Court. That December, the growing brood moved once again, this time southward to Nijmegen in the province of Gelderland, to an apartment at 59 Rozemarijn (Rosemary) Street, where they would reside for six years.

The van Halen brothers began their musical training early, each taking classical piano lessons from the age of five. The two also went on tour with Jan while he was on the road in the Netherlands and beyond with various jazz outfits, immersing themselves in a lifestyle with which they'd one day become acutely familiar.

"Growing up in Holland, when me and Alex were seven years old, we used to go across the border to Germany to clubs where he played," Eddie told *Musician* magazine. "That was just normal to me: eight years old, staying up to two, three in the morning, hanging in the club."

Though Jan's musical star was on the rise—he played saxophone with the Ton Wijkamp Quintet when they won the jazz competition in the "modern style" category at the 1960 Loosdrecht Jazz Festival—the family decided to emigrate to the United States in 1962. Relatives of Eugénie living in Southern California convinced her that, in addition to the glorious weather and endless sunshine, opportunity abounded there for Jan to continue his career.

The van Halens boarded the steamship SS *Ryndam* on the Holland–America Line at the Port of Rotterdam in the late winter of 1962. Traveling in tourist class, they had very little luggage for the trip, but they did bring an upright piano. Jan would be performing for passengers with the boat's band to help finance the voyage—and incredibly, given their young ages, Eddie and Alex would play the piano during the intermission. The former would later say they "were like the kid freak show on the boat."

After stopping at ports of call in France, England, and Nova Scotia, the nine-day journey ended when the boat docked in New York City on March 9, 1962. It was during immigration processing at the Port of New York inspection station that Jan changed the Dutch lowercase "v" in the family surname to uppercase, while Eugénie switched to the English spelling of "Eugenia." The newly christened "Van Halen" family then climbed on a train for a cross-country trek to California, spirits high, the fulfilment of the American Dream an imminent inevitability.

Unfortunately, the promise of success was not delivered upon with any immediacy. None of the family spoke English at first. They shared a three-room house with two other families, and they all had to sleep in one bed. Eugenia took a position as a maid; Jan found himself washing dishes at the Arcadia Methodist Hospital just to support the household, walking three miles each way as he couldn't drive a car. Later, he became a janitor at the Pasadena Masonic Temple and the Pacific Bell Telephone Company. Eventually, he would fall in with fellow immigrant musicians and spend his weekends playing in a band, which provided much needed additional income.

Alex and Edward were even worse off. They were relentlessly bullied by their peers, not just because of the language barrier but because of their mixed heritage, being as they were both Indonesian and Dutch. It was something that had plagued them in the Netherlands, where, as Eddie would later recall, Eugenia was considered "a second-class citizen" because of her nationality—but it only got worse when they moved to the States.

"That's the equivalent of a Black man marrying a white sorority girl in Tennessee or Rutherford, Mississippi, in 1958 . . . it was a big deal," David Lee Roth told Marc Maron in 2019. "Those homeboys grew up in a horrifying racist environment to where they actually had to leave the country . . . then they came to America and did not speak English as a first language in the early '60s. So, that kind of sparking, that kind of stuff, that runs deep."

"The school that we went to, it was still segregated at the time, believe it or not, and since we couldn't speak the language, we were considered a minority," Eddie said when he spoke at the Smithsonian's National Museum of American History in 2015, during its "What It Means to Be American" program. "My first friends in America were Black . . . it was actually the white people that were the bullies. They would tear up my homework and papers, make me eat playground sand, all those things, and the Black kids stuck up for me."

It also made for a sort of "us against the world" mentality that drew the Van Halens even closer than most brothers in everything they did. That unity would never fade, no matter how much others would see them argue with one another—in Dutch, mostly—as only the two of them knew how difficult it had been to face adversity like that on two continents.

Continuing with their piano lessons, Eddie and Alex began to clean up at local competitions as preteens, with both brothers taking the top prizes in their age groups at different points. Eddie in particular shone, as the contests didn't allow the usage of sheet music. He had faked being able to understand how to read music to his Lithuanian piano instructor for years, instead playing by ear with an uncanny ability to replicate what he heard. It would come in handy as he took first place over a series of years in the mid-'60s at the Southwestern Youth Music Festival in Long Beach.

The two grew their musical acumen and, inspired by the likes of the Beatles and the Dave Clark Five, Eddie decided he wanted to play drums. He saved up enough from his paper route to buy a $25 kit, while Alex had been taking lessons in flamenco guitar before shirking the classical route and getting himself an electric. The older sibling had his eyes on the drums, however, and he would jump on them while Eddie was delivering papers.

The oft-repeated history has become part of Van Halen lore, with each brother realizing they were better on each other's instruments. While it wasn't as instantaneous as the legend goes, it did happen fairly quickly. Decades removed from what became the swap heard round the world, Eddie would say without the slightest hint of jadedness that it was "destiny." And it soon became apparent that, though the pair were barely old enough, they were more than good enough to perform with Jan in a pinch, or as a novelty opening act. When they played with their father, Alex was on drums and Eddie handled bass.

"We would play at the La Mirada Country Club," Eddie said in a *Guitar World* interview. "My dad would play at the Continental Club every Sunday night, and we would sit in with him. He'd play at a place called the Alpine Haus off of San Fernando Road in the Valley, and we'd wear the lederhosen."

The two had been playing in bands together since elementary school—the Broken Combs were an early one—but they got serious about it in their teens. As huge fans of Cream, featuring bassist Jack Bruce, drummer Ginger Baker, and—most influentially for Eddie—Eric Clapton on guitar, they formed their own power trio, dubbed Trojan Rubber Company. Fellow Pasadena High School student Dennis Travis played bass with them from 1969 until he moved away from the area in late 1970. They formed another trio under the name Genesis in early 1971, with schoolmate Mark Stone soon joining on bass.

Dismayed to discover there was another band called Genesis when they stumbled across the U.K. prog-rock outfit's *Nursery Cryme* LP in a record store, Alex and Eddie soon came up with the name Mammoth. The three would deliver note-perfect renditions of songs by Black Sabbath, Alice Cooper, and, of course, Cream at local parties and the occasional "battle of the bands" competition. Eddie would reluctantly take on vocals much of the time, but soon enough Mammoth would find a full-time frontman in a wannabe singer who would not stop badgering them about getting a chance in front of the mic.

DIAMOND IN THE ROUGH

David Lee Roth was born on October 10, 1954, in Bloomington, Indiana, to Nathan and Sibyl Roth. Until the age of five, he had to wear a Denis Browne bar, which is used to treat clubfoot and developmental dysplasia of the hip. He was also troubled by multiple food allergies, and sugar drove him into spells of intense hyperactivity followed by unavoidable crashes. At age six, his parents sent him to a psychiatrist because they thought he had autism.

He didn't fit in with other kids his age—a trend that would never abate, for various reasons—and devoured music, television, and books to keep himself occupied, getting lost in a headspace only he could experience and understand. From that early age, Roth knew he wanted to be an entertainer. He wanted to perform for his supper and become a song-and-dance man . . . maybe make some movies like Cecil B. DeMille. Either way, his family was going to be the test audience, getting a mini talent show as they digested their evening meal.

"Every night after dinner, I'd start ticky-tack on the table with a knife and fork, singing TV commercials, acting out cartoons. And my folks would say to the company, 'Don't mind Dave, he's just doing what we call Monkey Hour,'" Roth told the *Washington Post*. "Well, I turned Monkey Hour into a career. I ticky-tack and I sing and I dance and I tell jokes and I'm having a ball misbehavin'."

He was given his first radio as a gift on his eighth birthday and would spend hours spinning the AM dial for two reasons, the obvious one being to absorb all the different kinds of music that would emanate from the small electronic box. More enrapturing, however, were the disc jockeys—the guys who had a seemingly bottomless well of anecdotes, words to say about an upcoming song, jokes to make listeners laugh; it was like a stand-up routine between the music and commercials. Dave was smitten with the innate capability the DJs had to think on their feet and dispense verbiage at will; it would inform his career as a singer and would later lead to a short stint in radio.

Jewish by birth, Dave began to sing while going to temple in Brookline, Massachusetts, a suburb of Boston that his family—including sisters Lisa and Allison—moved to while his father was finishing up schooling to become an eye doctor. They lived at 21 Alton Court while Nathan did his residency in ophthalmology at Boston City Hospital.

Roth also got a peek behind the showbiz curtain when visiting New York City to see his father's brother, Manny, who owned the legendary Café Wha?, a coffeehouse in Greenwich Village where musicians like Bob Dylan, Jimi Hendrix, and the Velvet Underground passed through, in addition to comedians and poets like Lenny Bruce and Allen Ginsberg. He spent summers there, soaking in the atmosphere, marveling at the talent that commanded the audience each night.

Some fifty years later, Roth would be the one in the spotlight at Café Wha? when Van Halen did an invite-only show at the tiny club in the early days of 2012. The singer recounted the first time he came to the venue and the city itself in 1961, and, in a rare moment of vulnerability, gave an indication from the stage of how much the moment meant to him, especially with ninety-two-year-old Manny looking on.

"It only took us fifty years to get this gig . . . it was easier getting into the Rock and Roll Hall of Fame than getting this gig," Roth joked as he tuned his acoustic guitar, before getting "real, real serious" and pointing out his uncle in the audience. "This is a temple. This is a very special place. And I am more nervous about this gig than I would ever be at the Garden. There's no hiding up here; there's no fake vocals, there no fake fucking anything."

When Nathan completed his residency, the Roths relocated to the West Coast, landing in Altadena, a part of Los Angeles County just north of Pasadena. Dave became fascinated with the music of the Beatles, the Rolling Stones, and the Beach Boys, while expanding his fantasies into comic-book superheroes, Blaxploitation films, and training in martial arts four times a week as a student of Senior Grandmaster Ed Parker, founder of American Kenpo Karate.

Nathan and Sibyl split up when Dave was seventeen, and his mother threw him out of the house during his second week of senior high school, leaving him to move in with his father. It was around this time that Dave saw the Van Halen brothers in Genesis for the first time, at a backyard party, and insisted he be their singer. He had the look of a frontman down, so was given a tryout, which he failed miserably—both times.

According to the book *Van Halen Rising: How a Southern California Backyard Party Band Saved Heavy Metal*, one final chance came when Alex hit a note on the family piano and asked Dave to sing it, which he couldn't. Equal parts frustrated, furious, and humiliated, Roth stalked off and vowed revenge on the Van Halens for the slight. He'd start his *own* musical group and take over the scene, stealing the thunder from Genesis.

Wasting no time, Roth swiftly put together an unremarkable five-piece who were godawful by most accounts, especially the singer's terrible vocals and over-the-top attempts at showmanship. Still, he had vision coupled with determination, and the band morphed into Red Ball Jet, named for the sneakers that were popular at the time and advertised with the slogan "Hi-speed shoes."

Honing their skills by practicing in his father's basement, Red Ball Jet—sometimes referred to as Red Ball Jets—covered a wide swath of music, from Chuck Berry to Ten Years After to Led Zeppelin. Come the summer of 1972, they were formidable enough to challenge the band now named Mammoth as crown princes of Pasadena's backyard party circuit.

"We were crosstown adversaries who hated each other with a vengeance," Roth told *WTF*, explaining how his band's material was simpler but more colorful and engaging to the audience, as Mammoth were more focused on their craft.

Even though they were getting more gigs and adding layers, with choreography, that others hadn't even considered, Red Ball Jet were not long for the scene. They had a look and a live presence, but Roth was under no illusions that they were on the same level as Mammoth when it came to being the masters of their instruments. "Our musicianship level, our musicality, between a one and a ten, was a solid five, a solid six on a good night," he writes in his autobiography, *Crazy from the Heat*. "There was no signature sound to it, but we had a helluva show. 'Cause I was already Diamond Dave."

Roth would eventually grow into one of the greatest rock and roll frontmen ever to live. His ostensibly off-the-cuff quips, stage raps, and nonstop acrobatics were credited with influencing an entire genre of singers in the '80s. But becoming "Diamond Dave" wasn't an entirely original venture. He lifted more than a page or two from James Mangrum, better known as "Jim Dandy," the vocalist for early '70s Southern-rock stalwarts Black Oak Arkansas.

Like Roth, Mangrum was blighted by less-than-perfect pitch but wouldn't be held back by it. He had an inborn desire to entertain, and he made up for his raspy voice and limited range by presenting an outlandish stage persona: Jim Dandy. He'd shimmy and shake, toss back his wild blond mane, throw roundhouse kicks to the sky at will, and make bedroom eyes to any young female who caught his gaze in the audience. Enthralled by Mangrum's moves, Roth took to filming Black Oak Arkansas live so he could later study the singer's movements and incorporate them into his own stage routine.

"He was there with a home movie camera and wanted to know if it was all right [to film]," Mangrum recalls in the documentary *The Van Halen Story: The Early Years*. "He said, 'I really dig the way you do a show . . . it's the kinda thing I want to be—sight as well as sound—I want to give 'em a show, I wanna make them happy, and you work hard.' [I said,] 'Take all you want!'"

Roth wanted it all, and he did take, liberally, from Mangrum, imitating the cadence of his onstage jabbering and taking what he'd learned in martial-arts training to mimic some of the same moves, while adding in a few new ones of his own. Roth's sprinkling in of a few original gymnastics didn't deter some from considering him a Jim Dandy clone in the early days, but it soon became a case where the imitation became more popular than the original. Diamond Dave can hardly be faulted for aping another's personality with the intent to make it a springboard into finding his voice and stage aura, which he did over time, and it's clear Mangrum doesn't harbor any ill will about it.

"Everybody asks me, 'What do you think of David Lee Roth stealing your thing?'" he says in the documentary. "He didn't steal nothin' from me. I learned from other people, too; I was just the first one with blond hair. He did cop a lot of the moves and poses, but he's got his own thing, man. I love watching him—he's entertaining to me."

Dr. Nathan Roth, acting as de facto manager for Red Ball Jet, had secured them a handful of high-profile gigs, including a particularly disastrous audition at the quintessential Sunset Strip nightclub, Gazzarri's. Between Dave's abrasive leadership mannerisms and an overall dearth of musical talent, by early 1973 the unit had dissolved.

Roth next dipped his toes into the singer/songwriter waters, doing covers and originals when and wherever he could, getting paid or getting experience. His goal remained to join Mammoth; despite the failed auditions from years before, he was undeterred. And, when the Van Halen brothers came knocking to rent out the PA that his father had purchased for him while he was in Red Ball Jet, Dave took advantage of the opportunity.

Each time Mammoth would rent his PA, Roth would pitch what he could bring to the band: flash, and the "right" songs to play that the audience could dance to—ones that would land them on the fast track to the Hollywood club scene. He'd taken to showing up at rehearsals with the PA to let them use it for free while bending Van Halen's collective ear, wearing them down until they agreed to allow him to sing a couple of songs during their sets.

Eddie had gotten tired of being a frontman. It wasn't a role he enjoyed, and he routinely blew out his voice while futilely trying to overpower the music with his vocals. He just wanted to play guitar. And everyone was exasperated at handing over money to Roth for the use of his PA while having to listen to his incessant yammering about what spoils lay ahead if they would just let him take the reins. It would be easier, and more financially beneficial, if Roth simply took over as Mammoth's vocalist. Hopefully he'd start singing better at some point, too.

Finally, by the summer of 1973, David Lee Roth was in a band with the Van Halen brothers.

The union got off to a rough start. Roth didn't know many of the songs Mammoth were doing—popular hits by Sabbath and Grand Funk Railroad that were completely alien to him—and he was pushing them to be more groove-oriented, maybe throw in some James Brown. The Van Halens initially resisted most of Roth's overtures, and soon they were second-guessing the decision to bring in a singer who left much of their hard-earned audience cold.

Then came an even bigger issue: they had to change their name. Another band called Mammoth, rooted in the San Fernando Valley, sent the Pasadena version a cease-and-desist order. There was no sense fighting it, so Eddie suggested retitling the group Rat Salade—a play on the jazzy instrumental "Rat Salad," a deep cut on the second Black Sabbath LP, *Paranoid*. The Dutch spelling of the word "salad" was a nod to the brothers' homeland.

"We played just about every Black Sabbath song," Eddie recalled during a joint interview with Tony Iommi in 2010, explaining his reasoning for wanting to use Rat Salade. "I used to sing lead on every Black Sabbath song we did—things like 'Into the Void,' 'Paranoid,' and 'Lord of This World.'"

Whatever the logic, Roth wasn't having it. He envisioned a moniker with more weight; something to make a person think about the meaning; a statement. He convinced the brothers their last name had just the right ring to it—sort of like how Santana did.

"I figured if we named it after a human being, especially Van Halen, it sounds strong. It sounds like it has power to it," he told *Circus*. "At the same time, a classical piano player could be a Van Halen. Also, in that way, the band can evolve. But if you call yourself the Electric Plotz, three years from now you're expected to sound like an Electric Plotz."

Along with the name change, Roth had begun insisting the rest of the band change up their style. "During their set, the Van Halens stood around like the guys in Nirvana," he said. "They wore Levi's cords with the boxer shorts stickin' out and a T-shirt, and just sort of stood there, but their music was spectacular."

Van Halen's notoriety kept building as the backyard parties began to get out of hand, routinely attracting attention from the local police. Sometimes they'd find themselves in the spotlight while playing onstage: not the kind a band wanted to be in, but because law enforcement had dispatched helicopter units to illuminate gatherings with thousands of kids in attendance. It was time to look at the clubs and take another shot at getting into a regular rotation.

Gazzarri's, where a disgraced Red Ball Jet had failed to make it past the audition phase a year prior, was the first spot where Van Halen got a break after securing a tryout via a loose relationship with a budding young management team made up of Mark Algorri and Mario Miranda, who just happened to be handling the book for the club. Almost from the outset, the band were drawing a crowd, upping their value in the eyes of the owner, Bill Gazzarri, the self-proclaimed "godfather of rock and roll," who didn't even like them at first. It gave the group credibility, and it would open more doors in other towns, but there was a weak link that needed to be addressed, and it wasn't Roth.

Mark Stone was spending more time getting stoned than learning songs. He was also intent to focus on his studies—he was a straight-A student—which didn't jell with the level of dedication Van Halen were seeking. His unreliability raised the ire of Alex on more than one occasion, which wasn't a good thing when the drummer and bass player should be in lockstep with one another. Stone would party to the point where he couldn't remember the songs, and it was affecting his ability to play live. Besides, he didn't like to sing, and there was an increasing need for backing vocals in the live setting—a task that fell on Eddie's shoulders.

While looking for a way to oust Stone, Algorri landed Van Halen an opportunity to lay down a demo through a cousin who was also a producer and had available studio time. Located on a ranch in Chatsworth, California, in the San Fernando Valley, Cherokee Studios is where the band recorded four songs: "Angel Eyes," "Believe Me," "Simple Rhyme," and "Take Your Whiskey Home." The latter two would end up on the group's third album, *Women and Children First*, in 1980. The demo was raw, though, and it didn't do anything for the group, so they proceeded with the excision of Algorri and Miranda, as well as Stone.

"We met one day, and they actually asked me to leave," Stone says in *The Van Halen Story: The Early Years*. "For a long time, it really hurt ... it was tough leaving that band, 'cause I knew they were destined for greatness ... they say, 'Don't leave before the miracle happens,' and I did."

Stone, who passed away from cancer in September 2020, remains a footnote in the history of the band. Most casual fans don't know his name—even Roth refers to him as "Mike" Stone in his autobiography—but his role in the budding success of Van Halen shouldn't be ignored, and it can't be taken away. He stayed in contact with Eddie over the years, and, when he died, the guitarist's son, Wolfgang Van Halen, took to Twitter to say, "Heartbreaking news to hear of Mark's passing. Met him a few times and he was a wonderful man. My heart goes out to his family."

SNAKE EYES

Michael Anthony Sobolewski was born in Chicago on June 20, 1954. Like the Van Halen brothers, he was the son of a big-band musician, and he followed in the footsteps of his trumpet-playing father, Walter, by picking up the instrument at the age of seven. The Sobolewski family—including Michael's siblings Nancy, Dennis, Robert, and Stephen—packed up and moved to Arcadia, California, in the late '60s.

Though he played trumpet in his high school marching band, Michael had taken a keen interest in the guitar as a teen, but he shifted over to bass as many of his friends were already having a go at the six-string. Following graduation, he signed up for classes to study brass instruments and piano at Pasadena City College, where Alex, Eddie, and Dave were also attending. The brothers were studying music theory, while Roth was taking theater courses.

Community college wasn't the first time Michael became aware of the three. He was playing bass and singing for another Pasadena outfit, Snake, and the power trio would sometimes find themselves playing the same circuit of backyard parties as Van Halen. He had seen them during the Mammoth days, too, when Eddie was still singing.

Early in 1974, Van Halen were headlining a show at Pasadena High School, with Snake as one of the openers. During soundcheck, they blew out their PA, so they asked Michael if they could use Snake's for the concert. He obliged, and while they watched him handle vocals and bass that night, Alex and Eddie thought they might have found their replacement for Mark Stone.

On the flipside, Michael had a positive impression of the band musically, but not so much of Roth's antics later in the evening. "I remember standing on the side of the stage, watching Edward and Alex play, and thinking, 'Wow, these guys are good,'" he told *Rolling Stone*. "Then Dave came up the side of the stage, and I forget what he was dressed in, some kind of a tux vest, but that was it, with a cane and a hat. He had long hair. I don't know if he had it colored, but I know he'd done something weird to it. And he said, 'How do you like my boys?' And I just went, 'Jesus Christ, get this guy away from me.'"

A scant couple of weeks later, Alex, Eddie, and Michael got together for an hours-long jam session that went so well that the Van Halen brothers asked him on the spot if he'd be interested in joining. Excited at the prospect of enlisting with a pair of wildly talented musicians and moving from backyards to clubs, he said yes, and the foundation was complete for the band who were set to conquer the Sunset Strip.

2

LET'S GET ROCKIN'

Van Halen were still playing keggers along with the steady gigs at Gazzarri's, but, by 1975, venues like the latter had begun to take precedence. The group canvassed Southern California, determined to win over audiences at any club or bar that would have them, playing a healthy mix of covers and the occasional original. They succeeded on most fronts, and were finding a groove with "She's the Woman" and "Take Your Whiskey Home"—songs they had written that fit in seamlessly with the covers.

"They were different because the early '70s bands, [who were] more retro rock and roll, they'd never heard a guitar player like that," remembered drummer Matt Sorum, who later joined the Cult and Guns N' Roses, but who as a young teen was playing on the scene at the same time. "[Eddie would] come up with an innovative style that was completely different than the Jimmy Pages and Jimi Hendrix and Eric Clapton and blues-based guitarists. The band was more aggressive; they had a little bit of a punk overtone to it in the early days. [Roth] wasn't doing a typical rock and roll rant. He was more of a circus barker. You could not deny his frontman abilities, even if he wasn't a great singer."

Yet, they were struggling to get anyone in the music industry to take a serious look at them. Legendary as Gazzarri's might have been, the club was hardly what one considered a hip spot in town—it was more like a dive you'd go to see some mediocre act interpreting Top 40 songs to the best of their ability. In other words, Van Halen were way overqualified. But it was easy money, and they brought in an abundance of girls, as well as the guys who would buy them drinks—which surely made Bill Gazzarri happy. Nevertheless, any hopes of landing a record deal were little more than wishful thinking, as those who had the power to do so rarely set foot in the place.

Then, in April 1976, scenester, music publicist, and "Mayor of the Sunset Strip" Rodney Bingenheimer popped into Gazzarri's on a night when Van Halen were playing. He was at once awestruck by their performance and baffled that such a talented band were playing an out-of-fashion dump. After the show, he asked the group if they played originals—and, if so, why weren't they hitting up the more respected Hollywood spots? They said they hadn't been able to make those inroads by themselves, so the diminutive Bingenheimer pledged to assist.

Not only did Bingenheimer get them into arguably the hottest club on the Sunset Strip, the Starwood, for a series of shows that June, he also told Gene Simmons that fall that Van Halen were his favorite unsigned Los Angeles group. The KISS co-founder was looking for a new act to take on and produce, so he and his bandmate Paul Stanley went to the Starwood on November 2 where they would have the opportunity to see this group with what Simmons thought was a horrible name.

He wasn't there just for Van Halen—or at all, really. A few days earlier, Simmons had gone to Gazzarri's to catch another outfit he'd been hearing quite a bit about, the Boyz. They too were a hard rock band who had a hotshot young guitarist in George Lynch. (He and drummer Mick Brown would both end up in the classic lineup of Dokken in the '80s.) Simmons was quite taken with the group and inquired about their next gig. The Boyz were playing the Starwood the same night as Van Halen in what would be more of a proper showcase for the former.

Simmons and his crew—which included model Bebe Buell, Stanley, Bingenheimer, and Lita Ford and Jackie Fox from the Runaways—showed up at the Starwood for the late set. The Boyz went on first, and, depending on who tells the story these days, were either a bit off their game or complete shit, or maybe Lynch was a standout in an otherwise stale performance. Well aware of how a show can go poorly, and perhaps still buzzing from the performance he'd seen a few days prior, Simmons went backstage when the Boyz were finished to mingle and chat up the band. Unfortunately for them, when Van Halen took the stage, the noise level of the bombast made it difficult to communicate without yelling directly in one another's ears. Plus, Simmons's interest was piqued by what he was hearing through the walls.

"Everybody's head just turned around like Linda Blair in *The Exorcist*: 'What is that?'" he told the *Los Angeles Times*. "When the solo came up, you couldn't believe your ears because all this music was symphonic, the melodies and the runs and the speed, all coming out of one guitar."

Simmons was *stunned* at what he was seeing. Here was this unknown band playing to a less-than-enthusiastic Wednesday evening audience like it was a sold-out Saturday night concert in front of adoring fans at the Forum. Between Roth's unapologetic preening and Eddie's blazingly nimble approach to the fretboard, Simmons was sold. The Boyz had become an afterthought within mere moments as he made his way backstage to talk to the members of Van Halen.

After exchanging pleasantries—and dispensing a lengthy lecture on how to not get swindled in an unrepentant industry—Simmons professed his love for the band, offered them a management contract, and said he wanted to help them professionally record a demo. Immediately. Plans were made to gather at a studio the following day.

The band met Simmons the next morning at Village Recorder Studios in Los Angeles, housed in a 1920s Masonic Temple just off Santa Monica Boulevard. Musically, the location had the distinction of seeing albums like the Rolling Stones' *Goats Head Soup* and Bob Dylan's *Planet Waves* come together there. Jim Morrison of the Doors had booked studio time on his twenty-seventh birthday in 1970 to record some spoken word and poetry that would later make up *An American Prayer*. More than a dozen tracks were laid down by Van Halen with Simmons at Village Recorder, all of them originals. Simmons excitedly called Bill Aucoin to tell him of the discovery, and the KISS manager, who was tangentially aware of the group, said to bring them back to New York to complete the demo by polishing it up with overdubs and additional vocals.

As proceedings moved to the famed Electric Lady Studios in New York City, time was running short: KISS were about to embark on a lengthy tour to support their just-released album, *Rock and Roll Over*, and despite Simmons's excitement over Van Halen, he couldn't pick them over his primary outfit, with whom he was scheduled to hit the road on November 24.

Ten songs were mixed for what came to be known among bootleg traders as the "Gene Simmons demos" and later "Zero," in deference to the first studio album by the band that was retroactively called *Van Halen I*. One of the songs from the sessions, "House of Pain," was much different musically and lyrically from the track of the same name that ended up closing *1984* several years later, having gone through a lengthy period of gestation. Initially, after each chorus, it contained the drone of the horn sound effect that would open "Runnin' with the Devil"—also on the demo—on the band's debut.

Two songs from the demo that would end up on later records true to their origins were "On Fire" (*Van Halen I*) and "Somebody Get Me a Doctor" (*Van Halen II*). "She's the Woman," "Let's Get Rockin'," "Big Trouble," and "Put Out the Lights" were adjusted musically, heavily reworked lyrically, and—save for "She's the Woman"—retitled for inclusion on the 2012 LP *A Different Kind of Truth*. "Woman in Love" and "Babe Don't Leave Me Alone" have never seen the light of day on an official Van Halen release.

Like any demo, the one Van Halen did with Simmons had its share of issues. Eddie wasn't used to overdubbing, and, frankly, he wasn't a fan of the process. The drumming by Alex was suppressed in parts, and Dave was noticeably straining in others. But all that could be worked out once an experienced producer was put in place and the situation wasn't so rushed, right?

It wasn't to be. Aucoin—with some insistence from Stanley that Simmons's focus on the group would detract from his commitment to KISS—passed on Van Halen. Simmons was shocked at first, but ultimately he understood. His band was peaking with the explosion of *Alive!* the previous year, *Destroyer* that March, and now *Rock and Roll Over*; jeopardizing their future for an unsigned act was too much of a risk, no matter how much he believed in them.

Rather than simply explaining to the group that Simmons needed to concentrate on KISS, though, Aucoin felt the need to lay into Van Halen, particularly Roth, telling them, "I don't think the vocals hold up." The melodies weren't there, and he didn't hear any hits. It was a blow to the ego of the band, particularly the singer—and one that Simmons felt terrible about. He ripped up the contract they had signed with him and said they were welcome to shop the demo around to potentially land another deal. And, just like that, Van Halen's hopes were dashed. They were sent back to L.A., while KISS boarded a plane for a seventy-date tour that would take them around the United States and to Japan.

It wouldn't be long, however, before the KISS bassist was back in their lives, for what Roth believed to be more nefarious purposes.

RADIO AND A RECORD DEAL

A dejected Van Halen, coming off the high of thinking they were on the fast lane to stardom with the backing of one of the hottest groups in music, had crashed back to Earth. Picking themselves up, there was no other choice but to return to the club circuit and plot the next move, which would see them look to the person who had gotten them into this disaster in the first place: Rodney Bingenheimer.

Rodney on the ROQ was a three-hour show hosted by Bingenheimer that launched that summer on the Los Angeles FM station KROQ. He took the freeform format to a new level, focusing on the punk rock and new wave that was coming up from the underground, exposing listeners to music they weren't going to hear anywhere else. Roth reached out to him in the winter of 1976, and on December 14, Van Halen got their first radio airplay.

Bingenheimer and Roth talked about the local scene for a bit, namechecking all the clubs the host had helped them get into, before the singer threw a jab at the city from which he and the band had recently returned. "Well, Rod, we all know what's comin' outta New York these days, and I think it's about time for L.A. to take their place on top here, and we're bound and determined to get something goin' around here." Then it was the moment Roth had come for, as Bingenheimer asked him to talk about the tape they were about to play.

"Well, we were playing one night and some of the fellas from KISS came down to see the band, who you brought along to see . . . a couple of days later, we were in New York City, doing a little tape recording down at Electric Lady Studios," he said. "So, what we have here is one helluva demo tape, and this is something that we're showing people around and people are being, you know, exposed to it—and this is the first radio play we've ever gotten . . . just the tape here, but we're proud to be on the ROQs of Los Angeles."

Roth wisely hadn't mentioned that the once-promising dalliance with Simmons had gone belly up as Bingenheimer spun "Runnin' with the Devil," complete with the horn sound tacked on at the beginning. Now Van Halen could add getting on the radio to their accomplishments for 1976, in addition to having a solid demo to shop around. They were also a major draw on the Sunset Strip, and they had begun to regularly play the Whisky a Go Go with the help of Marshall Berle, the venue's booking agent, who would end up playing a much larger role in the band's career moving forward.

The nephew of comedy legend Milton Berle, Marshall surreptitiously set up a showcase at the Starwood over a couple of nights in February 1977. One of the people he invited down was Ted Templeman, the executive vice president for Warner Bros. Records who had produced albums for many of the acts on the label, including the Doobie Brothers, Montrose, Little Feat, and Van Morrison. He had never heard of Van Halen, but he respected the ear of Berle, so he was looking forward to checking them out.

It's not like the group hadn't generated any interest from record labels. Reps from Mercury, A&M, and more had become aware of the buzz surrounding Van Halen, but when it came down right down to it, they didn't see the appeal—or, if they did, it was not enough to sign them. Templeman was different. His track record spoke for itself, and when he came out to see the band play, he was blown away, mainly by their guitarist.

"I saw Ed, and I was just fucking knocked out," he said in Greg Renoff's book *Van Halen Rising*. "He was the best musician I'd ever seen in person."

Templeman didn't go backstage and gladhand with the boys that night. Instead, he split with the determination to return the following evening with someone who had the power to sign the group. He came back with Warner Bros. chairman and president Mo Ostin, who wasn't afraid to put his stock in heavier artists, having signed the likes of Jimi Hendrix and Black Sabbath. Ostin had also brought the Kinks to the United States, and he was floored by Van Halen's muscular take on the English outfit's hit single from the summer of 1964, "You Really Got Me."

The pair from Warner Bros. met with a stupefied Van Halen, who didn't even know there were any label reps in attendance, let alone a chairman of one and a producer with the resume of Templeman. The two suggested Berle be instituted as manager, and for all of them to come in and sign a letter of intent the next day. Right after that, it would be off to the studio to get to work on a demo—this time for a prestigious record company that was eager to have them.

3

GET THE SHOW
ON THE ROAD

Recorded at Sunset Sound, the demos for Warner Bros. were done mostly live in just one afternoon in February 1977. Many of the twenty-five songs laid down would appear on the first two studio efforts from the band, or be reworked later, as their catalogue expanded. "Runnin' with the Devil" and "Somebody Get Me a Doctor" retained their titles; "Show Your Love" became "I'm the One," and "Bring on the Girls" turned into "Beautiful Girls." Later, "Voodoo Queen" would be retooled as "Mean Street," with an instrumental break lifted from "She's the Woman."

Various elements from other compositions would be cherrypicked for songs going forward, a lyric here and a lick there. Some wouldn't surface on an official recording until 2012's *A Different Kind of Truth*, while others remain on bootlegs—maybe forever—with varying degrees of quality, depending on how deep one digs for them, yet they're always several generations removed from the originals.

Even before Van Halen signed a letter of intent with Warner Bros. Records, Ted Templeman was unsure about David Lee Roth. While there was no questioning the singer's ability to command the stage and talk up an audience, there was serious concern that his vocals were not up to snuff. Could he hack it in the studio? And, if not, where would that leave the rest of the group?

Those were the doubts the producer was having when watching the band for the second time in as many nights at the Starwood, this time with Mo Ostin in tow. Incredibly, he thought that Sammy Hagar, who he'd worked with on the first two Montrose LPs, might be fill the spot perfectly. He never brought it up with the Van Halen brothers, but according to *Ted Templeman: A Platinum Producer's Life in Music*, he did mention it to engineer Donn Landee, who turned to him at one point while they were putting down tracks for the demos and whispered, "You gotta call Sam."

"He knew that Dave scared the shit out of me," Templeman says in the book. "Thinking back on that first go-around with Dave in the studio, I started wondering if I should stop talking about it and actually see about firing him. While he had his moments, he mostly just croaked along while the other guys played the most amazing shit."

Templeman had to weigh the pros and cons of pulling such a drastic move. The biggest obstacle was that the entire group had been signed to the label, and as a young gang, all for one and one for all, they might see an angling like that as an intent to sabotage. And, as he notes in *A Platinum Producer's Life*, it's not like Hagar was a sure thing. Lyrically, he was lacking—he couldn't hold a candle to Roth's witty and whimsical stanzas. Most importantly, what if Templeman put himself out there, convinced the band to bring in Hagar, and they didn't jell together? The whole thing could blow up in his face and sully a reputation he had been hard at work building since first starting with Warner Bros.

The decision was ultimately made to work with Roth instead of moving to replace him. Swayed by the frontman's intellect, Templeman took an unconventional singer and helped mold him into one of the greats by focusing on his strengths. Over the years, though, a fleeting thought by Templeman became an undeniable fact to many—even those inside the band.

"That's totally true," Michael Anthony told DJ Eddie Trunk in 2019 of the idea to replace Roth with Hagar. "Ted did make a suggestion at one point, yes." Hagar—who said he didn't find out until 1984, when Templeman produced his solo album *VOA*—backed up the claims. "I thought, 'Wow, nobody called me,'" he told *Classic Rock*. "If I'd heard Eddie Van Halen play, I would have said, 'Fuck yeah!' Mikey told me he knew about it. I guess Dave knew about it too. Maybe that's why he still doesn't like me."

Alex Van Halen's recollection jibes most closely with Templeman's; during the 1986 MTV documentary special *Van Halen Unleashed*, he said, "In '77, when we first signed to Warner Bros., the idea of having Sammy as a vocalist for Van Halen was tossed around—not by the band but by the powers that be. We didn't find out about that until three or four years after the fact."

ANOTHER KISS

Between the recording of the Warner Bros. demo and the first Van Halen album, Gene Simmons came back into the picture. The KISS tour to support *Rock and Roll Over* ended in April, following a Far East flourish with ten dates in Japan—the greasepainted rockers first trip there. There would be a couple of weeks of downtime for the band before they headed back into the studio in New York City in May to record their next album, and Simmons decided to soak up some California sun and pen some new songs. Two of them, "Got Love for Sale" and "Christine Sixteen," were written at the Sunset Marquis.

Simmons alleged he got the itch to head to Village Recorder to lay down bass, drum, and guitar parts on the demos for the pair of tracks, along with another song he had been working on called "Tunnel of Love." He needed a drummer and a guitarist, though, so he rang up a pair of siblings he knew to see if they'd be interested.

"In the middle of the night, I wanted to go in and record the three songs that I'd written," Simmons said in a promotional video to promote his 2017 box set *Gene Simmons Vault*. "I called up Edward—he likes to be called Edward: 'You guys want to help me put this demo together?' 'Sure!' And literally in the middle of the night, the Van Halen brothers came down, and it was a trio, the Van Halen brothers and Simmons. I guess the only time that's ever happened. We recorded those three songs in about two hours . . . and the solo Eddie played on ['Christine Sixteen'] was so wonderful that I, unfortunately for Ace, forced him to play note for note that solo."

That story—including the part about KISS guitarist Ace Frehley having to replicate the solo "note for note"—has been repeated over time in similar fashion. What's often left out is that, according to Roth, this wasn't a one-time thing. He says in his autobiography that Simmons would routinely ask Eddie to come down to the studio to play a solo on a new song.

"Turns out that Gene Simmons's true interest was in conscripting Ed Van Halen into their show in some form or another, get him to play on a record, get him to help write guitar solos, get him into the band," the singer writes. "I was always fiercely protective of what we were doing as a group, as a clan, 'cause there always going to be pirates, there's always going to be carpetbaggers, like Simmons. And I would show up with Ed at the studio. Simmons would look at me with horror. *Horror.* 'Cause I was on to his game way early."

Re-recorded versions of "Christine Sixteen" and "Got Love for Sale" would appear on the next KISS album, *Love Gun*, which came out in June 1977. A reworked "Tunnel of Love" ended up on *Gene Simmons*, one of the four solo LPs the four members of the band released in September 1978. All three demos with Alex and Eddie would be included in the aforementioned *Gene Simmons Vault*, an eleven-disc, $2,000 set featuring music and rare recordings from Simmons's career.

A RATT IN THE HOUSE

Stephen Pearcy kept hearing about this band up in Los Angeles. He was fronting and playing guitar for Mickey Ratt, a San Diego–based hard rock act. Making his way into a Van Halen soundcheck at the Whisky and then backstage to meet the guys, Pearcy—a self-professed gearhead at the time—became fast friends with Eddie, bonding with him over their shared love of guitars.

The show that night was hardly a full house, but it didn't seem to faze the group in the slightest. "Seeing them for the first time was a shock," Pearcy recalled. "They just had this arena mentality; they called it, as I do, 'big rock.' It was just like, 'Whoa! This is how it's done!' They gave a shit about their image, their sound—everything. That's what I learned from them."

Soon, Pearcy was making frequent trips to hang out with Eddie at his house and trade gear: "It was like going to a lesson every time we would go to his pad. He had all kinds of things goin' on." As a hub of budding musicians, Los Angeles didn't always have what the Van Halen guitarist needed in terms of equipment. Once, he was looking for an additional Vox AC30—Pearcy's "favorite toy"—but couldn't locate one in the area.

"Ed had one, but he needed another one at a Whisky gig one time," Pearcy said. "I happened to have one, and he was like, 'Bring it up,' and he ended up buying it. That kind of stuff went on all day long with him—we would trade stuff back and forth, buy stuff, you know?"

It was clear that if Mickey Ratt were going to make it themselves, they had to start thinking out of the old hat box. It wasn't just about the music anymore: there was an image to project, production to consider. You had to pretend like it was the big time even if it wasn't—yet. That's what Van Halen were doing, in a nutshell.

"I'd sit onstage, cross-legged, and watch them at the Whisky," Pearcy said. "There wouldn't be that many people there sometimes, but their production and the way they took care of everything was like an arena concert—it was crazy. You're looking at it, going, 'Well, that's it for the Cars and all these new-wave bands,' because they just changed the whole bar of everything. I knew right away."

Invigorated, Pearcy would go back to San Diego and tell his friends, "Hey, there's this band up there that's gonna be the next big thing—I know it. We gotta move up there, we gotta relocate."

It wouldn't take long before Mickey Ratt moved to Los Angeles to gig regularly on the Sunset Strip. Eventually, after dropping the "Mickey" part of their moniker, Ratt would become staples on the scene and one of the most popular outfits of the '80s, with hits like "Round and Round," "Lay It Down," and "Dance."

BUILDING A MONSTROUS DEBUT

August of 1977 saw Van Halen re-enter Sunset Sound to do it for real. At this point, the news had gotten out that the band had signed to Warner Bros. They were officially the kings of the Sunset Strip and the group to look up to on the scene.

"They worked hard, and probably a lot harder than other bands," said Greg Renoff, who painstakingly documented the early days of the group in the book *Van Halen Rising*. "Those guys played every weekend and played all that they could. Plenty of people work hard, but they didn't get discouraged enough to throw in the towel."

There had been endless opportunities for Van Halen to give up throughout the '70s, from the days when the brothers would be ridiculed for sticking with

Roth to the unfulfilled hopes presented to them by Gene Simmons. It all panned out, of course, but because of perseverance and talent above anything else.

"I think, number one, their dedication, and number two, musically, they were just better than the other bands around that time—all the other bands," Renoff said. "I had people who I interviewed for *Van Halen Rising* [tell me] about how when Eddie was fifteen, sixteen years old, one guy in particular who saw them basically playing at a basketball court . . . he was a little older—like eighteen or so—said, 'I'd seen plenty of guitar players at the Forum and Eddie was better than them.'"

The guitarist would prove as much in the short period of time it took in the late summer of 1977 to record Van Halen's debut. The sessions were loose and moved fast. Not many takes were performed of the songs, and many of the missed notes by Roth were patched in later. The singer would spend hours working with Templeman and Landee, trying to get it right after the rest of the band finished their respective parts and split for the day. His parts weren't perfect, but the authenticity he delivered was indisputable.

It's still mind-blowing on many levels that the melody Eddie Van Halen became most closely identified with could've been missed completely, perhaps simply remaining an afterthought of his live guitar solos. Templeman, walking back from getting a coffee, heard the guitarist's noodling and told Landee to record it. "I'm already rolling," his engineer replied. As significant a landmark as "Eruption" turned out to be, Eddie would remind the producer for years to come that he could've sharpened his playing on it.

"Even more mind-boggling to me is that Ed wasn't even going to show this piece to me or to Donn," Templeman told Renoff. "If I hadn't walked by at that moment, it wouldn't have ended up on the album. Now it's pretty much universally recognized as the greatest guitar solo of all time."

THE ERUPTION OVER TAPPING

One of the very few downsides to the release of "Eruption" is that it launched a decades-long debate on the roots of a technique and Edward Van Halen's role— if any—in it. At the crescendo of the piece, the guitarist begins tapping the index finger of his right hand on the frets, while, at the same time, the fingers on his left hand are doing hammer-ons and pull-offs—a dual approach where a player's fingers hold down a note, play it, and then push down or pull off on the fret or nearby ones. It made "Eruption" sound like a classical piece.

To listeners of the record, it was unlike anything they had ever heard, so therefore Eddie must be the inventor. Time has shown that isn't the case, and musicians have come out of the woodwork seemingly at every turn either to disparage Eddie or put themselves or guitarists they knew on a pedestal as the true architects of tapping.

"[Danny] Johnson was the first guy I ever saw doing that tapping the neck technique," Rick Derringer, of "Rock and Roll, Hoochie Koo" fame, told *Hit Channel* in 2020. "Eddie Van Halen said he used to come here and watch Danny Johnson and I, playing in the Derringer band, before they were even successful. So, my idea was that Eddie copied a lot of that tapping technique from Danny Johnson, who was in my band, and obviously 'You Really Got Me' was one of our encore songs for a long time. So, Eddie may have heard us playing that, too."

Jazz player Barney Kessel was supposedly tapping in the 1950s. Deep Purple guitarist Ritchie Blackmore opined that he saw Canned Heat axe-slinger Harvey Mandel doing it in Los Angeles in the late '60s. Steve Hackett, who played guitar for Genesis in the 1970s, said in 2012, "I'm the inventor of tapping on record . . . unless somebody did it in the 1930s, but I doubt it."

It turned out someone from the '30s was doing just that. Dubbed the "Wizard of the Strings," vaudeville act Roy Smeck can be seen doing two-handed tapping on a ukulele in various videos on the internet. But that's not far enough for some, who go back even further to the early nineteenth century, pointing to violinist and sometime guitarist Niccolò Paganini as the precursor to everyone. During the 1980s, though, it was something that was unheard of—and unseen.

"[Eddie] didn't show people; he'd have his back to the audience, so we couldn't figure it out," said Pearcy. "I mean, look, he pretty much took it to the limit—no matter who came up with it."

The funny thing is, Eddie wasn't pushing the idea that he came up with tapping. Still, that narrative would follow him around throughout a career where he never once indicated it was something he created, and musicians would get into heated arguments while trying to dissect the origins of the method. But for all the blowhards who want to get the credit for being the most right, there is absolutely no denying that Eddie Van Halen did more for tapping than anyone who even held a guitar before or since "Eruption" was first committed to wax.

The last word Eddie would have on it publicly came during a lengthy interview at the Smithsonian's "What It Means to Be American" event in 2015. "Before the internet, nobody could search things and whatever, but lately, everybody's going, 'Oh, Eddie Van Halen didn't invent tapping and pull hammer-ons and pull-offs' and this and that," the guitarist said. "I never claimed that I did. But I do know how, and when I figured out how to do it and—on top of that—I never really heard anybody do with it what I did, which is actual pieces of music."

4
ON FIRE

It was the night of October 15, 1977, and the first album by Van Halen was in the can. Recording had finished up a month earlier, and now came the waiting game before it was released the following January. The band needed to keep anticipation high for their debut by playing as few shows as possible, but they also wanted to properly say goodbye to one of their favorite haunts of the past year, the Pasadena Civic Auditorium.

Thousands of flyers had littered Los Angeles in the days prior, touting what was billed as a farewell concert: "Last Pasadena Performance Before U.S. and European Tour." During the first half of the set, right after bombarding the over-capacity crowd with "Runnin' with the Devil," David Lee Roth stepped up to the mic to briefly reminisce and then show his excitement about what was to come.

"You know, when we started out here, there weren't too many people . . . but now, now it appears that things have changed," the singer said. "And, as things change so very often, this is our last show here at the Pasadena Civic. But you know it's the end of somethin' and the start of another because, friends . . . I've been waitin' an awful long time to say: here's one off our first album, it's called 'Atomic Punk!'"

A rip-roaring set—heavy on selections from the upcoming record, like the ferocious blitz "Atomic Punk" and the raging shred of "Ain't Talkin' 'Bout Love," along with a couple that would appear on the next—concluded with an encore of "You Really Got Me." Right as Eddie's razor-sharp guitar riff began, bassist Michael Anthony seized the microphone to shout, "Ted Templeman, where are you?! This one's for you, baby!"

The producer was in the audience that evening, pumped at the reaction the group were receiving and hoping it would carry over when the album landed on shelves. Unfortunately, there would be an unforeseen delay in the coming weeks when the band were presented with a cover design by executives at Warner Bros. that left them aghast.

The band's name was spelled out in the top left as "Vanhalen" in pointed red letters thickly shadowed on the right in blue, while the "a" in both instances had a lightning bolt flourish. A bordered shot of the bandmembers, taken at night in Dr. Nathan Roth's yard, was cocked up to the right and mysteriously had Alex at the forefront while Dave is nearly in the background—with his eyes closed. A blue hue was present, offset by Alex's cream-colored jacket and Michael's muted—yet nevertheless conspicuous—yellow pants. Concerns were immediately brought to manager Marshall Berle, who fervently nixed the cover, which Eddie would later say was Warner Bros.' attempt to capitalize on the punk-rock movement and make them look like the Clash.

The release of the album would have to be delayed from January to February while a new photo shoot was scheduled at the studio of photographer Elliot Gilbert to capture action shots of the band while they performed. "It was just my assistant and me," Gilbert told *Cover Our Tracks*. "They came to my studio, which was kind of smallish, and I had them play one by one. They got louder and more and more crazy. They played songs for four or five hours, each one of them. The whole studio was vibrating with this collective sound."

The resulting cover of *Van Halen* is split into four squares; each member gets his own piece of real estate, while Eddie and Michael's instruments are enhanced by wobbly light trails. Alex is barely discernible through the smoke and movement of him playing the drums, and Dave is holding the microphone below his belt, head swiveled to the left. The singer is featured on the back cover in platform shoes bent backward into an impossible position. The inner sleeve is split into individual photos of the band, sweating like they had just finished a show—"spent, sexually spent," is how Gilbert described them.

Placed dead center of the cover is a shiny new, winged logo created by Dave

40

Bhang, a former in-house designer for Warner Bros. who had struck out on his own. Templeman, under the gun, approached him and asked if he would be able to complete something in less than a week. Having Gilbert's shots at his disposal, Bhang came up with the placement and typesetting for the font at the top of the album. Then Eddie offhandedly asked, "And can you design a logo for us too?"

The lore over the years went that the designer came up with the soon-to-be iconic emblem on the fly. The truth might be bit more complicated. Noel E. Monk, who managed Van Halen from 1979 to 1985, was in possession of a box left over from Berle's tenure in the position, and he came across something interesting while digging through it in 1981. Folded up multiple times was a poster of Jimi Hendrix, along with the guitarist's initials, "JH," that looked uncannily like the "VH" schoolkids around the United States had been trying to perfect for years. The angles, the wings—it was all there. He immediately came to the conclusion that the Van Halen logo had been ripped off from somewhere else.

"When I pulled that out," Monk recalled, "I was like, 'No—you gotta be kidding.'"

The poster Monk came across looks to be from an insert included in an eponymous eleven-LP Hendrix box set by Polydor first released in Germany in 1980. It therefore seems the designer of that was either trying to be cheeky or had taken umbrage at the sudden upsurge in popularity of Eddie and endless talk of him overtaking Hendrix in terms of status and influence. Sort of a "it takes more than a fancy logo to make a great guitarist" jab. It's unlikely there's anything more to it than that.

However, Bhang wasn't interested in any talk about the Van Halen logo and how it came to be when approached in 2021.

RUSHING TO RADIO

Warner Bros. might've been willing to push back the release of Van Halen's debut because of the artwork debacle, but they were forced to rush the first single to radio after Eddie demonstrated a bit of poor judgement in who he showed off the final mix of the LP to, including some members of the glam-rock outfit Angel. The band—who happened to be on Casablanca Records, the same label as KISS—liked what they heard, especially the cover of "You Really Got Me."

"The next morning, Ted Templeman called me up and said, 'Did you play that tape for anybody?' and I said, 'Yeah, I played it for all kinds of people!' He was pissed," Eddie later told *Guitar World*. "I didn't know—nobody told me not to play it for anyone. I guess they figured I knew. 'You asshole, why did you do that?'"

The producer had gotten word that Angel were about to head into the studio to record their own version of the Kinks tune, aiming to get it out to radio ahead of Van Halen's. Warner Bros. acted swiftly, pressing up white-label promo copies of the song and express-mailing them to thirty-five radio stations. Then they blasted out to record stores for in-store-play prints of a hastily arranged 12-inch EP—on red vinyl, with the jagged "Vanhalen" logo on the sleeve—that had "Runnin' with the Devil," "Eruption," and "Ice Cream Man" on one side, and "You Really Got Me" and "Jamie's Cryin'" on the other. Soon, "You Really Got Me" was being heard on 140 stations across the country, and the crisis was averted.

Several years later, Van Halen would slyly repay the stress caused by Angel, who, in a last-ditch effort to find success, released a 1980 live album they hoped would break them the way *Alive!* did for labelmates KISS. The recording, titled *Live Without a Net*, tanked spectacularly, and the band called it a day shortly thereafter. Come 1987, high on their smash LP *5150* the previous year, Van Halen would deliver their first official concert video, from which MTV would pull several songs and put them into heavy rotation, making it a popular seller. They decided to call it *Live Without a Net*.

THE DEBUT HEARD ROUND THE WORLD

Van Halen was released on February 10, 1978, and sold steadily on the strength of "You Really Got Me," with record buyers wondering if the original songs would be as impressive as the cover. Three weeks later, on March 3, the band opened their very first national tour in Michael Anthony's hometown of Chicago, at the Aragon Ballroom, supporting Journey. They were positioned at number three on the bill, playing a half-hour set before fellow opener Ronnie Montrose performed in promotion of his first solo instrumental album, *Open Fire*.

Word spread quickly about the wild partiers from Southern California with the brash sound and flashy guitarist, and soon enough audiences were making sure they got to the shows early to catch the band. Following a handful of headlining shows in the States and Europe, the growing popularity of Van Halen led to them landing as openers for Black Sabbath for a U.K. tour beginning May 16 in Sheffield.

"I couldn't believe the energy in them; Dave Roth doing bloody somersaults and God knows what else in them days," Sabbath guitarist Tony Iommi said in 2021. "I think they were really, really a great musical band and a very entertaining band, very exciting. I'd never heard anything like them—well, certainly like Eddie—when they played with us. It was such a different style from what I'd heard and a different technique all together. They just *worked*, and they were the first ones I ever heard like it."

Sabbath were wobbly at the time, with Ozzy Osbourne having temporarily left the band the previous October. The Sheffield gig was his first after he was briefly replaced by Dave Walker, an English singer who had previously had short stints in Savoy Brown and Fleetwood Mac. Now, with Osbourne back, it may have seemed on paper all was fine, but by the end of the year he'd be gone for good—or at least until a proper reunion tour almost two decades later. Suffice it to say, with the Sabs' original lineup on its last legs, the thunder was ripe for the stealing by Van Halen, who took full advantage.

June saw a short jaunt to Japan for seven headlining shows that went well enough. Then, on the way back, disaster struck. Arriving in Dallas via Los Angeles for the inaugural Texxas World Music Festival, the band discovered their equipment had gotten lost along the way. They were scheduled to help kick off the three-day event—dubbed "Texxas Jam"—over the Fourth of July weekend, playing early on day one on a bill topped by Aerosmith, with Heart and Ted Nugent among others also appearing.

Eddie had some of his guitars, which he had brought with him as carry-on, but everything else inexplicably ended up in Chicago, the city where the group's whirlwind tour had begun four months prior. Less than twenty-four hours remained until Van Halen's slot at the Cotton Bowl, the outdoor stadium playing host to an event that was expected to draw more than eighty thousand people—their biggest audience to date by far. Hoping an airline that had already proven unreliable would get everything to Dallas in time was too big of a risk, so the band set about renting what they could locally and borrowing from fellow musicians. Facing the adversity of jetlag, and, most importantly, playing with unfamiliar equipment—particularly Eddie, who was missing all of his pedals and amps—it wouldn't have been too surprising to see the up-and-comers wilt under the sweltering Texas sun. Instead, they killed it, drawing in every ounce of energy from those in attendance and giving it right back.

"The predominantly young crowd that jammed nearly every square foot of the Cotton Bowl on a 100-degree day went absolutely mad Saturday as Van Halen, first main act of the program, took the stage just before 1 p.m.," raved the *Austin American-Statesman*. "'We've only just begun,' said lead singer Dave Lee Roth, as a sea of uplifted fists greeted their first two songs."

The band's gear arrived in Dallas the next day, right before some headline dates that wound through the Southwest. But still missing was the cherished Marshall Super Lead amp Eddie had been using for years. By the time he arrived in San Diego, the guitarist was in desperate need of more equipment, so he phoned up Stephen Pearcy. The two had become friendly in recent months, with the Mickey Ratt singer and guitarist hyping Van Halen to all of his friends after coming up to Los Angeles to check out the band on numerous occasions.

"They were playing San Diego Sports Arena, and it was like a quarter of an arena—they block three-quarters of it off—and Ed calls me, and he goes, 'I don't have enough equipment, I need a bunch more cabinets!'" Pearcy said. "And I'm like, 'All right, let me make some phone calls.' Lo and behold, I called all my buddies, got a bunch of Marshall stacks together, went to the Sports Arena, and they played a gig and that was San Diego's introduction to Van Halen, and people finally knew what I was talking about."

PARACHUTING INTO GREATNESS

From late August to December of '78, the band were back supporting Black Sabbath, this time on their own turf, save for a brief two-week run in Europe. The Sabs were still punch drunk from round one with Van Halen opening, and the young upstarts were even more emboldened by their unchallenged rise in the hard rock world. Now they were looking for a knockout blow—especially as Sabbath were touring in support of their poorly received LP *Never Say Die!*

Having spent the year on the road upstaging not just Sabbath but most of the other headliners they opened for, Van Halen had one more concert trick up their sleeve. It was unveiled September 23, when the band took part in a multi-act mini festival—often incorrectly referred to as "Summerfest"—in Anaheim, California, where they were placed between opener Sammy Hagar and Black Sabbath, with Boston receiving top billing. Leading up to the event, Roth had come up a devious plan that would lift them even further above any other group—literally.

Following Hagar's set, a plane started circling above the 56,000-strong crowd who weren't really paying much attention—at first. Suddenly, a quartet of skydivers leapt from the airplane and opened their parachutes, which were emblazoned with the Van Halen logo. Eddie's guitar tech, Rudy Leiren, who also doubled as the band's announcer, took to the PA system and declared, "From out of the sky . . . Van Halen is coming into the stadium!!"

The crowd craned their necks in amazement at the skydivers who, as they came closer, obviously had long hair and looked just uncomfortable enough in their descent that they had to be novices. Right when it looked as if they were going to land directly on the stage, the four blew past it and were ushered into a van that took them into the stadium. Moments later, the parachutists bounded onto the stage, stripping off their gear to reveal it really was the band who had jumped!

It didn't take long for word to get around that Van Halen had parachuted into a stadium, with this already unbelievable stunt turning into an even taller tale by the time it circulated. The most prevalent account was that they touched down on the stage and immediately began the performance. A presentation is all it was, though—one that was orchestrated by Marshall Berle, who kept the hoax going by telling the assembled press that the group had been practicing for months.

In reality, professional acrobatic skydivers had been hired to make the jump and look like they were flailing away with uncertainty. When they landed and jumped into the van to transport them to the stage, the actual Van Halen were waiting inside, clad in full parachute gear. And poor Black Sabbath were saddled with another two months of them as openers.

There would be life left in Sabbath, of course. The very next year, after jettisoning Osbourne for Ronnie James Dio, they'd go on a powerful two-album run before devolving into self-parody for the rest of the '80s. And though the waning days of 1978 must've felt like a last gasp at times, Tony Iommi later recalled the positives of the union.

"I think having them with us, they learned quite a lot from us because they were new on the block and we'd already been round the block quite a few times by that point," the guitarist said. "I think by seeing the way we worked they picked on some of the things and ideas, and we all shared it with each other. Eddie and I talked a lot about music, about different things, Alex and [drummer] Bill [Ward] used to talk a lot ... it was a great combination, we had a good time with them."

AN IMMEDIATE IMPACT

For Southern California native Michael Sweet, Van Halen was an earth-shattering event in his life that year. He first heard "You Really Got Me" right around the time it came out, after his brother had been talking about the band.

"It totally blew my mind," he said. "It was hard to grasp what I was hearing and hard to take it all in. I had never heard a guitar tone like that, I'd never heard a guitar player play like that—I'd never heard a singer sing like that! Just the fire and the intensity ... it was life-changing for me. It became the soundtrack of my life really."

No matter what he was doing, Sweet was blasting Van Halen. Hanging at the beach on the weekend; driving in his car; heading up to the mountains to go skiing, Van Halen came along for the ride. They surpassed all other bands for him.

"They changed everything," he said. "They became the band that set the bar and you had to try to meet that bar, and most bands, if not all bands, just couldn't come close. Those are timeless songs; you hear them, and they just always feel great."

In the mid-'80s, when Sweet formed the Christian heavy metal outfit Stryper with his brother, Robert, they came to be known almost as much for their yellow-and-black color scheme as they were for their religious beliefs. Thinking back on it, Michael notes that his brother's drums were not only the same color but "very similar" to the pattern Eddie would later stripe his guitar with on Van Halen's second record.

"Van Halen had such an influence on us, consciously and subconsciously," he said.

Across the country in Columbia, Maryland, just outside Washington, D.C., the band's impact wasn't as immediate. William DuVall was a young Black kid in middle school, and he remembered a lot of "stoner, rocker, redneck kids" being into Van Halen.

"The very first time I heard of or about them was this one kid brought the first album to school and was playing it on a turntable that was in one of the classrooms," the future frontman for Alice in Chains recalled. "At first, I dismissed it, because these were the same guys that were bringing in music that had Confederate flag banners or whatever. Because of the messenger, I wasn't trying to hear it at first. This was also the height of the 'disco sucks' thing, which was troublesome on a lot of levels, because it was kind of a blanket dismissal of all Black music and rhythm and blues music."

DuVall was obsessed with the guitar, though, and it was only inevitable that his time with the band would come. "It wasn't until a little bit later that I really, really, got hit hard with Van Halen properly."

The singer would have plenty of time to come around, as the band were just starting a wild and awe-inspiring ascent both on the charts and into the consciousness of hard rock–starved American youth.

5

BOTTOMS UP

Van Halen cracked the Top 20 on the *Billboard* 200 on May 20, 1978, when it peaked at No. 19. Later that week, it went gold, having sold five hundred thousand copies; it hit its first platinum milestone, marking one million copies sold, on David Lee Roth's twenty-fourth birthday, October 10.

At the time of this writing, the last time the album was certified by the Recording Industry Association of America was in the summer of 1996, when it was confirmed to have gone ten times platinum. Less than three years later, the RIAA announced that any single title to have sold ten million copies would be awarded "diamond" status. *Van Halen* was among the sixty-two titles from forty-six recording artists that were celebrated at a certification ceremony in the spring of 1999.

Given that it has been nearly a quarter of a century since the LP was recertified, and so many incidents of note have happened in that timeframe—reunions, tours, and the passing of Eddie Van Halen, as well as the RIAA incorporating streaming into its numbers—the overall sales of the band's debut are likely significantly higher.

It's doubtful that the album has reached "double diamond" because of the advent of filesharing and so many years when streaming went unreported, but unless Van Halen's management or the label decides to pony up what is actually an insignificant amount of money for RIAA recertification—the estimated total will remain a mystery.

ROUND II

The roadwork had been put in, and Van Halen were officially the biggest rock and roll success story of 1978. There wasn't time to bask in the triumph, though, as Ted Templeman was quite literally knocking on the door for album number two less than a week after the tour with Black Sabbath ended. After rehearsals in the Roth basement, it was back to Sunset Sound to knock out the record.

A fully dedicated stockpile didn't exist this time, but enough songs were kicking around that would work perfectly. "Bottoms Up" and "D.O.A." had been set staples all through 1978; "Somebody Get Me a Doctor" appeared on the Gene Simmons demos and was an early candidate for *Van Halen* but needed some refinement, which came in time for the new album; "Bring on the Girls" was on the Warner Bros. demos, and was now rechristened "Beautiful Girls."

Going with the old adage "If it ain't broke, don't fix it," it was decided again to do a cover, with the Clint Ballard Jr. song "You're No Good" opening the record. Initially brought up by Roth, according to Templeman, the song had been a hit for the soul singer Betty Everett in the early '60s, and more recently for Linda Ronstadt in 1974. The idea was to make it sound much darker, which was accomplished by Eddie's arrangement, Dave's bloodcurdling screams, and Michael Anthony's ominous bass—once again the first instrument heard on the record.

"Dance the Night Away" was the polar opposite in theme and sound to follow "You're No Good," as it's one of the purest pop songs Van Halen would ever put down on record. Cobbled together in the studio, it's an example of magic being made on the spot. Most notably, the track doesn't really have a traditional guitar solo—rather, there's a breakdown, during which Eddie incorporates tapping harmonics. Released as the album's lead single, it would be the band's first entry into the Top 20, making it to No. 15 in the summer of 1979.

Though the record was largely completed by the end of the year, there was to be a late addition. While attending a New Year's Eve party at Templeman's house, Eddie picked up one of the producer's acoustic guitars and started replicating what he had done for years on an electric. Templeman was taken by surprise by the guitarist's ability to command the instrument with ease, so he had him come down to the studio to cut a brief acoustic interlude for side two, "Spanish Fly," on a nylon-stringed Ovation.

Van Halen II was released on March 23, 1979, and went platinum that May—the same month it topped out on the *Billboard* 200 at No. 6. The bold but no-frills cover, designed again by Dave Bhang, saw the "VH" logo turned into something befitting a superhero's chest. Set upon a deep blue backdrop, it's given a 3-D effect and a silvery sheen, with the colors pooling into a dark orange. As on their debut, the name of the band is placed at the top, in the same format, with a simple "II" added. The back cover has shots of the band members, with Dave doing a mid-air, gravity-defying split, Eddie and Michael pictured wailing away at their respective guitar and bass, and Alex pounding away at his kit—with his sticks on fire.

Among the inner sleeve images, Dave's display of photos stands out, with a set of nurses in above-the-knee skirts shown making their way to him as he sits awaiting cross-legged on a stool, his hair blowing back like a proper rock god. It's not just a typical male fantasy, either; the singer really did require medical attention, having broken a bone in his foot on the third try for the photo shoot for the back cover. Looking closely at the image reveals his right foot is bare and bandaged. Meanwhile, Alex is holding his sticks—still on fire—in one hand. Michael is shown in various poses with his bass, in one of them pounding on it with both fists. Eddie models what would become known as his "Bumblebee" guitar, which was made by Charvel. The black-and-yellow-striped instrument wasn't actually used on the record, but the guitarist liked its look so much that he wanted to showcase it before bringing it out on the road.

Another guitar that would make its debut in front of a live audience was a modified version of the black-and-white-striped Frankenstein that Eddie played and is pictured holding on the front cover of the first album. Commonly referred to as the "Frankenstrat," the six-string was a customized hybrid of a Gibson and a Fender.

While he was always tinkering with the mechanics of the instrument, one thing Eddie couldn't control was the rip-offs. It was one thing for some kid in the Valley to mock up his own guitar in the same color scheme, but seeing bands in the clubs doing it, and even music stores selling guitar-company copies at a higher price because they resembled the design, was driving him nuts. He decided to modify the pattern, and, in doing so, forever changed the way guitars were looked at going forward, simply by adding a color.

"The funny thing is, the black-and-white stripes, which was on the first Van Halen record, I don't know what made me think of that—at all," Eddie told *Guitar World* in a 2006 video interview to promote Fender's limited run of replicas. "I was just looking for something different."

Using his go-to Schwinn acrylic lacquer bicycle paint, Eddie used the color red before masking the guitar with tape and then "really went to town painting it all freaked out." The soon-to-be-iconic guitar, with its red background plus white and black stripes, took just two hours to complete. One of the ideas behind it was to make it difficult to copy, with additions being made to it regularly, like the reflectors on the back of the body, which the guitarist picked up at random truck stops on tour.

Today, the original red, white, and black guitar is stored safely in a vault by the Van Halen family. It's priceless, to say the least, but it would easily fetch millions at auction. It last appeared in public in New York, at the Metropolitan Museum of Art's "Play It Loud: Instruments of Rock and Roll" exhibit in 2019.

Like many of the things Eddie Van Halen came up with that turned to gold, the paint job had been a mistake—one he somewhat regretted. "Every time I look at it, I go, 'God, I wish I woulda left it black and white!'" he said. "It took on a life of its own."

HEADLINERS BEYOND HOME

Two days after *Van Halen II* hit the streets, the band began their first headlining tour at the Selland Arena in Fresno, California. "Hello, Fresno!" screamed Rudy Leiren, before the group launched into "Light Up the Sky," one of their brand-new songs. "Welcome back . . . on the first night of their second world tour . . . Van Halen!"

It was labeled the "World Vacation" tour driving home the point that a Van Halen show meant a respite from all that was afflicting those sufferers of a nine-to-five life. Boss got you down? Significant other cramping your style? Living in a one-horse Podunk town with nothing going on? The cops hassling you just because your hair is long, and you listen to rock and roll? Allow the mighty Van Halen to be your cure-all, at least for one night—or two, if you really need it.

The band were filling arenas throughout the country in places where they had been the opening act a year prior. Audiences at venues like the Philadelphia Spectrum, the St. Paul Civic, and the Masonic Auditorium in Detroit were now there for one sole reason: to see Pasadena's finest.

It also proved to show just how well the lifestyle of the road suited the group, as they turned it into an endless reason to celebrate. Van Halen had trashed the odd hotel here and there on their first tour—more out of obligation than anything else—but now they were starting to accumulate stories that would make them legends in the music industry, showing that not everything had been done before by the Who, Led Zeppelin, and the Stones. Sure, those acts broke the ice, but now was the time to come up with new ideas for debauchery, backstage madness, and behavior that would warrant an arrest, were it done by anyone not in a platinum-selling band.

The World Vacation tour was a time of a lot of drinking, a good number of drugs, and women everywhere. Fame had opened so many doors for the group, and they were happy to step inside each one. The boys were in their early twenties—a virtually indestructible age—they had a hit record, and none of them were married yet, so why not treat every night like a party? And if there happened to be a few thousand people who wanted to join in? Well, the more the merrier!

On April 8, less than a dozen dates into the 1979 tour, Van Halen co-headlined the second day of the CaliFFornia World Music Festival with Aerosmith, who, only nine months before, were at the top of the bill at the Texxas Jam while VH looked up from an opening slot. The leapfrog into sharing the pole position wasn't enough, though, and VH went back to the over-the-top handbook to see how they could best upstage the Bad Boys from Boston. This time, they planned on keeping it closer to ground level than the parachute stunt in Anaheim.

The hometown heroes had already taken over the backstage area at the Los Angeles Memorial Coliseum, presenting quite the spectacle, with things going on that would never fly today. Visitors to the cordoned-off area were greeted by two little people looking overly serious dressed in black, wearing bowler hats and long-sleeved shirts—with horizontal stripes on the arms—that read "Van Halen Security" across the chest, and a chimpanzee dressed exactly like David Lee Roth.

High above the stage on the grassy area underneath the famous Coliseum arches, in full view of the forty thousand people in attendance, was a strategically parked yellow Volkswagen Beetle. The idea was for an announcement to be made throughout the day for Aerosmith to please move their vehicle. It seemed like nothing more than a harmless joke, until Van Halen would come rolling out in the M4 General Sherman tank they had rented and obliterate the car, jump out, and run triumphantly down the steep steps to the stage. The band even did a dry run, with Roth saying in his autobiography, "That Volkswagen smashed flat like a bad textbook . . . everything just exploded outward . . . and of course we would then play our show and Aerosmith would have to make an entrance."

Calls were made on the day of the festival to have the Beetle moved as the tank sat under a tarp, sticking out like a sore thumb. The Aerosmith camp had gotten wise to the caper, though, and they had a maneuver of their own to counter with. The group, who would be closing the night, had obtained some footage of airplanes divebombing and destroying tanks that they planned to show right before their set.

Roth called off the hijinks, but he'd apparently irked his co-headliners so much that they didn't speak to him for decades. Thirty years and change later, in Australia, the singer appeared at a press conference along with Billy Joel and the entirety of Aerosmith to promote their respective appearances at the Stone Music Festival 2013. The latter group looked equal parts miserable and rankled as, perhaps unsurprisingly, Roth hijacked the proceedings. It also might have had something to do with the placement of the artists on the docket, which had Van Halen going on last.

A pause in the North American World Vacation tour came in the middle of June, when the band headed to Europe for two weeks of shows following festival appearances at the second Texxas Jam and the inaugural Day of Rock 'n' Roll in New Orleans, where only Boston and Heart were above them on the bill.

Warner Bros. asked manager Noel Monk and the group to head down to Johannesburg, the largest city in South Africa, between the end of some U.K. dates and the start of the second leg in the States. It wouldn't be to perform but simply to sit for interviews with local media outlets and meet and greet some fans and folks from the label, the latter of whom had worked tirelessly to promote the new record. Basically, it was to show the region that its support didn't go unnoticed.

Since they weren't going to play, there was no need for the entire foursome to go, so it was just Alex and Dave on the short sojourn to South Africa. Despite Van Halen's popularity in the country, they would never hold a concert there. However, the photo used for the cover of the band's very next album would be shot by a Johannesburg native, Norman Seeff—but not before drama reared its head.

6

EVERYBODY
WANTS SOME!!

Van Halen effectively avoided the dreaded sophomore slump with *Van Halen II*, establishing themselves as headliners by conquering cities across North America while advancing up the ladder on multi-band bills. The partying was heavy, but it didn't affect the performances. Coming off the road, though, it had to be all business as the band put together their all-important third album. The fans were on board, the label was confident, and it was time to deliver—again.

Stakes were higher for another reason going into the recording sessions with Ted Templeman at Sunset Sound in December 1979, with overdubs done early the next year in Paris. The songs would make up the band's first record of a new decade. The 1970s were about to be left behind, and much of the music from the era with them. There was a building backlash against so-called "dinosaur rock," made up of acts who had gotten complacent filling stadiums. The U.K. punk-rock scene was at a crossroads, with the Sex Pistols flaming out and the Clash breaking into the United States mainstream. Post-punk was already a thing, in the form of Joy Division and the Cure. And the voice of a generation, John Lennon, was MIA, on a self-imposed hiatus since 1975 while raising his son Sean. It had gotten so barren that kids looking for something new were reaching back to the Doors, who were suddenly hot again despite frontman Jim Morrison having died—or maybe faked his death—in 1971.

Eddie Van Halen was still getting compared to guitarists like the long-dead Jimi Hendrix and the might-as-well-be-dead Jimmy Page, whose recent LP with Led Zeppelin, *In Through the Out Door*, saw them go belly up in many a critic and fan's eyes—neither of which were a good look for a musician reinventing the instrument. And when it came to band contemporaries, KISS had done a disco song, for Christ's sake . . . and that's not the path Van Halen were going to tread. The music needed to speak to the youth, to touch on rebellion without causing destruction.

One of the ways they made an early inroad to the bedrooms of alienated youth was by appearing on a soundtrack—something that would be a rarity in subsequent years—to the 1979 cult teen film *Over the Edge* alongside the likes of Cheap Trick, the Cars, and more. Future Pantera and Down frontman Philip H. Anselmo was one of those immediately dazzled, particularly by Eddie's playing.

"I was still in grade school when I heard 'em [on *Over the Edge*], and they had Ramones on there and Van Halen doing the 'You Really Got Me' cover," Anselmo remembered. "I had never heard 'em, and it was a great album just to get into some new stuff as a youngster. Man, the first thing I ever remember was Eddie Van Halen's guitar tone. It sounded like a frickin' explosion; just so ripping, so fucking raw. Just listening to that one cover song you could tell, or you could only hope through hearing that, that they would bring it, especially in a live situation.

"They sounded alive on that goddamn recording; it sounded so energetic, and obviously, doing a little homework there, you did find out Van Halen kicked ass live and they were a party band, but a party band that real, experienced, and true musicians could listen to and walk away scratching their heads like, 'Jesus Christ, these dudes are upping the game constantly man'—every player in the band were fucking excellent. Just super bold and in your face and focused."

Showing up on *Over the Edge* and appealing to the only audience that really mattered in the adolescents, impressing the typically crossed arms and serious musicians in addition to giving the mainstream kids cause to get up and move in celebration—and not just under a mirror ball—Van Halen were primed to take advantage of the void waiting to be occupied.

A NEAR PHOTO FINISH

Released on March 26, 1980, *Women and Children First* filled all the right holes in the musical landscape while avoiding any stylistic landmines. The LP peaked at No. 6 on the *Billboard* 200 on May 17, two days shy of the anniversary of *Van Halen II* achieving the same feat.

The record tapped into the feelings of disaffected youth on its sole single, "And the Cradle Will Rock…"—which also featured a heavily distorted Wurlitzer electric piano fed through a Marshall amp—and embodied testosterone-fueled, grab-a-bottle-and-a-lady-while-looking-for-a-fight Saturday nights with "Romeo Delight." An instant anthem came in the form of "Everybody Wants Some!!," a fist-pumping concert highlight if there ever was one, notable for Alex Van Halen's jungle-like tom-tom beats but more so for David Lee Roth's Tarzan-inspired yelps over them, and his crude spoken-word seduction, in which he tells a girl to leave on her high-heels and likes the line running up the back of her stocking.

A trio of tracks—"Take Your Whiskey Home," "Fools," and "In a Simple Rhyme"—were compositions the band had from earlier in their career. Bits and pieces from catalogued material were also used for a lyric here and a lick there, but the well was running far from dry; the band had also been writing new music on the road, and fresh stanzas were perpetually flowing.

For the first time, there wasn't a cover song on a Van Halen record, but the cover of the LP itself apparently caused a near disaster within the band. Roth relays a story in *Crazy from the Heat* of cold-calling famed fashion photographer Helmut Newton in Los Angeles and asking him to shoot the group. The German-born photog was impressed by the singer's bravado, inviting him to the hotel where he was staying and quickly declaring, "Do you know what, David? You are my new favorite blond. I would love to shoot photos of you." The two decamped to the frontman's house and did a session that produced a soon-to-become-infamous portrait of a shirtless Roth on his knees while chained to a diamond-mesh fence. And that's where the singer's story ends.

Cut to many years later, when *Cuepoint*, the music arm of the website Medium.com, published a lengthy piece by *Van Halen Rising* author Greg Renoff that told quite a different tale, complete with photographic evidence from that December 1979 day that proves the entire band attended the shoot and took part. When they arrived arrived at the estate grounds, however, the others were dismayed to see Newton already taking elaborate solo shots of Roth.

A Warner Bros. in-house art director—who said the label had negotiated the shoot—asked that he focus on capturing some of the other members, but it never clicked when he did, so the photographer returned his lens to Roth. Eventually, the rest of the group left, and Newton continued to shoot the singer.

The Van Halens were livid with Roth and saw this as evidence that he wanted to be the star, with the others his backing band. If they used the photos Newton took, it would show clear favoritism toward the singer instead of representing them all as equals. Roth argued that having such a prestigious photographer associated with them was essential to raising their profile above other acts, but no one else was buying it. Noel E. Monk claimed the rampant discord over the situation never happened.

"They haven't got a clue," the manager said, laughing. "Someone was in my office and [said] there was a photo shoot which almost broke up the band. God knows where that came from. [People] make these stories up and I don't understand; do they think everyone is stupid?"

Regardless, the decision was soon made to bring in Norman Seeff instead. The South Africa–born photographer had worked with the likes of KISS, Ike and Tina Turner, and Frank Zappa, and he was noted among musicians for being able to capture a positive mood in his images, even if one didn't exist in real life. That would be needed now more than ever, so he was hired.

It's unclear how the Helmut Newton pictures might have changed things up in terms of the artistic representation and perception of *Women and Children First*, especially given how iconic Seeff's black-and-white front and back cover shots have since become. The former, framed by deep green with light grey borders, has Eddie leaning back while wailing away on his guitar, with the others crowded around him. The back cover shows the four members of Van Halen standing together, looking as cocksure as ever, with the guitarist pointing confidently at the camera, holding his ragged Ibanez Destroyer, Dave framing Alex's face with one hand, and Michael Anthony blowing smoke from a joint. It's easily their most famous photo as a group.

Joyous as they may have seemed, the images concealed a growing divide within the group. Roth even got his wish, in a way, when the others begrudgingly conceded to have the shot by Newton of the singer tied to a chain-link fence blown up to poster size and inserted into the first million vinyl copies of the album.

LIGHTING UP THE SKY

On March 19, one week before the new LP landed in record stores, Van Halen began the "1980 Invasion" tour—sometimes called the "World Invasion" tour and nicknamed by the band the "Party 'Til You Die" tour. It spanned eight months and crisscrossed North America, with a monthlong run in Europe, where the band were becoming frustrated in their inability to break the Continent. They didn't have the same drawing power there as they did elsewhere, so they decided it wasn't worth it to keep going back, taking the region off the docket for a number of ensuing touring cycles.

The boasting and criticisms of the band for being "out of control" were good for business, but Van Halen entered a U.S. touring scene in 1980 that had become quite strict in the wake of a concert tragedy some months earlier. On December 3, 1979, the Who were about to play the Riverfront Coliseum in Cincinnati when a stampede to get into the venue saw eleven people killed and several others seriously injured. A confluence of misinformation, apathetic law enforcement, staffing issues, and festival seating had led to the deaths, and it left promoters and security on edge.

On April 24, 1980, less than five months after the catastrophe, Van Halen played the same venue. The city of Cincinnati had done away with general-admission seating—a ban that would be held in place for nearly twenty-five years—and was keeping a close eye on all possible rowdiness in the wake of the Who incident, ready to clamp down on even the slightest perceived indiscretion.

Late in the set that night, ending the *Van Halen II* cut "Light Up the Sky" after Alex's drum solo, Dave intoned (as he does on the studio version), "Light 'em up!" For added effect in the live setting, he repeated the phrase, which some in the audience took to mean, "Light up whatever you have to smoke, illicit or otherwise." The problem was, *everything* fell under the umbrella of illegal, as the crackdown by officials included a ban on smoking and any open flame, like a lighter, in the arena. Some 100 concertgoers were thrown out by venue security for violating those restrictions, and 177 were arrested on drug or alcohol charges, according to police. "It was the worst crowd since the Who concert," Sgt. Richard Tessendorf told the *Cincinnati Enquirer*. "The crowd Thursday night was incited more by the band than most."

Roth was charged with encouraging the audience to violate the fire code, paid a $5,000 bond, and was let go that night, promising he'd return the following week for an arraignment. Thankfully, the tour would be back in the state for a show at the Richfield Coliseum in Cleveland, so it was a mere detour on the way back from two shows at the Cobo Arena in Detroit. The singer received a court date in the summer to fight the charge.

Later that day, Roth didn't seem affected by the hoopla, joking on the radio station WMMS that the band were on the escape from Cincinnati after DJ Kid Leo informed listeners the boys had arrived just out of court. "Ah, the people got crazy, man—that's what happens when Van Halen gets onstage," Roth said. "It was the end of 'Light Up the Sky,' everybody was having a good time and we finished the song, and I didn't feel like finishing right then, so I just kept going, 'Light 'em up! Light 'em up! Light 'em up!'"

"Light Up the Sky" stayed in the set and the tour rolled on. An unrepentant Roth would make the episode sound like it was just another adventure in the life of Van Halen—which, in truth, was on the mark. At the end of the day, though, it was about feeling like nothing could stop the band—or the audience.

"It's excitement," Roth told North Carolina DJ Allan Handelman that summer. "People are gonna walk out of a Van Halen show, they're gonna feel like the building can fall on them ... feel like a car can hit 'em. I like that feeling, dude, and I get it every time we play."

That July, the charges against Roth were dismissed after a request by the Cincinnati DA, who wasn't able to prosecute because of a lack of clarity in the law and how it was broken.

NO BROWN M&M'S

As strict as officials were in their respective jurisdictions, there was some rigidity in the Van Halen camp as well. It would ultimately lead to the most mythologized example of rock-star ego, excess, and entitlement—with all the speculation and reports on the origins incorrect until Roth set everyone straight years later.

What remained uncontestable, though, was this: there were to be absolutely *no* brown M&M's in the Van Halen dressing room under any circumstances—it was right there in black and white in the band's tour rider (a printed, detailed list of requests and demands made by an artist ahead of each performance). And, if there were brown M&M's found on the premises, the dressing room would be summarily trashed.

Word spread of dressing rooms destroyed, causing thousands upon thousands of dollars in damage. Once, after a show in March 1980 at the University of Southern Colorado, Van Halen allegedly caused $10,000 of destruction—a number that rose to double, then triple, and finally quadruple that amount by the time it hit music magazines and television and radio news segments.

How the "no brown M&M's" clause integrated itself into the tour rider of the band has been the subject of endless theories over time. The first recorded appearance of such an order came in Van Halen's hometown, when the *Los Angeles Times* reported on the aftermath of the Cal Jam II music festival in March 1978. According to an event staffer, one artist had asked for dishes of M&M's—but no yellow ones, necessitating someone pick through and remove them. It wouldn't be a stretch to imagine Roth reading that passage and a thought bubble popping up with a lightbulb inside, to be filed away for a later date.

One of the earliest theories had Van Halen putting on an awful performance and M&M's being the last thing they saw before going onstage, so that had to be it. Why were the brown ones singled out, though? Well, no one could answer that, of course, raising an immediate red flag.

Speaking of red, another rumor had Van Halen taking a cue from KISS and then bringing it to another level. KISS, you see, supposedly required in their rider that all the *red* M&M's be removed from the backstage area, because of the red dye scare of the 1970s.

The synthetic dye FD&C Red No. 2, also known as amaranth, was said to cause cancer and be a contributor to fetal deaths, according to a study conducted in Russia in 1971. In 1976, the Food and Drug Administration officially banned the additive, which at the time was being used daily by millions of Americans. Mars, the company that owns M&M's, excised the color red from its palette the same year the FDA began to prohibit Red No. 2. The move by Mars was purely to quell public concern; its red M&M's actually used Red Dye No. 3 and No. 40, both of which were considered safe. KISS may have preemptively played the "better safe than sorry" card, but there's no record of it. (Incidentally, Mars reintroduced red M&M's to the market in 1987, and, in 2009, partnered with KISS and Walmart in a promotion that put the band's painted faces on the candies. The colors on which they appeared? White . . . and red.)

Printed as fact in newspapers around the country as other potential reasons were suggestions that the members of the band believed that brown M&M's were "very bad luck" or caused cancer, or they weren't aesthetically pleasing, or simply because the band could. The folklore had gotten to where Van Halen weren't even the band in question any longer; it was the mandate of Duran Duran, or Savage Garden, or "a demented rock star who refused to perform" if he found brown M&M's in his dressing room. Promoters also spoke of employees having to sift through ten—sometimes it was fifteen—pounds of the candies just to make a three-pound bag with no brown offenders.

When David Lee Roth released his autobiography in 1997, all was finally explained—supposedly. The band had intended, the singer writes, to make the whole thing "seem like it was a complete act of self-indulgent extravagance." Below the surface, however, there was a method to the madness—keeping an eye on a very minor entry in the tour rider would inform the band whether the rest had been heeded. Upon walking into a dressing room, it could be discerned right away if there were any brown M&M's at play—and, if there were, who's to say that much more important line items hadn't also been ignored?

"Guaranteed you're going to arrive at a technical error," Roth writes. "They didn't read the contract. Guaranteed you're going to run into a problem. Sometimes it would threaten to just destroy the whole show. Something literally life-threatening."

"We figured that if a promoter took the time to remove all the brown M&M's from the bowl before putting them in our dressing room, it was far less likely he'd screwed up any of the other, really important stuff," Noel Monk writes in his own book, *Runnin' with the Devil*. "It gave the promoters a headache and made us look like a bunch of dickheads, sure, but it saved me time, and it prevented something going wrong for the band."

A criticism of this explanation is the people responsible for putting out food for the band aren't the same ones who hang the lighting truss, who aren't the same members of the crew who position the pyrotechnics. Therefore, it could be assumed that the whole justification by those in and around Van Halen at the time might be nothing more than a rationalization for obscene behavior.

One thing is certain. Van Halen did indeed wreck the dressing room at the University of Colorado in 1980, to the tune of approximately $1,200, because they found brown M&M's backstage. The higher figure of $10,000 came from the damage done to the school's recently installed flooring, which was made from tartan—a spongy material made from rubber granules—and couldn't withstand the weight of the band's stage. Had promoters read the tour rider, they would've found the weight listed and known in advance what might happen.

ONE DAY BROWN M&M'S WERE ALLOWED

When twenty-year-old Valerie Bertinelli was visiting her family in Shreveport, Louisiana, in the summer of 1980, Van Halen were also coming to town, and her brothers, Patrick and David, were determined to meet the band. They planned to utilize their actress sibling as the key to the backstage kingdom: after all, she was one of the most recognizable faces around, thanks to her starring role as Barbara Cooper on the hit sitcom *One Day at a Time*, which was then at its peak in the ratings.

The Bertinelli brothers made a deal with the local rock radio station, where their sister would go backstage as part of a promotional stunt and give each bandmember a bag of M&M's, brown ones included. Unfamiliar with the group, she had picked up a copy of *Women and Children First*, and the picture of Eddie on the back cover caught her eye. Come the night of the show, she met Alex and Michael and ceremoniously presented them with the gag bags of candy for the radio station cameras. She got a quick wave from Eddie, then went to watch the concert, with the two staring at one another for the duration.

After the show, tasked with the second half of her promotional duties, Valerie met Dave. He claimed to have no idea who she was and had no interest in her, intimating in his book that this is the reason that she subsequently "fixed her eye very seriously on the door to Ed's dressing room."

The reality of her intentions was much less devious than the singer implied, given that Eddie and Valerie would hit it off and soon become inseparable.

He would regularly fly her out to shows, and they'd spend all of his free time together. Ignoring the tabloid press, who were having a field day with the on-paper mismatch of the girl next door and the rock and roll wild man, within four months the couple were engaged.

Dave, already quietly discouraged by the emphasis given to his guitarist by the music press, simmered at the attention the young couple were receiving in the mainstream media. It was interfering with the spotlight the frontman commanded and demanded, deepening a palpable rift between him and Eddie.

7

SO THIS IS LOVE?

Eddie Van Halen and Valerie Bertinelli were engaged on the same day John Lennon was assassinated by Mark David Chapman, December 8, 1980. It wasn't exactly a harbinger for things to come, but there certainly wasn't an easy road ahead of the pair. Just one month prior, the guitarist had been slapped with a paternity suit by a groupie with whom he claimed he had never even had sex.

The case against Eddie was dismissed following a paternity test that absolved him. David Lee Roth, however, was given an idea by the circus-like atmosphere inside the Van Halen camp over the litigation. He approached Noel Monk and said he too needed to shield himself from the money-hungry hangers-on who would like nothing more than to sink a hand into the growing fortune in the singer's pocket. He might have offhandedly said he'd pay for it as "Everybody Wants Some!!" faded out on wax, but he didn't plan on doing so in real life. And he was the frontman—the chief focus of the group—and so the most susceptible, right? Therefore, Dave wanted to be insured against such scenarios as the one Eddie had just faced.

The famed insurance marketplace Lloyd's of London was known to have written a variety of unusual policies, including those that covered the legs of actress Marlene Dietrich and television host Mary Hart, as well as Elizabeth Taylor's diamonds and Bob Dylan's voice. When it came to celebrities, the weirder the item insured the better, as it showed a position of importance. Roth asked Monk to get in touch with Lloyd's and get some paternity insurance.

"I said, 'David, I'm not quite sure that's gonna run,'" Monk recalled. "He said, 'Oh no, no—you can do anything.' I called up the top, the Lloyd's of London, and they started to laugh at me! I said, 'Come on guys . . . just a million dollars in insurance.' They said, [sarcastically] 'No problem Noel . . . but maybe next year.' And, of course, they would never do that. And we said, 'Well if we can't get it, then let's put it out.'"

So, Monk leaked to the media that Roth had gotten insured by Lloyd's of London for one million dollars to protect him against any paternity cases—and, to this very day, it's reported as fact. It was once as ubiquitous in stories about the band at the height of their popularity as the brown M&M's. A leering, fifty-eight-year-old Roth continued to perpetuate the rumor in 2013, while speaking with the *Huffington Post*, but he spun the tale slightly so that it was his male member—which he cringingly referred to as "Little Elvis"—that was the star of the falsehood.

"It's still [considered] a fact of life that David got paternity insurance, which never happened," Monk said. "That was written about, and people discussed paternity—no one is smart enough to call Lloyd's of London and see if you can get it. I mean, *you* get paternity insurance and then the story's correct. Rumors rule the day in bullshit rock and roll."

FRUSTRATIONS AHEAD

Van Halen finished the tour for *Women and Children First* in mid-November 1980 and went right back to working on their next record at Sunset Sound. At the same time, Eddie and Valerie were preparing to be married—an event neither his brother nor his singer approved of. With the typical stress of upcoming nuptials combined with a lack of immediate support from those closest to him, the guitarist ended up creating some of the darkest music of his career.

During the recording of the album, which took less than two weeks in total, Eddie would return in the middle of the night with engineer Donn Landee to re-record his parts or tweak the music in general. He'd later claim no one else even noticed the changes he'd made. Part of it was to gain greater control over the material, while another reason was that was where he felt most comfortable; in the studio, working on music.

The tone of what was to become *Fair Warning* was bleaker than anything else the band had done. Sure, there are the usual moments of levity—notably the exchange between Roth and producer Ted Templeman during the breakdown of "Unchained"—but, overall, there wasn't much to smile about. "On the whole album I was angry, frustrated, and loose," Eddie told Smashing Pumpkins' Billy Corgan in an interview for *Guitar World* in 1996.

Never is this more evident than on the creepy "Sunday Afternoon in the Park," for which the guitarist used a cheap Electro-Harmonix Mini-Synthesizer to create a sonic landscape that wouldn't be out of place on the soundtrack to any one of the low-budget horror movies of the era. Elsewhere, the in-your-face nature of songs like "Sinner's Swing" and "One Foot Out the Door," and the chugging riff of the aforementioned "Unchained," show an almost aggressive side to Eddie's playing.

Roth lyrics weren't his most carefree, either. He was writing about rough-and-tumble neighborhoods and porn queens who used to be prom queens; even the tried and true "live life to the hilt" refrains are tinted toward the downtrodden, as on "Hear About It Later," which could've been a celebratory anthem about not having any money but still having a good time, but somehow felt a bit bleak. Like on the funk-blues of the kiss-off "Push Comes to Shove," there's a smoky pall cast over the proceedings.

None of which is to say *Fair Warning* is a letdown or a bad record. It's the complete opposite, really—many hardcore fans consider it the best in the band's catalogue and the highpoint of Eddie's playing. If anything, the themes of alienation and rage contained within are what drew fans to identify more closely with it. There was no denying that art was imitating life, and the band façade was cracking like the stucco on the VH logo pictured on the inner sleeve of the LP.

INSIDE THE "MAZE" OF *FAIR WARNING'S* COVER ART

It isn't much of a coincidence that the artwork chosen to adorn the album wasn't the essence of sunny, either, though even Alex Van Halen, who came across the original piece and had the idea to use it, couldn't have imagined just how deeply it would align with both the music and the feelings of disenchantment within.

The image on the cover was actually spliced together from elements of a much larger and more involved piece by William Kurelek. The Canadian artist, born in 1927, painted *The Maze* in 1953, during his stay in two psychiatric hospitals in England for depression and mental illness that was manifesting itself into physical ailments and led him to attempt suicide. Psychotherapy— including electroshock—wasn't working. He was unable to convey accurately to doctors what was driving his unhappiness, so he took to what he knew best and painted what he was feeling.

"*The Maze* is a painting of the inside of my skull," Kurelek later wrote, dissecting the composition in his autobiography. The piece shows a closeup of the artist lying in a wheatfield, his head and neck split open from behind to reveal seventeen compartments of his psyche, making up a narrative of seven larger partitions. Each of the cranial sections displays a scene in his life, from youth until death, with perspectives on coming of age, personal relationships, and politics.

The front cover of *Fair Warning* uses four fragments from *The Maze*. The primary one—on the right, with "Van Halen" overlaid in a cream-colored typeface—shows a man in a cap punching a prone boy on the ground while people look on and point. Pulled from the childhood section of Kurelek's painting, it represents a fear he had of bullying and ridicule from his fellow classmates, even though it never transpired.

Clockwise to the left is a man making a kicking motion, but, upon closer inspection, a pair of feet from the recipient of the action is also visible, while people behind the man bask in the glow of a fire as snow falls outside. Also taken from the childhood space, this image characterizes Kurelek's fear of rejection by his father, contrasted with the safety of a warm and welcoming home. Concurrently, it's a commentary on his European parentage—his father came from Bukovina, an area between Romania and the Ukraine. This was a time when mothers and fathers felt their children were indebted to them for giving them life, and any rebuke of that construct resulted in swift disownment.

At the top left of the cover are two slivers from the "Museum of Hopelessness" part of *The Maze*, an area Kurelek said depicted "the uselessness of effort in a meaningless world." The first shows two marionettes embracing and kissing, though they are simply going through the motions: they cannot feel anything as they are made of wood. Then there is a standing man ramming his head into a brick wall, which is what Alex originally wanted to use as the cover. Though it is an action of futility, Kurelek saw it as courage.

The back cover of *Fair Warning* incorporates three more images from *The Maze*. At top right, Kurelek is the man on the conveyer belt headed to death, with the clock showing he is one third of the way there. Strapped down, there is no way to avoid the pending end of life. Below that, and from the same area of the painting, is a man with an exposed skeletal arm, which he is comparing to a drawing of a skeleton. What's not seen is that he has stripped his own arm of flesh and, despite being in a room with coffins and dead bodies, is using the secondhand information of the drawing to see if he is mortal.

Filling the left-hand side of the back cover is the portrayal of a half-naked Kurelek in a test tube, being prodded by doctors who each think they know what is best for him. He's on display, with a depth of professionals in the background waiting to get their chance at examination, and those who have done so already writing down their diagnoses.

The parallels between the Van Halen brothers and what Kurelek felt while putting together the painting are astonishing in retrospect, though there is likely no way either Alex or Eddie could have known to what degree. *The Maze* was created in 1953, the year Alex was born. Kurelek was twenty-six when he made it and incredibly depressed, seeing painting as the only way to get his feelings out. That's the same age Eddie was during the creation of *Fair Warning*, a period where he was unhappy, and the manner with which he dealt with his unhappiness was to work on his music.

In addition, Alex and Eddie had been subjected to endless bullying as children because of their mixed heritage, both in Holland and when they came to the States. They looked up to their father, Jan, with infinite reverence, completely buying into the mid-European ideal of making their parents happy above all else.

Finally, the model of the painter in his mid-twenties encased in glass like an exhibit is how the Van Halen brothers must have felt, with all eyes on them and everyone wanting a moment of their time, their money, or to get into their heads to see what made them tick. Correlate it to fans, management, and media—all seeing it as their right to own a piece of the band—and it was the exact same thing.

COKE AND OAKLAND

The wedding of Valerie and Eddie took place on April 11, 1981. It was a lavish affair, with over four hundred people in attendance, but it was beset by turmoil and second-guessing leading up to the date. Dave turned down an offer to be a groomsman, and he wouldn't even sing at the reception, despite having done so several weeks prior when Michael Anthony married his high school sweetheart, Susan Hendry, and Van Halen performed.

Dave would infamously detail in *Crazy from the Heat* how his gift to Eddie for the affair was a custom-made white tuxedo; at the post-ceremony party, he writes, the two were doing coke together in the men's room of the Beverly Hills Hotel, "taking turns holding each other around the waist so we don't plunge headfirst into the toilet from dry heaving." Noel Monk adds in his book that he came upon the newlyweds sequestered in a bathroom, with Valerie holding her new husband's hair back as he vomited into a toilet.

It wasn't much a surprise, then, to find out the guitarist passed out in his hotel bathroom that night, while his bride was zonked out in her wedding dress on the bed. There wasn't much time for a honeymoon, other than a brief getaway to Santa Barbara, as *Fair Warning* was released a couple of weeks later, on April 29, 1981, and a tour commenced the second week of May.

Had there been any lingering doubts that the band had fully arrived, the five-month run squashed them. Though it was the first time a tour in support of a Van Halen LP was limited only to North America, it was full of two- and three-night stands in arenas, coast to coast. Sales of the record weren't nearly as strong as Warner Bros. had hoped, but it did make it to No. 5 on the *Billboard* 200 on June 13, as the band closed out a trio of gigs at the Oakland Coliseum.

The concerts in Oakland were professionally filmed—commissioned and paid for by the label and the band—though to what degree has been a mystery in the ensuing four decades. Three complete songs, "Hear About It Later," "So This Is Love?," and "Unchained," are widely available and have received airtime on music video channels over the years. However, Roth said in a 1982 interview that the initial two nights of filming were "an abysmal failure" and that all the footage was culled from the third show; Anthony told the Van Halen News Desk he didn't think the full set was recorded.

Why there's so much interest in the Oakland video is because there's very little good-quality footage from the early years of the band, on the road or otherwise. There are a handful of poorly lip-synced television showings, but nothing that cuts deep into the incendiary live shows for which they were known. The *Fair Warning* tour, widely accepted to be Van Halen at their most ferocious, would be the logical point to try to mine something archival. Unfortunately, it turns out the three songs used as videos are it.

"In those days, with videos, the labels always wanted [footage] of the three songs they figured were going to be released as singles," said Bruce Gowers, who directed the clips. "You normally went out and shot the projected three singles off the album, and that's exactly what we did with Van Halen."

Gowers, who also directed the video for "Dance the Night Away," remembered shooting over two nights, capturing the songs live in front of the audience the first night and at soundcheck the next, with cameras placed on the stage to get closeups that weren't possible the night before.

"An amazing lack of foresight on a lot of people's parts there," marveled William DuVall. "It goes to show how often labels don't know what they have. You've got the cameras here; you've got the sound crew—why not just roll it on the whole gig? 'Cause you just never know what's gonna happen—especially with a band like that. Why not just roll the whole show? This is an era just before MTV, just before home video becomes a real thing. It's *right* before all of that. It is really frustrating because that was a missed opportunity."

HEARING ABOUT IT LATER

Still living outside of the nation's capital, DuVall would flip between two radio stations: 98 Rock out of Baltimore, and DC101 out of Washington, D.C. The latter had Howard Stern as its local DJ, appealing to any child wanting to hear the outspoken outrageousness of the future King of All Media. DuVall set his clock radio alarm to go off in the morning straight to one of the stations; there was no ring or buzz first. One day changed everything.

"This particular time, it was DC101, and I swear, the radio came on just as 'Unchained' was starting. I was like, 'Oh, shit.' That was when I really got hit," he said. "That was where I finally made real room for Van Halen and was like, 'I have to deal with this now—I have to do it.'"

DuVall saw the band as part of a three-night stand at the Capital Centre on the notorious 1981 tour for *Fair Warning*, one where those who missed it, missed it.

"I remember little things that just kind of blew my little twelve- or thirteen-year-old mind," he recalled. "Like, Roth at one point was pointing out in the crowd and was signaling to a stagehand behind him. And next thing you know, a handler comes running out and scurries down into the crowd and a couple minutes later you see him scurry back—onstage—with the girl from the crowd that was picked. And I'm going, 'Did that just happen!?! They're around women! And they're doing that in front of everybody!' He's just pointing, and a guy runs out there and gets the ... and just runs her right across the stage, back to—I'm like, 'Whoa. That was really something.' Like, 'Wow man ... this dude; it's his world.'"

Musically, it was Eddie who had the most impact on DuVall. He remembered being "flipped out" by the intro on "Mean Street," and, when he saw it performed live as part of the guitarist's solo, he found it reminded him of Graham Central Station's Larry Graham and the bassist's slap technique.

"From my perspective, growing up when and where I did, as a Black kid who was into all sorts of music, to really get my attention, you had to have some kind of funk in your playing," DuVall said. "That was just in the air at the time. My immediate touchstones had a lot of swing, they had a hard pocket. Once I got into Ed and Van Halen, one of the things I really liked about it was how great a rhythm player he was and how much funk he had in his playing."

Later, DuVall moved to Atlanta and formed the hardcore punk band Neon Christ. A guitar obsessive, he pointed to the genius of Eddie being about not just soloing but deeper elements too. "A lot of his fills are the best shit," he said. "He knew how to get in and out even between the lines of the lyrics. There's fills that he does that's some of the greatest guitar playing I've ever heard, and it literally lasts maybe three seconds. In the cover of 'You're No Good,' after they come back in after the breakdown and they hit the chorus again, he does this one fill [sings the guitar part] and I still, to this day, I will listen to that and just go, 'Man, what the fuck was that motherfucker doin'?!' I turned my son on to Van Halen because of stuff like that."

Yet in the hardcore punk scene of the '80s across America, the vibe was totally different—especially lyrically—than what a former SoCal backyard party band were going on about. Kids were trading in or outright trashing their Aerosmith and Led Zeppelin records because they were now connecting to something that felt more meaningful in punk rock. DuVall claims that didn't matter—they were still fans.

"Van Halen was one of those bands that a lot of different people from a lot of different walks of life could agree on, just because they were fun and their talent was so undeniable, especially from the guitar player," he said. "Like, you don't even have to like this music, but you have to understand, and you have to realize that this is uncommon what this guy's doing. Even if you weren't gonna obsess over it and live your life by it, you could still go, 'Oh yeah, well, you know, they're great.'

"They ascended to a level that was impossible for anyone who's gonna even pretend to be serious to deny," DuVall continued. "You could not deny what was happening there and be taken as a credible voice in any music scene. We can allow for the fact that musical taste is subjective and all that stuff, but if you are in a guitar-based band . . . you had to deal with Van Halen. There's no way you were going to disrespect it or dismiss it."

Obviously, at the core of that was Eddie and his innovative playing. "There's very few musicians that are strictly instrumentalists that have this kind of broad appeal while still being a virtuoso at their instrument; to the point where they become almost pop culture touchstones just being an instrumentalist," DuVall said. "That's really rare. Even Louis Armstrong. He was a virtuoso, but he sang. Eddie Van Halen had almost that level of broad appeal. He was a rock musician obviously, great rock band, but Eddie himself, he kind of transcends that over the years."

DuVall, who now fronts the Seattle hard rock outfit Alice in Chains, looked back fondly and felt lucky to have caught Van Halen when he did in the summer of 1981. "To see the band during the *Fair Warning* era, that's hard to beat," he said. "It was just such a steamroller, and those guys were doing that night after night no matter what condition they were in. It was a great age to get blown away by something like that—it set the bar really high [*laughs*], it really did."

"The first time I heard *Fair Warning*, it felt like I was listening to a live record," added Phil Anselmo. "It was just so fun, so great. That was like a serious badass album in my opinion. Just a lot of finesse and attitude. Van Halen was different. They get lumped in the hard rock category, because I think in spirit and in songwriting and in attitude, they were very much hard rock, but Eddie Van Halen, what he did for heavy metal guitar tone and sounds . . . it's outrageous, man."

The relatively short trek of some eighty-odd dates ended with two shows at the end of October opening for the Rolling Stones. Taking the stage at the sold-out Tangerine Bowl in Orlando in front of 120,000 fans over both nights was a highlight of the tour. Then it was off to Europe for a quick series of promotional appearances in hopes of maintaining a presence in countries like Germany, Italy, and Spain.

It was announced in mid-November that *Fair Warning* had gone platinum—the fourth Van Halen album in a row to do so. By now, the continuous album/tour/album/tour cycle was wearing on everyone, so a short hiatus was agreed upon, with no set date for return to the studio. A good, solid rest to recharge was in order . . . unfortunately, it just wasn't in the cards.

8

WHERE HAVE ALL THE GOOD TIMES GONE!

Sales of Van Halen's albums were on the decline each time a new one was released. Obviously, not every one was going to be a blockbuster like their self-titled debut, but at some point the numbers needed to level off. Warner Bros. hadn't declared code red just yet, though—especially given the band's prosperity as a touring unit—and was appeased by the group's decision to head into the studio at the end of 1981 to record a cover to be released as a standalone single in early 1982, ahead of taking some time off.

David Lee Roth and Alex Van Halen had also been storyboarding a music video—even before a song had been laid down. It would be the first concept video by the group, and the pair expected it to give them a foothold within the growing MTV audience. Previously, in delivering the three Oakland clips, the idea had been to shirk what had become commonplace: artists trying to get fancy in front of a bland backdrop while miming to a track. This time, however, Van Halen were going to go to the opposite end of the spectrum by presenting a mini movie that was loosely tied to the music.

Roth originally wanted to do a version of "Dancing in the Street," the song made popular by Martha and the Vandellas in 1964. The Kinks had also released an incredibly bland version of the song the following year, but given the success Van Halen had with "You Really Got Me," it made sense to go down that avenue again. Eddie Van Halen couldn't get a handle on an interpretation of the song, though, and rather than continuing to argue with Dave, he suggested another song that had been a hit in 1964, Roy Orbison's "Oh, Pretty Woman."

The group brought the idea to Ted Templeman, who didn't think the cover was right for them but produced it anyway. He also recalled Alex and Dave being more consumed with the video idea than anything else. They knocked out "Pretty Woman"—the "Oh" part of the title would be absent from the single— and two additional compositions. "Happy Trails" was the theme song from *The Roy Rogers and Dale Evans Show*, the acting couple's short-lived variety hour from 1962. Van Halen had been doing the track for years as a tongue-in-cheek four-part harmony piece; it even appeared on the Warner Bros. demos. The other track was a minute-and-a-half instrumental, titled "Intruder," devised for the sole purpose of providing a musical cushion to the video.

Filmed over a period of one day under the boozy and drug-induced conditions that were typical of the time, the "Pretty Woman" video features a pair of little people sexually accosting a woman who is shown standing up and tied between two stakes in what looks to be an Old West town. A hunchback witnesses the assault and makes phone calls to four characters: Michael Anthony, who is dressed as a samurai warrior; Alex as a Tarzan-like aboriginal; Eddie as a cowboy; and Dave as Napoleon. The first three arrive on the scene to rescue the woman—Michael and Eddie on horseback, Alex on foot—before Dave pulls up in a white stretch limo. When he steps out, the woman breaks free of the little people and runs toward her rescuers, pulling off her wig and revealing herself to be a man, offering up a sideways smile.

Inexplicably, the song rocketed up the charts and made it to No. 12 on *Billboard*'s Top 100 by mid-April. Wasted, though, was all the thought and excitement put into the video. It aired on MTV a handful of times in the spring of 1982, but when offended viewers lit up the station's phonelines and affiliates began to complain, the "unsuitable" clip was pulled. Executives at the channel pointed to the transvestite theme as the reason why it was banned.

Whether the video was getting airplay on MTV was beside the point when it came to how Warner Bros. viewed "Pretty Woman." The band had a legitimate yet wholly unexpected hit on their hands, and the label needed an album to go along with the single. Then there was going to have to be a tour.

"And we're going, 'Wait a minute. We just did that to keep us out there, so people know we're still alive,'" Eddie told *Guitar Player*. "But they kept pressuring, so we jumped right back in without any rest or any time to recuperate from the [*Fair Warning*] tour and started recording."

This threw a complete wrench into plans for a much-needed vacation, and the added pressure from the label wasn't going to make the upcoming sessions easy on the group and the already strained relationship between its members.

"By '82, it was starting to bleed," manager Noel Monk said.

GOING DOWN

So rushed were Van Halen to record the new record that they had to abandon the usual confines of Sunset Sound, which wasn't available, and go to the label-owned Warner Bros. Recording Studios—usually referred to by its old name, Amigo Studios—in North Hollywood. Much of the album was thrown together—there's no other way to put it. Eddie told *Guitar Player* journalist Jas Obrecht he figured, why not add in a few interesting instrumental pieces, which Dave objected to, saying, "Fuck the guitar hero shit, you know, we're a band." Templeman thought otherwise, incorporating the haunting "Cathedral," which resembled a church organ more than a six-string, into the LP, to join "Intruder" and a short intro to "Little Guitars" as entries without vocals.

Recorded in just twelve days, *Diver Down* was released on April 14, 1982. There have been constant complaints in the years since its release about the number of covers on the album—five in total, when you factor in the minute-long "Happy Trails"—and the fact that it contains just seventeen minutes of original material, but what else could the band do? They refused to put out songs that weren't ready, like "Big Trouble" and "House of Pain," old Gene Simmons demos that had been worked on briefly but needed significantly more time to be fleshed out. The demo well was no longer that deep, either: "Hang 'Em High" was a carbon copy of the Warner Bros. demo's "Last Night" with a fresh coat of lyrics added.

Covers-wise, the feel-good take on "Dancing in the Street," resurrected after Dave pushed for it a few months prior, would be a candidate for the song of the summer when it dropped as a single in 1982. Eddie later complained that he wanted to use the Minimoog synthesizer that's heard throughout the track for a

Van Halen original, but he was overruled. The guitarist spliced a solo from the demo of "Young and Wild" into an inspired version of the Kinks' "Where Have All the Good Times Gone," which had an exclamation point added to the title for emphasis.

The most interesting cover—perhaps in the entire Van Halen catalogue—came in the form of "Big Bad Bill (Is Sweet William Now)." Written in 1924 by Milton Ager and Jack Yellen, it was recorded that year by vaudeville performer Margaret Young and subsequently by Peggy Lee, Ry Cooder, Leon Redbone, and others. Dave heard the track on a Kentucky radio station and not only suggested it to the band but asked if Alex and Eddie's father, Jan, would lay down a clarinet solo. A decade earlier, Jan had lost a sizeable piece of a finger on his right hand in a work accident that stopped him performing professionally. He was nervous to play on the record but jumped at the chance to share a musical moment with his sons. His woodwind skills fit right in with the breezy nature of the song, which features Alex playing the drums with brushes.

Diver Down was an odds-and-sods collection that shouldn't have worked but did. The juxtaposition of wildly contrasting rhythms and tempos was something no other rock band would dare, even if Van Halen did so out of necessity. Michael and Eddie—the latter expressly, and on numerous occasions—have dogged the album in the press, and that's primarily because of the covers. The four originals—with vocals—were overshadowed by them and relegated to deep cut status, but any one of them is representative of a highly creative unit about to peak.

Though it was eye-catching in bright red, with a diagonal stripe of white, the artwork on *Diver Down* didn't appeared to have had much thought put into it—unless you listen to Dave. The band's name and album title are superimposed in bold, black text at opposing corners over the scuba flag design used in North America to indicate that there is someone below the surface of a body of water.

"It's for when they start doing any activities underwater—something going on that's not immediately apparent to your eyes," the singer told *Sounds*. "You put up the red flag with the white slash. Well, a lot of people approach Van Halen as sort of the abyss. It means, it's not immediately apparent to your eyes what is going on underneath the surface."

The back cover has the flag colors inverted and transparent over an image of Van Halen celebrating in front of sixty thousand people at the Tangerine Bowl during one of the shows they opened for the Rolling Stones the previous October. It was a smart way to make the band look like a bigger draw than they actually were, co-opting the headliner's audience as their own.

Two months after its release, on June 12, 1982, *Diver Down* made it to No. 3 on the *Billboard* 200—the group's highest showing to date. It had gone platinum by the end of the month, and it would go on to double the sales of its predecessor, selling more than four million copies in the United States alone.

HIDE YOUR SHEEP ... VAN HALEN IS COMING TO TOWN

There are three avenues of thought as to the origins of the name of the 1982 Van Halen tour, which ran from mid-July to mid-December. The first is that it was a play on the old saying to alert people that trouble was coming to a neighborhood: "Lock up your wives, hide your daughters!" The second stemmed from the story of a farmer in the Midwest, who, when told Van Halen would be coming to town and asked if he would be hiding his daughters, replied, "Hide my daughters? Hell, I'm gonna hide my sheep." The third is that it was a tongue-in-cheek response to a run of dates by AC/DC called "Hide Your Daughters."

"So many people had input on the art and merch, names, and ideas, I really am not sure [where it came from]," Monk said. "The idea was, hide your women and even your sheep when VH comes to town."

Regardless of its etymology, "Hide Your Sheep!" was a stroke of brilliance aimed squarely at an increasingly pearl-clutching society that was, much as had been the case in the '50s and '60s, turning its attention toward rock and roll music as the corrupting influence on its impressionable youth. The Van Halen road crew even donned shirts featuring a sheep in a garter belt and high heels, her eyes covered by a black bar.

The run would be confined once again to North America, with Roth making an offhanded remark to the U.K.-based magazine *Sounds* about the band's lack of live presence there. "I love England," he said. "It just appears England isn't enthusiastic about Van Halen."

Despite two of the bandmembers now being married, Roth was determined to keep the party image alive. *Life* magazine came out to see the group during a three-night stand at Cobo Hall in Detroit for a multi-page photo spread that ran in November under the banner headline "*Life* Visits Van Halen on Tour: Rock's Rowdiest Rogues." The feature was the absolute ideal for every teenager with posters of their favorite band adorning the bedroom walls and wondering how rock stars really lived. One series of images shows a woman tugging Roth's pants down as she hoists herself up on the stage, only to be forcibly removed by security. He's holding up a pair of women's panties that have been tossed his way in another, with a hand-in-the-cookie-jar look on his face. And then there's a set showcasing the debauchery and wanton destruction in the singer's hotel room, using a "before and after" motif.

The ancillary text in the *Life* pictorial stated how Alex was the one who was most destructive with inanimate objects while noting that Michael liked to start food fights. Eddie was portrayed almost as a loner, preferring to spend time pre- and post-show with his instrument, not surrounded by people. Dave was the star subject, of course, but for all of his bluster he revealed something quite telling when he said, "People always ask me if we behave this way at home. I tell them this *is* our home!"

This was the fifth year in a row that the band were on the road for the bulk of the twelve-month calendar, and they weren't that young anymore. The routine was beginning to wear in all the ways one might expect—and then some. Eddie got so frustrated at a drunken Alex one night that he punched the wall in his hotel room, resulting in a severely sprained wrist and leading to the postponement of three shows in the New York City market. Thankfully, 1983 was going to be the year 1982 was supposed to be, with some time apart from one another, a bit of vacation, as little drama as possible, and then a relaxed approach to a new album.

No problem.

TOP The van Halen family aboard the steamship *SS Ryndam* in late winter 1962, on the way to America. *Author's collection.*

ABOVE Flyers from several of Van Halen's early performances in Southern California during 1975–1976. Note the opener on the middle flyer: "Red Ball Jett," a different version of David Lee Roth's pre-VH band. *Courtesy of Jack Strong.*

LEFT A 1953 magazine ad for Red Ball Jets, "The Hi-Speed Sport Shoe" from which David Lee Roth got the name for his pre–Van Halen band. *Author's collection.*

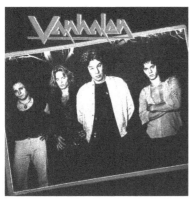

TOP Goofing around at the Eiffel Tower in Paris, May 1978. *Photofest.*

ABOVE LEFT The original 1977 Warner Bros. cover design for Van Halen's self-titled debut album. It was rejected by the band for, according to Eddie Van Halen, trying to make them look like the Clash. *Courtesy of Jack Strong.*

ABOVE RIGHT A trade magazine advertisement touting the success of Van Halen's debut single, "You Really Got Me." *Author's collection.*

TOP Eddie Van Halen during a quiet moment backstage at the San Diego Sports Arena, December 3, 1978. *Colleen Bracken.*

ABOVE LEFT A poster from the inaugural Texxas World Music Festival—better known as Texxas Jam—held in 1978 over Fourth of July weekend. *Author's collection.*

ABOVE RIGHT Michael Anthony, Alex Van Halen, and David Lee Roth head to the stage on the final date of their first world tour, December 3, 1978, at the San Diego Sports Arena. *Colleen Bracken.*

RIGHT David Lee Roth and Michael Anthony onstage at the 1979 CaliFFornia World Music Festival. *Ralph Hulett/rockretrospect.com.*

BELOW Eddie provides Dave with a light onstage at the San Diego Sports Arena, October 6, 1979. *Colleen Bracken.*

ABOVE LEFT Poster included with an 11-LP Jimi Hendrix box set released in Germany in 1980. Note the striking similarity to the *Van Halen II* logo. *Author's collection.*

ABOVE RIGHT Alex Van Halen pounds a beer before preparing to do the same to the drums at the San Diego Sports Arena, October 6, 1979. *Colleen Bracken.*

BELOW LEFT Eddie onstage in 1979 with the yellow and black "Bumblebee," which would later be buried with slain Pantera guitarist "Dimebag" Darrell Abbott. *Colleen Bracken.*

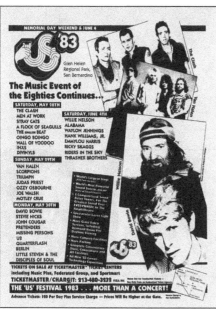

ABOVE David Lee Roth onstage at the US Festival. *Ebet Roberts.*

LEFT A newspaper ad for the 1983 US Festival where Van Halen headlined "Heavy Metal Day." *Author's collection.*

OPPOSITE PAGE A pair of photo outtakes from the *Women and Children First* era. *Norman Seeff.*

ABOVE Backstage at the Monsters of Rock festival at Castle Donington in Leicestershire, England, August 18, 1984. *Eddie Malluk.*

RIGHT Poster promoting the release of *1984* playing on the themes examined in the George Orwell book of the same name. *Courtesy of Jack Strong.*

BELOW RIGHT The original Western Exterminator Company logo (*left*) was tweaked slightly by Van Halen and used as the mascot of their *1984* tour, appearing as the stage backdrop and on various pieces of merchandise. *Courtesy of Western Exterminator/Author's Collection.*

VAN HALEN IS WATCHING YOU!

1984

9

SECRETS

Right after the "Hide Your Sheep!" tour ended in early December 1982, Van Halen got an offer to extend the jaunt by heading to South America, a region where they had never performed before. The monthlong run dubbed the "No Problems" tour began with three-nights in Caracas, Venezuela, on January 14, 1983, and ended with a pair of shows in Buenos Aires, Argentina, in early February.

South American audiences were treated to some loose sets, with the band having fun rolling back the clock to their club days by dropping in covers like Eddie Cochran's "Summertime Blues," ZZ Top's "Beer Drinkers & Hellraisers," and even Elvis Presley's "Heartbreak Hotel." They also played "Little Dreamer," which hadn't appeared in a set since the tour to support the band's self-titled debut back in 1978.

Since there was nothing else on the docket for the immediate future, David Lee Roth and the band's head of security, "Big Ed" Anderson, stayed behind when the dates were finished to trek deep into the Amazon rainforest. The singer details the expedition in *Crazy from the Heat*, describing how he contracted a bacterial infection that left him fifteen pounds lighter a week later, "dreadfully ill," and receiving dodgy medical attention. The pair survived, partied all night with the natives, traded cigarettes for boat usage, and swam with piranhas to bathe. It was a life experience very few ever get to have, but if there's one bug Roth had caught with success, it was an enthusiasm for travel. He has regularly traversed the globe to explore faraway places with a loose collective of likeminded individuals dubbed "The Jungle Studs," hitting up spots like New Guinea, Tahiti, and the Himalayas.

What gets lost to time and the inclination of most to weave tall tales in the case of Roth's trip to the Amazon in 1983 is how it came to an end. Shortly after returning from the "No Problems" tour with three-quarters of Van Halen, manager Noel Monk received a proposal from Apple co-founder Steve "Woz" Wozniak for the band to headline one of the nights in the second installment of a multi-day concert, the US Festival, set to take place over Memorial Day weekend. Monk was about to turn it down, but then Woz revealed the payment would be a cool $1.5 million, and not accepting it would've been foolish.

Roth later said he found out about the single-day payout when Monk somehow reached him via shortwave radio in the Amazon and quickly jumped on a twin-prop plane with a few geologists from Germany to get back to the States pronto. And this is where things get a little suspicious, in terms of timing and more. The lore has always been that no one knew where the singer was or how to reach him—that he was missing somewhere deep in the jungle, and there was a virtual all-points bulletin put out as the band had already accepted the offer, and what were they to do without a frontman? One permutation of the narrative goes that Roth was found, near-death and hallucinating; then brought back to civilization, where he received immediate medical attention; and returned to Van Halen like a conquering hero at the last minute to save the day.

One of Roth's favorite catchphrases is, "Who am I to get in the way of a good rumor?" While it works wonders on the talk-show circuit, it's a bit easier to hash out when basic math is involved. Were the legend true, he would've spent some fifteen weeks roughing it below the equator before making the superhuman rebound at the US Festival. During that time period, something like that wouldn't be that hard to believe as there were no real ways to track someone like today; but reports from the period said Roth was vacationing for anywhere from three to six weeks. He says in his book it was two months before he made it back to New York, to be treated at a hospital for "tropical diseases." Even the longest of those three variations would put his return to the U.S. at sometime in mid-April, approximately six weeks before the gig.

Why any of this matters is because Van Halen were about to headline the biggest show of their career, which quickly turned infamous, and the underlying reasons need to be discerned. It's clear that Roth got back with more than enough time to recover from the conditions plaguing his system post-safari. There might have been a little rust to shake off, but come the US Festival, the band should have been well-rehearsed and primed to take their rightful place among their peers—at the top. He certainly wasn't stumbling out of a prop plane at death's door and right onto the stage . . . but it made for a great story.

STUDIO WORK UNDERCOVER

During the fiasco of making and then touring in support of *Diver Down* in 1982, Eddie Van Halen did two things that would drastically alter the course of the band's trajectory forever. First, he broke ground on a home studio, although the freestanding structure on his Coldwater Canyon property was submitted to Los Angeles County inspectors as a racquetball court, since zoning laws didn't allow for a music studio to be built on personal property.

Eddie and engineer Donn Landee were behind the creation of the studio, which they decided to name "5150" after the Welfare and Institutions Code in California that allows for the "detention of a mentally disordered person for evaluation or treatment," resulting in the placing of said individual in a seventy-two-hour hold at a psychiatric facility. When he first saw the studio in its beginning phases, longtime VH producer Ted Templeman thought it was great—for a home studio. He had no idea what Eddie's ultimate intentions would be with it.

Templeman was also somewhat responsible for the next occurrence in the Van Halen universe. One night, he was sitting at home when he received a call from fellow producer Quincy Jones, who was in the studio working on the follow-up to Michael Jackson's solo breakthrough LP, 1979's *Off the Wall*, and was looking for Eddie's phone number. Jones rang up the guitarist a few weeks later, reaching him while he was working on 5150. A bad connection led to Eddie thinking a fan had somehow gotten his number; he hung up on the producer twice, the second time calling him an asshole. The third time, they could finally hear each other, and Jones asked Eddie if he'd be willing to lay down a solo on one of Jackson's songs. Flattered, he agreed without hesitation.

"Certain people in the band at that time didn't like me doing things outside the group," Eddie told the *Independent* in 1993, adding that no one else in the band was around at the time. "So I thought, well, they'll never know. Seriously: who's going to know that I played on a Black guy's record?"

Turns out, nearly everyone in the free world would know.

Eddie went over to Westlake Recording Studios in L.A. the next day and listened to the track, which was called "Beat It." He had the engineer rearrange a chunk of it and took two passes at an improvised guitar solo. When he was finishing up the second, the guitarist relayed to the *Independent*, Jackson arrived at the studio and said, "I love the high fast stuff you do." Worried the singer might not like the change he'd made, Eddie was relieved to hear him say, "Wow, thank you so much for having the passion to not just come in and blaze a solo, but to actually care about the song, and make it better."

"Beat It" was released right when Van Halen returned from South America, on February 14, 1983. It was the third single from Jackson's *Thriller* album, debuting at No. 78 on the Hot 100 and propelling the LP to No. 1 on the *Billboard* 200 for the first time. The video—incorrectly rumored in advance of its release to feature an appearance by Eddie—premiered on MTV in March, pushing the song to No. 1, where it would stay for three weeks. The song ended up selling some seven million copies; the album became the best-selling record of all time, at sixty-six million strong, and is credited with being one of the most important crossover hits in music, crumbling the boundaries between Black audiences listening to Jackson on R&B stations and the majority white one catered to by rock radio. Eddie's solo was the sole reason for the track breaking into the rock format, and he famously didn't receive a cent for his contribution.

"Eddie wouldn't take a dime for doing 'Beat It'—that happened," Monk said, still marveling, decades removed from the situation. "Fuckin' idiot. [*Imitating Eddie*] 'Oh . . . I love Michael . . . Michael loves me.' 'Yeah, you're doin' it for nothin'—I'd love you too.' [Jackson's] got the dumbest, most brilliant guitar player on the face of the earth—why wouldn't you love this guy? I asked him, 'Please, take just a half a point'—do you know what he woulda made with half a point? To me, it was ridiculous."

The guitar solo on "Beat It" is a flat-out showcase for Eddie Van Halen. It's thirty-two seconds of blazing fretwork, full of the tapping and vigor for which his playing was already legendary among rock fans, now suddenly exposed to the whole world, coming in like a Trojan horse to unsuspecting ears. He did make one request to Jones: don't credit his work on the song, because he didn't want the other guys in the band to know. It was an impossible secret to keep, though, and the members of Van Halen were not happy when they found out. Alex agreed with Monk that not taking any money for it was ridiculous.

Dave, who heard the song blasting out of a pickup truck at a 7-Eleven and initially thought it was someone ripping off Eddie, saw it as a final straw of sorts, and a reason to reverse course on hammering the point that everything should be kept "in-house" and not participating in projects outside of the group. Backhandedly, he would tell *Rolling Stone*, "What did Edward do with Michael Jackson? He went in and played the same fucking solo he's been playing in this band for ten years. Big deal!"

Inside, though, he was simmering. He later wrote in his memoir, "It was at that point I said, maybe I'll do something on the side as well."

"OUR BIGGEST SHOW—THEY FUCK UP!"

The first US Festival took place in 1982 over Labor Day weekend, at Glen Helen Regional Park in San Bernardino, California. It was put on under the banner of Wozniak's newly minted Unuson Corp., which was short for "Unite Us in Song," hence "US," and not the abbreviation for the United States as many assumed, given the capitalization. The idea was to right the wrongs of the Altamont tragedy in 1969 and have a real go at a "Woodstock West." Woz lost a reported $12 million across the three days of performances, but he wanted to try again in the final days of May 1983, over the Memorial Day holiday. This time around, it would span four days, each with a different musical theme. Saturday was "New Wave Day," followed by "Heavy Metal Day" and "Rock Day," with "Country Day" staged the next weekend.

Van Halen were slotted in on Heavy Metal Day, which was set to draw three hundred thousand people. Below them on the bill were Ozzy Osbourne, Judas Priest, Scorpions, Quiet Riot, Triumph, and Mötley Crüe. Monk had included a "most-favored-nation" clause in the band's contract, which stated that no other artist could be paid more than them at the festival. When Rock Day headliner David Bowie needed an extra $50,000 to be supplemented to his own $1.5 million deal to transport equipment from England, the same amount was automatically added to Van Halen's check.

On the Sunday of the show, backstage was buzzing about Van Halen for all the wrong reasons. A park-trail sign leading to their half-acre compound behind the scenes to prepare for the show had been altered to read, "Van Halen Trail: No Virgins, Journey Fans, or Sheep Allowed on Trail!!!" The band had turned it into a go-to zone for anyone looking to lubricate themselves with all manner of drink and substances.

One person who shouldn't have partaken in the festivities, but did, was Roth, who had shown up absolutely wasted to his media interviews. "He was drunk and coked up, laughing at every joke he made," recalls MTV VJ Mark Goodman, who interviewed the singer for the channel, in the oral history *I Want My MTV*.

Roth wasn't in much shape to be diplomatic about what happened the night prior, after New Wave Day headliners the Clash threw a tantrum when word got around about what Van Halen were being paid—which far exceeded their own $500,000 compensation. At a hastily arranged press conference, they picked a fight with Wozniak over the outlandish amount: "At least he could give 10 percent back to the community and to the poor people," singer and rhythm guitarist Joe Strummer said. The British punk outfit then announced they wouldn't be taking the stage unless Apple gave $100,000 to charity, but they were ultimately talked down from the demand.

Strummer was apoplectic by the time the Clash's set started—nearly two hours late—with the band's backdrop now reading, "THE CLASH NOT FOR SALE." He pulled out all the stops to get a reaction out of the crowd, talking up social justice and furiously shouting, "You make, you buy, you die—that's the motto of America!"

Looking back, this was a band falling apart for all to see. At one point, Strummer was about to go into another one of his rants when lead guitarist and singer Mick Jones cut him off by playing the opening riff to "Know Your Rights." The group got into a fistfight with security when leaving the stage, and the US Festival ended up being the final Clash show for Jones, who quit the band four months later.

The next night, as Van Halen's set time approached, Roth appeared at a press conference of his own, even more inebriated than he had been during the afternoon, alternately standing behind or sitting on the table in front of the assembled media. When asked about Strummer, he said, "The thing that the Clash don't understand, and the thing that a lot of these bands don't understand, is that you can't take life so goddamn seriously, honey!"

Across two hours, Van Halen put on their very best and worst on the US Festival's massive stage, which the organizers boasted was the largest in the world, with a wingspan of 432 feet. Right out of the gate, during the second verse of opener "Romeo Delight," Roth screamed through the 400,000-watt sound system, "I forgot the fucking words!" The crowd—a majority of whom were unaware that the singer had been doing a version of this schtick since the 1982 tour—roared approvingly.

Roth seemed to sober up as the show progressed, but he remained wildly offkey. He rambled on and on between songs, and at times visibly lost his train of thought. Other instances, he'd point the microphone to the audience to sing a chorus—except it would be during an instrumental break. His usual rapid-fire one-liners may have suffered from some "alcohol translation" issues, but he could still be depended on for verbal gold. Following a long slug on a bottle to rapturous applause, the frontman said, "I wanna take this time to say ... that this is real whiskey here. The only people ... who put iced tea in Jack Daniel's bottles is the Clash, baby!"

Musically, the show was more on point, but it wasn't without flaws. Perhaps forgetting how big the stage was, Michael Anthony strayed too far in one direction during his bass solo and detached the cable by accident. He played it off by throwing the instrument down and acting angry with his bass tech when he came out with a new one, shouting while the two shoved one another. Eddie had some slight flubs, but they were all minor compared to his typically jaw-dropping solo spot. The band also did a breakdown during "Somebody Get Me a Doctor," where they debuted a portion of a forthcoming song, "Girl Gone Bad," before Alex and Eddie did a guitar-versus-drums battle, capping it off by bursting into Cream's "I'm So Glad."

Toward the end of the performance, Roth came out in a completely bonkers outfit replete with a long and flowing top that looked like it had been funneled through a paper shredder and capped off with a fur-and-feather collar. When he whipped it off during "Ain't Talkin' 'Bout Love," his pants were revealed to be black leather studded chaps with white fringes running down the sides. A leather studded "tail" saw to it that his entire rear end wasn't exposed, but both cheeks were prominently displayed.

The authorities weren't kind to Van Halen in the aftermath, either, putting a large amount of blame on their shoulders for the mayhem that took place on the festival grounds, the capacity of which was three hundred thousand, but on Heavy Metal Day it swelled by another fifty thousand, with some estimates putting it even higher. Some fans were treated for broken ribs and arms, while others collapsed from lack of oxygen in the rush to get closer to the stage. Upon leaving the grounds, fans tore down fences, and some deliberately crashed their cars into police cruisers. One person was beaten to death, and a security guard was left with a fractured skull. A newspaper columnist posited that the band's behavior was lower than tying firecrackers to the tails of dogs and should be looked into by a grand jury.

In a press conference, San Bernardino County Sheriff Floyd Tidwell said that Roth encouraged the crowd to commit violence: "There are a couple of bands that never need to come back to our county: Van Halen, for example."

The US Festival was a disaster on all levels except the one that mattered: it increased the storied stature of Van Halen. Nobody cared that David Lee Roth was shitfaced and nonsensical, or that Michael Anthony's bass cut out, or that Eddie had a muffed note in "Cathedral." When the set was broadcast on the cable channel Showtime that August, as part of a four-night special on the festival, it gave further confirmation to music fans that the band were having just as much fun in concert as those in the crowd were, making them more authentic than the synthesized new wave crap they were being told was the next big thing.

For better or worse, the '83 US Festival stands as the most viewed and bootlegged complete Van Halen show from the era. There have been calls for it to be officially released—an unlikely hope, given the subpar quality that night of a unit who were known for scorching live performances. Fans got their hopes up in late 2013, when an official home video of the fest was announced. Sadly, VH were one of a few top-tier artists who weren't represented on the single DVD release, alongside Ozzy Osbourne and David Bowie.

It certainly wasn't for lack of effort that they didn't appear. "We have been trying for years to obtain them, and yes, we are still trying," Unuson CFO Carlos

Harvey said. "We would like nothing more than to be able to provide the fans with a total compilation that includes the top songs performed by every artist and also would love to release the full performance of each artist individually, but unfortunately, despite much effort, it seems that some artists just don't want their performances seen."

In retrospect, it was the first in a series of incidents where Van Halen totally botched a high-profile situation, either by their own doing or due to the cruel hand of fate taking control. There they were, in front of the biggest audience they would ever play to, and it's remembered more for the camp behavior of a blitzed Roth than the highlights.

"I never saw them, no matter how fucked up they were, do a bad show—except the US Festival," said Noel Monk, laughing. "Our biggest show—they fuck up! The five or six hundred other shows I saw? They were brilliant—they never fucked up! They were always brilliant."

10

I'LL WAIT

Right as preparations for the US Festival were getting underway, engineer Donn Landee and Eddie Van Halen dropped a bombshell on Ted Templeman, telling him they wanted to record the new album at 5150 Studios instead of Sunset Sound. This turn of events made no sense to the producer, as Eddie's home studio wasn't close to being finished, it was too small, and there was the potential for things to get too comfortable in the space, stretching out the entire process needlessly.

Templeman did not exactly come around to the idea of working at 5150, but he more or less acquiesced because his engineer and Eddie were so enthused by the space. Things got rocky, though, when the guitarist presented a bunch of new pieces of music that weren't guitar-based at all: instead, they were synthesizer-led. The skeleton of "Jump" was in there, and neither the producer nor David Lee Roth was excited about it. To the former, it was much too poppy for his liking. In his mind, he had signed a hard rock band—not a keyboard-driven act.

THE KEYBOARDS COME OUT TO PLAY

Over the years, there's been a bit of a mythology built up that Roth and Templeman were anti-keyboards. Eddie has said on numerous occasions that the singer told him to stick to playing the guitar. That may very well have been true, but even the staunchest rock and roller couldn't deny how catchy a number "Jump" was turning into. The singer quickly put together the lyrics, which he assured Templeman were not about suicide, but rather about taking a chance and risking it all, even with the crippling insecurity often driven by the fear of failure. He changed his tune somewhat when it came time to promote the album, telling Lisa Robinson for *Rock Video Magazine* that it had to do with it being a leap year first and foremost. Then he relayed a story about how he was watching the news and saw a suicidal man on the Arco Towers in Los Angeles and all the people below were yelling for him not to jump. Roth said he thought to himself the opposite—let the guy jump—but wanted it to be a positive piece as well. Many years later, while in Japan with Van Halen in 2013, he told the television program *Song of Soul* that "Jump" was about moving ahead with little hesitation.

"Aw, you 'might as well' . . . let's just not even have the verb 'jump,'" the singer said. "Might as well! It's a commitment to a forward space. There's no wasted days, there's no timing moves like in chess. Maybe the only rationale you can use is, 'Hey, I might as well.' That may be all you need to propel you into your next big move in your life—or the next big mistake. Either way, at least you have a life worth living, a life well lived in."

Another track that utilized synthesizers was "I'll Wait," but for whatever reason the lyrics weren't coming to Roth when it came time to record it. He was struggling so much that he asked Templeman to call up hit songwriter Michael McDonald, who the producer knew from working with the Doobie Brothers, to see if he might be interested in collaborating.

"I met David Lee Roth at Ted's office. That was, uh, an interesting experience," McDonald told *Ultimate Classic Rock*. "He kinda liked what I had going, so we sat there in the office with the demo playing on a cassette recorder, singing lines and melodies."

McDonald's contribution to the song would turn into a bit of musical trivia as time went on, due to his name being left off the credits of the album and single. Whether it was on purpose or not, it damaged the trust between him and Templeman, as "I'll Wait" became a hit and McDonald was due a large share of royalties. Eventually, the singer's attorneys had to get involved, but by 2000, when Warner Bros. launched its Warner Remasters series of compact discs, the slight looked to have been rectified.

"I guess they thought I was Santa Claus, because I had to go chasing them a little bit on that one," McDonald said, laughing. "It's probably one of the most played things I've ever written, just because it's Van Halen. That album sold three or four million copies right away, which was a really big deal at the time."

Unfortunately for McDonald, when Rhino reissued the record for its thirtieth anniversary in 2015 on 180gram vinyl, it was once again missing his name.

STUDIO MADNESS

While "Jump" and "I'll Wait" were completed early in the recording sessions, the rest of the music dragged along. It wasn't due to a lack of material, though—in fact, it was the opposite. Eddie kept coming up with music, encouraged by Landee, while Templeman was applying pressure to finish it so they could get to mixing. This went on for weeks, and it began to wear on everyone involved. The executives at Warner Bros. wanted the final product so they could get the new LP by one of their marquee artists on shelves by the end of the year, and Roth was tired of sitting around—this was a band who used to make records in days, but now it was up to six months plus.

Finally, Eddie gave in. The music was mixed by the end of October 1983 and ready to be mastered. Then things really got out of hand when Landee and Eddie suddenly commandeered the tapes and refused to give them up. The back-and-forth quickly developed into something akin to a comedy routine, albeit a tragic one. Templeman would show up at 5150 for the master tapes to take them to Sunset Sound to mix, and Landee would run out the back door with them while Eddie stalled the producer and told him he had no clue where the tapes were. When Templeman left, Landee would return, and the pair would go about pulling all-nighters, fueled by cocaine and alcohol, trying to get what they heard in their heads as the perfect mix.

It was now November, and a widespread marketing campaign by the label to hype the record release at midnight on December 31 had to be scrapped, as it wasn't going to make the deadline. Left with no choice, Templeman went into Sunset Sound and began to mix the album from scratch, using the analogue safety copies, which was hardly ideal. One day, out of nowhere, a crazed-looking Landee showed up, "manic and all messed up, sweating and crazy," according to Templeman's book. He had the masters and was threatening to throw them into the ocean. Cooler heads prevailed; Landee got some sleep, then returned to master the album properly in the right frame of mind.

WATCHING—AND BEING WATCHED

MCMLXXXIV—soon to become more commonly known by its Arabic numeral translation, *1984*—was released on January 9, 1984. It debuted at No. 18 on the *Billboard* 200 and made it to a peak position of No. 2 that year on March 17. The title was a nod to author George Orwell's 1949 novel about a dystopian future, *Nineteen Eighty-Four*. The band even co-opted the phrase "Big Brother is watching you" into advertisements for the record, which declared, "VAN HALEN IS WATCHING YOU!" It was of course concurrent with the calendar year the album was released in, too, as noted in confident print ads that predicted, "This is their year."

Musically, *1984* was slick and primed for mainstream attention. Most of the songs were polished and catchy; like "Everybody Wants Some!!" and "Unchained" before it, "Panama" had a callout chorus for the audience to latch onto. Full of mischievous double-entendres about pistons popping and shiny machines, the song's breakdown features a cameo by Eddie's 1972 Lamborghini Miura S, which he brought to the studio to lay down the rumble of the engine. "Hot for Teacher" doles out a nonstop fretwork shuffle, sees Dave at his most comedic, and features a relentless thump of the bottom end, with Alex Van Halen's assemblage of four bass drums used to create a firework-like blitz.

The pop sheen of *1984* was a surprise to many fans who'd last experienced Van Halen at full capacity on the dark, unconventional, and somewhat sinister *Fair Warning* nearly three years prior, but not so much to those who dialed into the seemingly throwaway cover ditties of *Diver Down*. This LP was a sign of a new era, with the only leftover of days past being "House of Pain," tacked onto the end of the record, with Roth's lyrics now an ode to BDSM. There were no covers at all, either—though Wilson Pickett's "In the Midnight Hour" had been tracked—proving Van Halen were no longer just a backyard party band; they had evolved with the times and as musicians, becoming innovative for the pop world while still appealing to the heavy metal parking-lot crowd who blasted tunes out of souped-up, small-block Camaros when heading to the drag races on a Saturday night.

The idea for the *1984* artwork was originally for it to show four chrome women dancing in various stages of undress—think something along the lines of Aerosmith's 2001 effort *Just Push Play*. The concept was brought to artist

Margo Nahas, but she declined, as the design would be too cumbersome. The label asked her husband, fellow designer and art director Jay Vigon, to bring by Nahas's portfolio to a band meeting anyway. Alex, Eddie, and Dave came across her drawing of a cherub smoking a cigarette and were struck immediately by it. Nahas was hired. To come up with a completely new work of photorealism, she spent an afternoon taking pictures of her friend's two-year-old son, plying him with candy cigarettes after putting gel in his hair and taking numerous shots. The final product adds wings to the baby, who's shown glancing to his left with a cigarette in his right hand. It ended up as one of the more iconic and notorious rock album covers of all time, with much of the critical focus on the sacrilege of having a baby smoking, no matter how harmlessly it was staged.

Per usual with a new release, Van Halen wasted no time getting on the road to support *1984*, kicking off what was simply titled the "Tour of the World" just over a week after the LP came out. Most North American cities saw them play two- or three-night stands over some one hundred dates, heading to each gig with eighteen trucks hauling their stage and equipment. Eddie later said the lighting rig on the trek was made up of two thousand lights, as opposed to the normal five to seven hundred.

The *1984* tour even had a mascot. Adorning the stage backdrop, as well as T-shirts and backstage passes, was a curious image of what looked to be a cartoon of a character in a top hat, wearing a tuxedo and sunglasses, pointing his index finger forward in a "hold on" manner while brandishing a hammer behind his back. "The Little Man," it turned out, was the logo for the Western Exterminator Company, a pest-control service with offices up and down the California coast and in Arizona. The business was established in 1921, and a decade later an artist by the name of Vaughn Kaufman created the logo icon first known as "Kernel Kleenup."

Van Halen had gone looking for a sponsor to offset the costs of their lengthy tour but, according to Roth, "nobody wanted us," and they were turned down. "I guess our image was wrong. So, we decided that we'll be the first band to sponsor a company," the singer told *Rock Video Magazine*. "So, we took the logo from the Western Exterminator Company in Los Angeles—a little man with a top hat and a big hammer behind his back—and we put him on the T-shirt and the program and on the merchandise, and he is the tour logo."

Sponsoring a company, pulling out all the stops, and selling out arenas for multiple nights in major metropolitan cities showed there was no bigger rock act in the country than Van Halen. There was, however, a bigger show on the road that year: the Victory Tour, featuring the Jackson brothers and led by the white-hot sibling Michael, with his solo album *Thriller* having spent thirty-seven weeks atop the *Billboard* charts. Just as VH were winding down their run, the Jacksons were getting started, meaning they only had the opportunity to cross paths once, in Dallas.

The Victory Tour included three dates—July 13, 14, and 15—at Texas Stadium, while Van Halen were doing three nights of their own at Reunion Arena on July 14, 15, and 16. Showing up in town a day early to catch the Jacksons spectacle on July 13, Eddie and Valerie went to the concert together while Dave went on his own, grabbing his floor seat and drawing the stares of starstruck concertgoers as he did. The encore began with "Beat It," and Michael Jackson brought out Eddie to reprise his guest turn on the solo and play for the whole track. It would be the only time Eddie performed live with Michael.

One month after the end of the final North American leg of the Tour of the World, Van Halen went to Europe to perform live concerts there for the first time since 1980, as part of the Monsters of Rock package tour. They appeared second to AC/DC on a bill that also featured the likes of Ozzy Osbourne, Dio, Mötley Crüe, Y&T, Gary Moore, and Accept. The tour ran over five dates in England, Sweden, Switzerland, and Germany, from August to September.

It was hard to measure the success of Van Halen on their return to the region as they were buffered by artists who were more well-known there. But there was no question that Stateside, a huge part of their rise was due to an increasing exposure on MTV. The band took the "this is their year" slogan to heart and assaulted the eyes and ears of the network's viewers. They didn't just make videos out of obligation for the quickly changing times and to keep up with the Culture Clubs and Def Leppards—instead, they sought to own the art form.

11

JUMP

Van Halen had yet to conquer the all-important video medium—primarily MTV, shorthand for Music Television—but they were determined to do so come 1984. Following the "Pretty Woman" fiasco, they had little presence on the channel, other than the occasionally played Oakland live clips from the *Fair Warning* tour. Despite his less-than-sober state at the US Festival, one moment of clarity David Lee Roth had while being interviewed by MTV came when he said Van Halen were hard at work on their new album, and that there would be a number of hit singles and videos—"probably something that they'll show on the channel this time." Even at his most arrogant, there's no way the singer could've been aware of the heights the band were about to reach on the cable network.

In April 1983, shortly before the US Festival, MTV was reported to be present in 15 percent of American television homes, allowing it to be reported on for the first time by the Nielsen Homevideo Index national ratings, where it achieved the highest twenty-four-hour rating ever for a basic cable service. Michael Jackson's short film for "Thriller" debuted in December 1983 with off-the-charts buzz, and forecasts said the next year was going to be a big one for the network. Estimates were exceeded in 1984: the channel went public with an IPO in the summer, and it revealed a 37 percent increase in subscribers through the year to 25.4 million households. The National Association of Record Manufacturers (NARM) showed its appreciation to MTV for reviving a long-stagnating record industry by bestowing it with a Presidential Award in 1984. There wasn't a better time for Van Halen to infiltrate than on the heels of their most accessible album to date.

"Jump" was the band's first and only No. 1 single, topping the *Billboard* Hot 100 for five weeks beginning in February 1984. There's little question the low-budget clip, directed by the band and Pete Angelus, pushed it to the slot once it went into heavy rotation on MTV. Depending on who you believe, it cost either $600 or in the neighborhood of $5,000. Reams of additional footage were shot—later repurposed for the "Panama" video—but the decision was made to cut the material down to a simple performance piece, shot on handheld 16mm cameras at the Complex, a tiny theater on Hollywood's Santa Monica Boulevard.

"We didn't want any of the stuff, like, standing on the edge of a cliff with a picture in the background or fireballs thrown at you," Alex Van Halen told *Rolling Stone*. "We just wanted personality."

It was a small-scale maneuver that paid off, with Van Halen snagging three nominations and a win for Best Stage Performance in a Video at the first ever MTV Video Music Awards in 1984. This was a period when videos were costing an average of between $30,000 and—at the "Thriller" end of the pond—$1 million. To break out ahead of their peers in the manner they did kept up the outlaw mentality the group cultivated.

"I loved it because it was them—it was so perfect, just stripped down," said Nina Blackwood, one of the original MTV VJs. "You see that nut David Lee Roth, it showcased him—I thought it was great. It matched the song, the song is so uplifting, the video is uplifting and fun . . . I gotta say, with that song and video, I always think of my VJ little sister, Martha Quinn, because Martha really thought she was gonna marry David Lee Roth."

Blackwood, whose half-Dutch heritage may have accounted for drawing her more to Van Halen than other rock bands, said that in the golden age of MTV, there was no disputing how influential Van Halen were "across the board." "Where do you even start?" she asked hypothetically. "David Lee Roth kind of set the stage for blond-haired frontmen wearing spandex—even though, of course, he's way more than that. And how can you deny the influence of Eddie Van Halen? I absolutely love him as a musician. He's my favorite guitar player.

Even though his technique was so incredible, what he did with his solos fit the song. It wasn't overplaying, it was just this incredible, unique-that-you-never-heard-before type of playing."

The second single to be turned into a video was "Panama," which saw the band going the more traditional route of a performance clip. Filmed primarily over two nights at the Philadelphia Spectrum in March 1984, it was intercut with the shelved footage from the "Jump" shoot, much of which was pulled from the inner workings of Roth's ego. He's spotlighted cruising down the road on a motorcycle, somersaulting over Anthony while wearing a shirt airbrushed with his own face, doing a kung-fu routine with a sword, sliding down a fireman's pole and singing with two other versions of himself, and goofing off with Alex in his customized 1951 Mercury convertible. Everything in it was staged for the cameras—even the singer getting arrested at a hotel.

The "Panama" clip marked the debut of Anthony's Jack Daniel's bass, which he cobbled together from various bass parts and decorated with the logo of his favorite Tennessee whiskey. It was also a unique way to circumvent MTV's strict rules against product placement in videos. Less fun for Michael was when he was hung from a cable for a goofy part of the shoot where each member swung from it doing something different, Dave flying by with a boombox on his shoulder, Eddie hanging upside down by one foot in one scene and coolly strumming his Frankenstrat in another.

"They said, 'Mike, why don't you go first?'" he recalls in *I Want My MTV*. "They strapped me in a harness under my clothes, and it was totally—how would you say?—I mean, it almost castrated me, the way it was wrapped around my legs and groin. My nuts were, like, in a vise. These straps were coming right around my ball sac. As soon as I did it, then you got Al swinging and drinking a beer, and Eddie swinging while Al and Dave yank on him."

"Hot for Teacher" was the final single to be released from *1984*, and it finished checking the boxes in terms of video types from the LP as it was conceptual in nature. Angelus later joked that the pizza for the shoot cost more than the entirety of the "Jump" video. It typified the humor of the group and became a favorite on MTV, with child actors playing younger versions of the bandmembers, looking and acting a lot like their adult selves, getting into trouble, being driven mad by the opposite sex, and living for the time of the day when partying would commence—when class was dismissed. The recurring character was Waldo, voiced by *Saturday Night Live* alum Phil Hartman, the quintessential outcast student with thick glasses and squeaky, greased-down hair, wearing a sweater vest and bowtie. So popular was the video that the name Waldo became synonymous with "nerd." Perhaps most hilarious was the dance routine by Van Halen, choreographed by Roth, for which the band—notably Alex—could not keep in step with one another.

It was reported as fact for decades that Janet Jones, the dancer, actress, and future wife of hockey superstar Wayne Gretzky, played the blonde physical-education instructor who strips down in the lunchroom, but it was actually Lillian Müller, a 1976 *Playboy* Playmate of the Year and budding actress. Donna Rupert, Miss Canada 1980's runner-up, was the chemistry teacher in the blue bikini, strutting in front of a chalkboard. And, in a bit of subversive humor that slid past standards and practices, each number written on the board corresponded to a letter in the alphabet so that, when read backward, it said, "HOLY SHIT."

The clip's images of scantily clad women—in the roles of teacher, disciplinarian, and sex object—were a magnet for criticism from conservatives and the uptight sect known as the "Washington Wives," spouses of the political elite in Washington, D.C. The video was referenced in a *Newsday* piece written by Tipper Gore, co-founder of the Parents Music Resource Center (PRMC), under the headline "The Smut and Sadism of Rock." In it, she quoted Thomas Radecki, then chairman of the National Coalition on Television Violence, who said, "Van Halen's 'Hot for Teacher' features a schoolteacher doing a striptease on top of desks while elementary schoolboys ogle at her. When my eight-year-old asked me, 'Why is the teacher taking off her clothes in school,' I started paying attention to the videos my children watch." (It should probably be noted that Radecki, a psychiatrist, was later sentenced to between eleven and twenty-two years in prison for exchanging prescriptions drugs for sex with young female patients who were addicted to heroin and painkillers, including one who bore his child.)

On September 19, 1985, congressional hearings took place to hear out all those who had gotten into a stir over music lyrics. There was nothing legislative about it, as chairman Senator John C. Danforth noted in the opening statement;

it was simply a forum for those who were up in arms to complain on a national stage, making for some of the most interesting television C-SPAN has run to date.

First to speak was U.S. senator Paula Hawkins, a Republican from Florida and chair of the Senate Subcommittee on Children, Family, Drugs, and Alcoholism. She held up a series of blown-up "offensive" album covers like Def Leppard's *Pyromania* and W.A.S.P.'s *Animal (F**k Like a Beast)*, before adding "values in rock videos, which are viewed by the kids" to the mix. The hearing, it turned out, wasn't going to stop at analyzing lyrics.

Hawkins gestured to a television for the first reprobates, and the video for "Hot for Teacher" began playing. When it was stopped—right in the middle of Eddie's solo—scattered laughter and applause broke out in the chamber, leading Danforth to furiously bang his gavel and say, "None of that. No. Now, wait a second, Senator Hawkins, just a minute. Now, this is a very large crowd today, we have allowed people in beyond the capacity of this room. We're not gonna have any demonstrations, no applause, no demonstrations of any kind."

"I thank the chairman," Hawkins said. "The title of that tape was 'Hot for Teacher' . . . and we will give each senator a copy of the words if they'll promise not to distribute them beyond their own possession."

"I gotta say, I thought it was kinda much ado about nothing," said Blackwood. "On a personal level, honestly, I didn't give it much thought. In hindsight, yeah, I think a lot [of the videos at the time] were [sexist], but it wasn't outside of the 'male rock star' thinking. It was sex, drugs, and rock and roll—that's kind of what the whole thing was about. The groupies, the backstage, carrying on and all that. It really was in the fabric of it all. For 'Hot for Teacher' specifically, I didn't even think about the teacher; I was laughing about Waldo. I was laughing about David Lee Roth with the cap on, driving the school bus. I really like that song—because it's fun. I didn't go, 'Oh my god—look at the teacher! She's doing a striptease!' I didn't think of it."

"People like them come along every eight to twelve years, peddling this nonsensical hysteria about lyrics ruining our kids," Roth would later tell *Playboy*. "But we can't ignore Tipper. She's sawing away at some of the basic tenets of our great society. I don't want to trade off my constitutional rights to someone who feels capable of censoring my reading and listening material. She wouldn't want me censoring hers."

THE LOST WEEKEND

MTV was known for just two things in the mid-'80s: a steady, near-nonstop serving of pop and rock music videos, and off-the-wall contests tied in with the hit music of the day. Among them was a chance to score a party house in Indiana, which would be painted pink in honor of the John Cougar Mellencamp hit "Pink Houses"; "Win a Date with Prince"; a "Cruise to Nowhere" with Mötley Crüe to the Bermuda Triangle; and even a giveaway of Jon Bon Jovi's childhood home in New Jersey. None of them came close, though, to the popularity of the "Lost Weekend with Van Halen."

"We shouldn't call it a contest, because we don't know what's going to happen to the winner," went a voiceover in a commercial for the contest, which required nothing but a postcard to be sent to the MTV studios in New York City by a date in March 1984 for a chance to win. More than a million entries were received, and twenty-year-old Kurt Jefferis from Phoenixville, Pennsylvania, had one of the thirteen postcards he'd sent in picked out of the batch.

Mere weeks after being declared the winner, Jefferis and his friend Tom Winnick were ushered in a limo from their suburb outside of Philadelphia to the airport and boarded a private jet to Detroit, where Van Halen were performing two nights at Cobo Hall. The band brought Jefferis onstage during one of the shows to congratulate him, then smashed a sheet cake in his face and sprayed him down with champagne. It looked like the ultimate dream come true, but behind the scenes was quite a different story.

The 2020 documentary short *Lost Weekend* goes into depth about just how treacherous things got as Jefferis drank with the band, smoked some pot, and even snorted "a little cocaine off David Lee Roth's pinkie." What the band and MTV staff didn't know was that Jefferis had had a recent fall down a stairwell that left him with a blood clot on his brain and resulted in a three-month hospital stay, during which he was close to death. Following the injury, he underwent a speech-therapy course to learn to talk again, and he was taking anti-seizure medication three times a day. He shouldn't have been drinking at all, let alone partying the way Van Halen did.

"It got to the point to where I think it was freaking some people out," Winnick said. "That's when I think I came clean with the MTV people about the accident."

A decision was quickly made to separate Jefferis from the festivities—a move that may have saved his life. Had he fallen or suffered a blow to the head, it could have put him right back in the hospital—or worse.

"The rush was unbelievable," Jefferis said. "I didn't tell MTV about my accident because I didn't think anything of it. I was the grand-prize winner, and I was going to go experience a lost weekend with Van Halen. I guess I would consider myself a very lucky dude."

The footage shot by MTV was nearly unusable because the majority of backstage hijinks were nixed by Van Halen management, with enough left over for about ten minutes of quality follow-up television. That was plenty, though, to put the contest—and the band, for that matter—further into legendary standing for the channel's viewing audience.

It wasn't just the videos and contests, either. There were interviews, tour date announcements, and on-the-road check-ins as Van Halen seemed to be everywhere on MTV in 1984. When Frank Sinatra was preparing for his debut on the channel in late July, with the title track to what would be his final proper studio album, *L.A. Is My Lady*, Quincy Jones hit up his old pal Eddie Van Halen for another favor. This time, the producer didn't want the guitarist to put down another solo, but rather to appear in the video—and could he bring along his lead singer?

"L.A. Is My Lady" opens with Eddie and Dave coming out of a backstage area, awkwardly shaking hands before making their way through a crowd of fans and into a waiting limousine. Once inside, the latter starts digging through a bag and says, "I got something new. It's the latest, it's the greatest, a little bit of Frank!"

"Frank?" Eddie asks, puzzled.

"A little Frank Sinatra for ya here," Dave replies.

The guitarist encourages him to "Pop it in!" as they lean back to watch.

Although it featured a bevy of guest stars in addition to Eddie and Dave—from Dean Martin to LaToya Jackson to Missing Persons—the clip ultimately fizzled. Maybe it was because the song, meant to capitalize on the hype surrounding the Olympic Games, which were taking place that year in Los Angeles, wasn't that good. It didn't help that it was such an obvious attempt to lure in a younger crowd for Ol' Blue Eyes. The targeted audience inwardly balked and tuned it out. Still, it showed just how in demand and valuable Van Halen were across all divides.

These forays into the deep waters of Music Television paid off, as by the end of the year *1984* was approaching the five-times-platinum mark. When Roth appeared as the self-described "Toastmaster General of the Immoral Majority" to co-host MTV's *4th Annual New Year's Eve Rock 'n' Roll Ball* alongside VJ Martha Quinn, he was in fine form to drop one-liners over four hours in front of a live audience. He mentioned he had a message from "Edward and Alex and Michael" for viewers, urging them to make resolutions before the clock struck midnight. But as the evening wore on and the drinks flowed, talking about Van Halen was the last thing on his mind. He had something else to promote, and it was obvious just how separated the frontman had become from his soon-to-be-former bandmates.

12
HOUSE OF PAIN

Van Halen rightly predicted 1984 would be their year, but it was also the apex of the band: sold-out shows coast to coast, a top-selling album on the charts, constant airplay on radio and MTV, and the bane of parents watching their kids draw the VH logo everywhere as the sounds of "Jump" and "Panama" rang out incessantly. Behind the scenes, though, things were less than triumphant. What should have been a celebration of a banner year and how far they had come as a group was a mess of ego, isolation, disenchantment, and division on almost all fronts.

While on tour to promote the album, Eddie Van Halen was continuously coming to manager Noel Monk to complain about David Lee Roth and the singer's unrestrained self-centeredness. Alex Van Halen was starting each day with a beer and would routinely drink himself into oblivion. But it was the perennially happy-go-lucky guy, the unsung hero of the Van Halen sound, who was the first to feel the brunt of the decay inside the band.

It had long been speculated that Eddie and Dave—but mostly the former—wanted to replace Michael Anthony with Billy Sheehan, wunderkind bassist from Talas, the Buffalo power trio who had opened up a series of dates for Van Halen on the 1980 Invasion Tour. During a 2020 interview with the podcast *The Metal Voice*, Sheehan confirmed he had been offered the position three times over the years, the last in 1984, before later clarifying that no "official" offer had been made by the group.

Unable to land the change in bass position they wanted, Alex, Eddie, and Dave approached Monk and said they wanted to cut Michael out of the royalties, but not just going forward: they wanted a backdated contract drawn up stating that he wouldn't receive anything from *1984*, which at that point had sold millions of copies. The reasoning was that he hadn't contributed musically or lyrically to the album. Monk dutifully had lawyers draw up the agreement, and, much to his surprise, the bassist signed it. He had given up his partnership in Van Halen, and he would thereafter make his money from touring and merchandise only. It wasn't a pittance, but compared to what the others were pulling in, the reduction was an immense financial blow, no matter how it's looked at.

"The thing that probably hurt me the most is how they treated Michael," Monk said. "You have this incredibly brilliant guitar player—probably one of the most brilliant guitar players ever—if you're that good of a guitar player, why do you have to downgrade an okay bass player who fits in, who has an incredibly beautiful voice? What is the point in knocking him? He was a real integral part of the band. That voice was seminal to the band. He was a fun guy, and he played a good bass."

Years later, and after further financial demoralizing, Eddie would finally excise Anthony from the band. "He loved being in Van Halen," Monk said. "For Ed to continue to beat on this guy . . . it's beyond me."

1984—?

In mid-1984, Ballantine Books released *Everything You Want to Know About . . . Van Halen*. Written by Gordon Matthews, it was one of those cheap, mass-market paperbacks publishers put on shelves to quickly capitalize on the latest pop-culture sensation. It's not inherently bad, and it didn't pretend to be anything than what it was: a short-on-substance account of the band that any teen would be willing to pick up for $2.95 at the local drugstore while browsing the latest issue of *Tiger Beat*.

There's something intriguing, though, in retrospect, about the title of the last chapter: "Van Halen 1984—?" Matthews couldn't have conjured in his wildest dreams what was to take place over the next several years. What may have started in 1982, with the breakneck pace and pressure of *Diver Down*, the drunken US Festival, or the sudden explosion of fame that came with being one of the hottest acts on MTV—that question mark was about to turn into a whole lot more than a frivolous bit of punctuation wondering what the future might hold.

JUST A GIGOLO GONE SOLO

Bolstered by the sense of control he was beginning to feel, with his home studio turning into the *band* studio, and further emboldened by the praise he was getting for the "Beat It" solo, Eddie Van Halen began to step out more to work with people separate from the band. He linked up with Brian May for the *Star Fleet Project*, a mini-EP resulting from a jam session the Queen guitarist held with some of his musician friends over a two-day period.

Eddie recorded a trio of musical compositions for Valerie Bertinelli's made-for-television movie *The Seduction of Gina*, and when director Cameron Crowe approached him to score *The Wild Life*, the thematic follow-up to the smash-hit film *Fast Times at Ridgemont High*, he was more than happy to take on the role of musical director. An instrumental, "Donut City," appeared on the soundtrack, but the movie tanked and failed to appear on most people's collective radar.

Eddie also gave a piece of music to the filmmakers of the subsequent blockbuster *Back to the Future*—a track done completely on the sly and not confirmed for decades, as the band said they didn't want their music used in the film. It can be heard in the scene where Michael J. Fox's character, Marty McFly, is shown putting a cassette into a Walkman to terrify his future father with sonic torture. At first glance, the tape reads "Van Halen," but upon closer inspection it has "Edward" written in small print on the top left of the label.

Dave had already thrown in the proverbial towel when it came to forsaking outside projects. Eddie's flirtations with seemingly anyone who came calling led him to thinking he'd mount his own expeditions, completely removed from the Van Halen umbrella. So, when the band were riding on the supersonic Concorde jet to their short run of shows in Europe in August 1984, the singer revealed his plans to put out a solo EP of covers. The songs were originally made famous by the Lovin' Spoonful ("Coconut Grove"), the Beach Boys ("California Girls"), Louis Prima ("Just a Gigolo / I Ain't Got Nobody"), and the Edgar Winter Group ("Easy Street"). Roth had begun recording the music earlier that summer with Ted Templeman, and it was slated to be released the first month of the new year, with a single coming in mid-December.

For his part, the producer said he didn't envision the EP, titled *Crazy from the Heat*, as encroaching on Van Halen in the slightest. If anything, it was a way for Roth to scratch an itch to do music that would never work within the parameters of his primary outfit. And it would give the rest of the group a moment to take a breather, without pressure from the record company. After all, the singer was the hyperactive one, and if this was a way to keep him busy, what harm could it do?

"I believe that he didn't have any interest in leaving the band when we worked on *Crazy from the Heat*," Templeman says in his book. "If I'd gotten even the slightest sense that he saw this as step one of David Lee Roth's post–Van Halen solo career, I wouldn't have done the record. I never, ever wanted to do anything to threaten the future of Van Halen. I can't emphasize this enough."

LIFE GOES ON ... WITHOUT ME

"I picture myself as very firmly in a rock and roll band," Roth told writer Lisa Robinson ahead of the release of *Crazy from the Heat*. He added that his hands were full with Van Halen, who he said would be heading into the studio in January 1985. Those sentiments were echoed during the first week of the new year when he appeared as a guest on *Late Night with David Letterman*, days after the video for "California Girls" premiered at midnight on MTV's *4th Annual New Year's Eve Rock 'n' Roll Ball*.

The more press he did, and the more numbers *Crazy from the Heat* put up, the further speculation was fueled that Roth was striking out on his own beyond the EP. It wasn't just in the tabloid rock magazines like *Circus* and *Hit Parader*, which for years had been saying the band were done. This time it felt different. Even go-to industry publication *Billboard* ran a headline that screamed, "Van Halen's Roth: Maybe It's Over," though the corresponding article hardly indicated such.

Yet as 1985 wore on, and Roth's star kept rising, reports were growing to inescapable levels. The singer had certainly shown he was bankable as a solo artist. "California Girls" was a hit on MTV, and the single ended up going to No. 3 on the *Billboard* Top 100 in March. The "Just a Gigolo / I Ain't Got

Nobody" medley did the same, peaking at No. 12 in June. The EP itself had sold a million copies by the summer and made it to an impressive No. 15 on the *Billboard* 200. Then Roth appeared on the cover of *Rolling Stone*. Now he was talking about making a movie.

Finally, the dispatches started stating as fact that the unthinkable had happened: David Lee Roth had left Van Halen.

Mythical as the story about the breakup has become, much of it is untrue. First, Roth didn't announce his departure on April Fool's Day. It's a convenient tale that likely got legs the way jokes on April 1 do—or did—and never stopped. It's not like today, when something can be fact-checked in seconds, usually by going straight to the source on an artist's social media page. But because what many remember as a then unverifiable April Fool's prank, an already rampant rumor, and the official confirmation Dave was out all occurred within a somewhat close window, the sands of time have meshed them together. The truth of the matter is the general public didn't find out the news until the last week of July 1985, when the August 15 issue of *Rolling Stone* landed on newsstands. It wasn't reported with breathless fanfare or worthy of a cover mention, but rather relegated to the "Random Notes" section that was more focused on whispers that Eddie and Valerie were headed for divorce. It was there, almost as an aside, that the guitarist gave an update on Van Halen.

"The band, as you know it, is over. Dave left to be a movie star, I don't give a fuck what he says," Eddie said, adding the frontman asked him to pen a score for the film. "Me, I'm lookin' for a new lead singer, 'cause I've got so much material ready to go—stuff Dave probably wouldn't have wanted to sing. . . . If he can't scream over it, he has trouble. I just sat around and waited for that guy, from December till now. Now he's got the nerve to blame it on me. It's weird that it's over. Twelve years of my life, putting up with his bullshit."

"You know you're successful when you implode," said Ratt's Stephen Pearcy. And that's exactly what happened.

GOODBYE DAVE, HELLO . . . ?

The timeline of Van Halen's split with David Lee Roth has never really been very transparent. It's not that surprising, and it happens with a lot of bands from the era that didn't feel the need to put out a press statement about everything that was going on in private—and there was quite a bit of action in the band's camp in 1985. All of it involved more than one person, so it's no wonder the accounts vary greatly.

Noel Monk had seen the writing on the wall in drunken conversations Eddie had had with him during the 1984 tour, and he knew that Alex was going to make a move at some point to relieve him of his managerial duties. He wasn't surprised, then, when the group called a meeting in February and told him he was being fired from his position—but, as a consolation, offered him a role to book their next tour.

"The way I saw it was, '84 was the year we finally broke," Monk said. "I saw us going another five or eight years before David's ankles went out. I think that we had a huge future ahead of us—this was gonna be the biggest band in the world, playing stadiums across the world. We didn't do it. We did not live up to my expectations. We were three years away from being the biggest band in the world."

Sometime that March, Dave and Eddie had a face-to-face. Supposedly, the former said he had a multi-million-dollar deal with CBS Productions to make and star in a film based on a script he had with the same title as his EP, *Crazy from the Heat*. He asked the guitarist if he would score it but was turned down. The two decided to part ways, shed some tears, and shared a hug. Honestly, that's what makes the most sense, too. They had been through a lot together, and no matter how much either secretly thought they'd be better without the other—Eddie not having to deal with the singer's ego, Dave not having to share the spotlight with the guitarist—it had to be bittersweet. But as so often happens—especially when there's something to promote and the media gets its collective ink in things—stories change and expand, and the insults come out.

Dave said he got tired of sitting around waiting for the band to make new music. That isn't completely true—at least not in the sense he tried to sell it. He was frustrated with the time he spent waiting for Eddie, who was deep into cocaine and alcohol addiction, to finish with the recording of *1984*. Between the tour for that album, which ended in September 1984, and the announcement of the breakup in the summer of 1985, Roth was in total solo mode. He was on the talk-show circuit, making videos, and plotting his entry into Hollywood.

Eddie said *he* was tired of sitting around waiting for Dave to finish with his solo outing and his movie-star aspirations, and he didn't want to be in Roth's backing band. This aligns more with the truth, but according to the band's former lighting director, Pete Angelus—who by that time had linked up in a creative partnership with Roth, under the name the Fabulous Picasso Brothers, to do videos and the *Crazy from the Heat* film—Van Halen had agreed in the spring of 1985 to take a one-year hiatus. When Eddie came out saying Dave had quit, it was a shock to both Angelus and Roth.

"It rolled into a lot of very negative feelings, because I think Dave felt betrayed," Angelus says in *MTV Ruled the World*. "I don't know how the Van Halens felt betrayed, because they had agreed to it. Maybe they felt betrayed because he wanted to pursue something in film. But it rolled quickly into some very negative areas."

"When I left Van Halen, it was not something that I was delighted to do," Roth writes in his autobiography. "I was not celebrating. I was not relieved. It was one of the scariest moments in my life. I perceived that Van Halen was heading towards catastrophe . . . I am not Mr. Not Guilty at all, but the chemistry between us was becoming morbid, it was becoming threatening and nonproductive. You can hear it in the music, it started turning melancholy right after I left. That's great, there's plenty of room for melancholy music, but it's not my personal constitution."

The members of Van Halen did not just consider Roth out of the band; by the dawn of summer, they were looking at other singers. *Rolling Stone* correctly reported in June that Patty Smyth, who sang on the hits "Goodbye to You" and "The Warrior" while fronting Scandal, was working with the group. She'd recently struck up a friendship with Eddie and Valerie, but she was also pregnant and living in New York at the time. That had a lot to do with her decision to turn them down, but so did the hard-partying lifestyle, which Smyth was not into—she didn't even drink.

"It's all semantics, because if [Eddie] had said to me, 'Let's make a record,' then I would have said yes to that," she told *Stereogum* in 2020. "But joining the band—to me, then, 'Oh god, they fight all the time, him and his brother, and I don't want to get into a volatile situation.' And I was probably heavily hormoned out because I was eight months pregnant, so there was a state of mind that I was in of how I need to take care of myself. But I regretted turning him down. For a long time, I regretted it."

Also getting a call around that stretch was Steve Perry, the frontman for Journey, who was in the midst of some solo success with the 1984 LP *Street Talk*, which spawned five singles, including the smash hit "Oh Sherrie." He wasn't sure where Journey were headed next—if anywhere—with his involvement. While he was never offered the position by Eddie and didn't even get to jam with the band, he was intrigued by the idea.

"I don't know what Eddie's intentions were when he called me," Perry told *Rolling Stone*. "He was just saying, 'Let's get together and play.' It wasn't a promise. It was just, 'Why not? Let's see what this sounds like.' As I said, I think representing their legacy up to that point would have been something vocally that I don't think I was really suited to doing. It's a different kind of singing. David had something vocally that I would say was in kinship with Louis Prima."

Van Halen began to toy with the idea of doing an album with a different singer on each track—an all-star rock and roll precursor to Santana's 1999 collaborative masterstroke *Supernatural*, perhaps, with the hottest frontmen of the period. The label was also beginning to pressure Eddie to do his own solo effort. Then, a storybook turn involving a high-end car-repair shop, a vocalist between recordings, and a sense of immediate kinship altered the course for the band and took them down a road with which they weren't familiar, but which they were game to drive down with the pedal floored.

13

I WANT SOME ACTION

Nobody seemed to be a good fit for the vacancy at the microphone in Van Halen. They were damned if a carbon copy of David Lee Roth was going to be enlisted, but going too far left of center—by, say, getting a female singer— would alienate a diehard fanbase already split between Roth and whatever VH were going to come up with next. Eddie Van Halen was voicing all of those concerns to various friends and acquaintances—including his car mechanic who, of all people, came up with a solution.

Claudio Zampolli was no ordinary grease monkey. A former test driver and development engineer for the luxury sportscar manufacturer Lamborghini, he had moved to Southern California to open up a series of repair shops for exotic Italian automobiles. Eddie had owned several of those over the years, and he'd spent a bunch of time at Zampolli's shop in Van Nuys, often just shooting the breeze.

Eddie wasn't the only musician the mechanic knew; Zampolli had even appeared in the opening scene of the video for Sammy Hagar's 1984 hit "I Can't Drive 55." Catching the guitarist's eye one day was a nice-looking Ferrari 512 waiting for a tune-up, so he asked about it. Zampolli said the car belonged to Hagar, and he suggested Eddie give him a ring about singing for Van Halen.

Right then and there, that's what he did.

FILLING THE VOID

Samuel Roy Hagar was born on October 13, 1947, at Monterey County Hospital in Salinas, California, where his parents were living at the time. His father, Bobby, was a bantamweight boxer in his younger days who had more losses than wins, and later ended up with what we now call PTSD following a stint in World War II, having been drafted to serve as a paratrooper. His mother, Gladys, was born in Los Angeles and was homemaker to Sammy and his three siblings, Robert, Bobbi, and Velma.

When Sammy was two, the family moved south to Fontana in San Bernardino County—a steel mill there was hiring, and Bobby needed to find steady work. Bobby was a mean drunk who would regularly get into fights around town, and he spent a lot of time in the local jail. He beat on Gladys, too, and eventually, when Sammy was ten, she left him and took the kids with her. As Hagar got older, he'd sometimes see his dad, now a homeless drunk, around town. He'd eventually die in the back of a police car after getting arrested at just fifty-six years old.

Hagar trained from a young age to follow in his father's footsteps in the boxing ring, but once he heard the Beatles and then the Rolling Stones, he knew music was his destiny. He started singing and playing guitar before making the move to San Francisco, where he met guitarist Ronnie Montrose, who had just left the Edgar Winter Group and wanted to do something different: hard rock that kept an edge while being fun at the same time. Hagar was the perfect frontman for the task.

The band, also named Montrose, landed a deal at Warner Bros. with the help of Ted Templeman, who produced their 1973 self-titled debut and its follow-up, *Paper Money*. But while there were some very fine songs across the pair of records, like "Rock Candy," "Bad Motor Scooter," and "I've Got the Fire," the timing wasn't right for the group to break into the market. The music was too heavy to keep in regular rotation on AM radio, but not revolutionary-sounding enough—like a Black Sabbath, for example—to create a large following on the underground of FM radio.

Having failed to gain the attention he sought over two albums, Ronnie decided to get rid of Hagar and start anew. The singer was signed to Capitol Records and began a fledgling solo career with a label unsure of what to do with him, releasing five records there from 1976 to 1980 that failed to gain the traction or popularity he was experiencing on the road. One thing Hagar did figure out during the time on Capitol, specifically on his eponymous sophomore effort, was how much he liked red. He really, *really* liked red. It wasn't just his favorite color—it was becoming a way of life.

Hagar describes the allure of the shade in his 2011 book, appropriately titled *Red: My Uncensored Life in Rock*: "Red is fuzzy, if you look at it. You light red with a red light, it doesn't have hard edges, like most colors. It turns into fuzz. It isn't like a defined circle. It gets deep. It looks soft. Yet it's aggressive as hell. It's blood. And it's energy. It means so many different things. Red is my color. It means everything for me. I dream in red."

Geffen signed Hagar—who was now proudly carrying the nickname "Red Rocker"—and released the 1982 LP *Standing Hampton*, which spawned the hits "I'll Fall in Love Again" and "Piece of My Heart," a cover of the song made famous by Janis Joplin. It also included what would soon become one of the most popular live staples in his catalogue, "There's Only One Way to Rock." Later that year, he dropped another album, *Three Lock Box*—his first album to crack the Top 20 on *Billboard* at No. 17. It also yielded his highest-charting single as a solo artist, "Your Love Is Driving Me Crazy."

What really put Sammy Hagar on the map was "I Can't Drive 55," the lead single from his 1984 album *VOA*, which saw him reunite with Templeman. It was inspired by a real-life incident where the singer was pulled over for going 62 in a 55-miles-per-hour zone in New York State. Hagar later said he was scribbling down the lyrics as the officer was writing the ticket.

The song needed a video if it was to reach mainstream audiences, and Hagar delivered with an entertaining accompaniment for what was a textbook anti-authority screed. Enlisting Zampolli to play himself, the clip shows Hagar speeding down the road in his black 1982 Ferrari Berlinetta Boxer, crossing the double yellow line on the highway, being arrested, facing a trial by jury, and finally getting tossed in jail. Of course, the strength of the music allows Hagar and his band to break out and speed away from the chasing police cars.

As with all of the videos from that time, one thing that sticks out is Hagar's choice of dress. He's wearing a sleeveless yellow jumpsuit with straps across the chest, stomach, and legs. His bandmates, meanwhile, wear black jumpsuits with red strap accents.

"I did that for a reason," Hagar explained. "I know it seems crazy, but the album was called *VOA*—'Voice of America'—so I wanted to have a military thing goin', but I was so tired of everyone wearing the same . . . rock had turned into that torn-up, leopard-skin, all the stuff that Van Halen kinda wore—that shit. I wore it in the *Three Lock Box* era—that was my look. Then they came with it, then Poison came with it, then Mötley Crüe. It was all these people doing all these radical things, and I thought, instead of leaving my band to their own version of that look, I said, 'We're wearin' fuckin' uniforms.' [*laughs*] I thought it was funny because it was sort of an R&B thing—it was fun—and people got it. It was like, 'Wow, we have a look.'"

That much was true, and visually apparent during the jail scene at the end of the "I Can't Drive 55" video, when there is a brief moment that recalls the Temptations circa 1967, with Hagar doing his best David Ruffin, leading the rest of the group in a finger-snapping, fist pumping strut. But the biggest question on people's minds: were the straps the singer was decked out in functional?

"Oh yeah; you could tighten them, loosen them, like if you had a big meal the night before and you had a little gut on you, you could loosen up the gut a little bit—it was great," Hagar said. "That was just a big old baggy frickin' mechanics jumpsuit, basically, with a bunch of straps all over it, totally strategically put where you could tie it up close around the legs, tighten it up around the hips, you know? It was definitely cool."

MEET THE BAND

Hagar and Van Halen had crossed paths over the years, appearing on the same festival bills here and there. It was at one such event at Anaheim Stadium, in September 1978, that he and Eddie first met, with the guitarist approaching the singer backstage to tell him he was a big fan of Montrose.

"I thought he was just one of the nicest, sweetest, humblest rock stars on the planet," Hagar later told *Ultimate Classic Rock*. Cut to several years later, and Eddie was approaching him again, but this time to see if he was interested in a job to replace Roth. Yet it was the frontman who left a bad taste in Hagar's mouth, even way back when.

"I was a fan of the band . . . and the music, I always dug it," he said. "I wasn't a fan of Roth's image. If I would've never seen him, I could've handled his vocal style and his attitude was great; he had a great rock and roll attitude—and it kinda fit with the music. I always thought it was a little weird because the music was so good, and he was a little bit too clowny sometimes with the lyrics and sometimes with just his vocal antics."

"They had such a heaviness, but they were really poppy at the same time; I thought that was really cool," Hagar continued. "But when I would see that guy and the way he was suckin' his jaws in and his stances and his attitude and raps it was like, 'Oh my god, who is he trying to kid here?' He was playing the role of a rock star to the bone, and I never liked that role too much. I wanted to be more like a musician and an entertainer. I wanna get up onstage and make you feel happy and have some fun, keep your eyes on me, charismatic—all those things—but I didn't want to be some kind of a caricature of myself or a clown. He bugged me—and that's all I can say."

Having just come off a lengthy tour to support *VOA*, Hagar was in no rush to get back to the grind right away. Still, he was intrigued by the prospect of fronting Van Halen—as long as they weren't looking for a direct sequel to Roth.

"When Eddie asked me to join the band, I thought, 'Well, I'm kind of interested, but I ain't gonna be one of those guys. Don't expect me to put on those clothes and go out and be that guy,'" he said. "And it was like, 'No, no, no, man.' And when I got with Ed, Al, and Mike, they were so down home and we had such a common family bond; all of us had alcoholic fathers, the Van Halens and me, and we were kind of raised poor, and we struggled, and we had all those things in common. We really bonded—it was great."

Shortly after Eddie called him, Sammy went over to 5150 Studios to find that the guitarist, Alex Van Halen, and Michael Anthony had been up since the night before, which they had spent jamming while drinking copious amounts of alcohol and likely partaking in other substances. When the singer arrived, the jamming part continued, the four riffing on what would become "Summer Nights" and "Good Enough." Feeling like they had finally solved their vocalist conundrum, the band offered the gig to Hagar, who remained hesitant due to the level of partying happening before his eyes, and because he was looking forward to taking some time off to decompress. At home later that night, though, he popped in a cassette of the day's proceedings, and it all clicked. He wanted in.

THE SUITS WANT A PIECE

Van Halen were coming off the best-reviewed, highest-charting, and fastest-selling album of their careers; Warner Bros. was incredibly unhappy when Roth left and not sold on bringing in Sammy Hagar to replace him. Relatively speaking, the guy had only recently seen success on the charts, while Van Halen were on a record streak of platinum albums for the label.

David Geffen, the founder of the record company that bore his name, wasn't thrilled about letting Hagar go, either. He'd fought to get him out of the Capitol Records deal just a few years before, and he was only now just seeing it pay off; letting go one of his marquee acts wouldn't happen without a fight. There was also the matter of there being three records left on the singer's contract. "There was a lot of nice energy about it, and there was a lot of controversy goin' on, and there was a lot of politics between the record labels," Hagar recalled.

Geffen Records held all of the cards. Not only did the label have the talent Warner Bros. wanted to abscond with, it also had a distribution deal with Warner Communications that was set to expire at the end of 1985. Ultimately, an agreement was ironed out where Hagar would deliver one more album to Geffen, and the record company would also get a cut of the sales—rumored to be 50 percent—of his first LP with Van Halen.

Then there was the issue of that very name. Warner Bros. had a lot invested in "Van Halen" as a major moneymaker. If the upcoming union tanked, it would sully the brand while driving down revenues for anything the label did in the future, including with the band's back catalogue, like with reissues or hits collections. To avoid a potential black eye, they suggested rebranding the group "Van Hagar." Ted Templeman in particular said he wouldn't produce the next record if they didn't come up with a new moniker.

"At first, I was flattered," Hagar told *Classic Rock*. "But then I thought, 'Fuck that—this is Van Halen! I'm joining them. We're not starting another band.'"

Eddie and Alex agreed, with the former balking at the idea of taking away an identity that was fundamentally their birthright to retain. *Van Halen Rising* author Greg Renoff said, "The Van Halen brothers, I think with good reason, never wavered from the belief that it was *their* band."

"They invited Roth to join *their* band," he added. "I think that was part of the anger that went on when they felt that Roth was using Van Halen as a platform [during *Crazy from the Heat*] to promote himself—which he was. That doesn't mean it was immoral or some high crime. From their perspective, they thought that this guy wouldn't work with them on the record, whether that's accurate or not, in early 1985, and the whole time he's out there promoting his solo record, and then decides he's gonna walk away in the summertime and go make a movie."

Subsequently, it was settled upon that the name would stay the same, though the tag "Van Hagar" would forever be used as a term of both endearment and derision by music fans, journalists, and haters of the group with Sammy at the forefront.

ROTH RIDES AND SAMMY ARRIVES

David Lee Roth hadn't slowed in coming up with the kind of over-the-top antics he'd perfected in Van Halen, often with harmless trickery involved. In September 1985, his latest stunt involved driving across country in his 1951 Mercury lowrider—red with white trim, as made famous in the "Panama" video—following a $5,000 bet with Templeman that he could make it from Los Angeles to New York City in three days, with the top down and going no faster than fifty-five miles per hour. If all went as planned, he'd be arriving in time for the second annual MTV Video Music Awards, where he was the most nominated artist of the night.

Prior to taking off on the journey, he was asked what he thought about the rumors of his replacement. He quipped, "Sammy Hagar's been making good records for years, but Van Halen's been making history."

According to Roth, after a press event kick-off in Los Angeles, he drove the car a few miles before loading it onto a flatbed to transport it to Baltimore, while he flew on a low-budget airline in coach to meet the vehicle before resuming the drive to Manhattan. He appeared there on the Wednesday before the awards show, bedraggled but triumphant, with a few days' stubble and looking like he hadn't showered. That night, after a shave and a change of clothes, he was presented with the Gigolo of the Year award at the Palladium. It was the only award he took home, as he lost all eight entries in the five other categories in which he was nominated at the VMAs that weekend.

Roth didn't seem too unhappy about the goose egg, claiming in his book he "spent the night in the bathroom with the Go-Go's, doing everything you can imagine and then some."

"Honestly, we have talked about that extensively and none of us can remember that happening," said Go-Go Jane Wiedlin. "I am not saying it didn't happen, because those were the wild days, but I don't remember it happening. I do remember at the Tropicana it was female mud wrestling or oil wrestling— some crazy thing when you just go out for kicks and do something stupid. I remember seeing him at that, but that's only because I can actually remember seeing him in sort of a nonmusical setting, and I don't remember ending up in a bathroom stall—that's for darn sure. But, you know, he might have a better memory than me. It's kind of a big blur."

While Roth may or may not have been getting into some debauchery with the Go-Go's, Hagar was at the other end of the spectrum, set to play the inaugural Farm Aid, organized by Willie Nelson, John Mellencamp, and Neil Young to provide relief for struggling U.S. farmers. The show at Memorial Stadium in Champaign, Illinois, was broadcast live on the Nashville Network (TNN), with Hagar providing a contrast to artists like Johnny Cash, Alabama, John Denver, and Tanya Tucker.

"I'm not playin' no country up there, and I'm not adapting my set to anything," Hagar told *MTV News* earlier in the day. "I'm goin' up there and rockin'."

Newspapers had reported the event would be where the "new" Van Halen would be unveiled, though the reports were somewhat off the mark. Following renditions of "There's Only One Way to Rock," "Three Lock Box," and "I Can't Drive 55," Hagar brought out Eddie to perform a crude and slapdash version of Led Zeppelin's "Rock and Roll." Before the song had even started, the frontman put the censors to the test after a fan threw him a homemade sign fashioned on a bedsheet. It was too cumbersome for the singer to unravel and figure out what it said, so he called on the guitarist to assist.

"Come on Eddie, what's this say—can you read?" he asked, leading Van Halen to say something off microphone, which Hagar then repeated. "My dick's too small? Goddamn, how'd they know that? Oh shit . . . okay, well . . . sorry about that. Me and the old lady get along pretty good."

At that point, TNN was getting ready to pull the plug on the broadcast because of Hagar's obscenities, even though the network had to have known it had a golden moment, with two of the top figures in popular music sharing the same stage.

"We didn't have time to work nothin' up," Hagar continued, "And Eddie and I were sittin' at his house, bullshittin', and we just looked in the newspaper and it said Eddie was gonna jam with me. And I thought, 'Well, shit, I didn't know that.' So, at the last minute, we decided to go ahead and do it. We don't know any songs as a band, so we're just gonna jam a couple songs that we all grew up on—okay?"

At the conclusion of "Rock and Roll," Hagar praised Eddie by shouting, "The king! The king!" as the guitarist went into a solo. TNN decided that would be the best time to end the broadcast, cutting away after twelve hours of performances but missing out on the announcement from Hagar—and a cover of the Troggs' "Wild Thing"—that he had in fact joined Van Halen. Backstage after the performance, he said, "It ain't gonna be the old Van Halen or the old Hagar. It's gonna be new stuff, and it's gonna be magic."

14
GET UP

A press release from the Van Halen camp hit the wires at the end of October 1985, officially announcing Sammy Hagar had joined the band as frontman and second guitarist. Glossing over the turmoil and uncertainly of the preceding months, it said, "Sammy's was the first and only name we considered."

Interestingly, and somehow flying under the radar, the new Van Halen made their first public appearance together at the 1985 MTV Video Music Awards. Neither the band nor Hagar were up for a prize or there as presenters, but they showed up as a united front with their wives in tow. Heading into the show, Hagar told *Rolling Stone* the group had ten songs in the can, with Eddie Van Halen echoing, "And at least three albums' worth of material written." Brother Alex then made a quip about the music being "all cover tunes of Barry Manilow."

The smart betting was on an LP by a reconstituted Van Halen being a disappointment. Even though David Lee Roth had been shut out at the VMAs, he was touting a movie deal and looking for a new band. His stock was still rising. Eddie was a once-in-a-generation talent, for sure, but there was no way he could bring in the "I Can't Drive 55" guy as a serious swap for a frontman who was inspiring legions of kids to try jumping off their beds and touching their toes, and teens to dye their hair blond and start singing for a band. What was Sammy doing, other than encouraging people to drive fast and get a ticket?

Fans of the group were still shellshocked, too. The news spread much, much slower in those days, but by the winter, everyone knew what had happened, even if the "why" remained murky. But things seemed to be moving at a faster pace in Van Halen because they had a head start: they'd been working on music since the summer.

Ted Templeman had already told the band he wasn't going to work with them unless they changed their name. When they refused, he committed to working with Roth on his next album. Eddie felt confident in his and Donn Landee's abilities to produce the new record, given the work they had done together on *1984*.

That didn't fly with the Warner Bros. brass, who demanded a "name" producer be brought onboard. Hagar called up Foreigner guitarist Mick Jones, who he'd known since the early '70s. Bringing him in placated the record company and provided fresh ears to hear what the band had been working on for months. Jones was able to polish, assist on some arranging, and push Hagar to deliver some of the best vocal performances of his career. But that's not to say it was all a tranquil walk in the park at 5150 Studios, which became the official Van Halen base for recording. In fact, even with a new singer and a new producer, the circumstances were just as chaotic and insane as during the *1984* sessions.

"We went through some crazy times," Jones told *Ultimate Classic Rock*. "The engineer locked himself in the studio for a day and threatened to burn the tapes. It was a real standoff, you know? It was touch and go whether the tapes were going to survive. It all ended up great, and everybody ended up [being] really cool and happy with what had happened, but it was pretty exhausting. It all paid off in the end."

"HELLO BAAAY-BE!"

Van Halen's new era began when the single "Why Can't This Be Love" was released on February 26, 1986, along with the announcement of a North American tour to support the upcoming LP, *5150*. The synthesizer-led track quickly rose to the top of the rock charts, and by spring it would peak at No. 3 on the Hot 100—the highest position a song with Hagar would reach. The album would be another story, surpassing that mark and astounding the doubters.

5150 landed on shelves on March 24, 1986, and entered the *Billboard* 200 at No. 13, continuing a precedent whereby every LP by the group entered the charts higher than the last. Three weeks later, though, Van Halen had their first No. 1 album. It was a momentous accomplishment that also elicited a heavy sigh of relief, no matter what degree of confidence everyone involved claimed to have in the music with Hagar.

The cover of the record was a play on Greek mythology and the story of Atlas, who bore the weight of the world on his shoulders. The *5150* LP replicated that idea, with a musclebound man holding a mirrored sphere displaying the new-look VH logo, the wings converted into rings. The back cover shows the man crumbling under the weight of the globe, which is split in half, revealing the members of Van Halen rising out of a green-tinted mist. Atlas was portrayed by bodybuilder Rick Valente, who got the part after a casting call at the famed Gold's Gym in Venice Beach.

Reviews, for the most part, were positive, with the comparisons to the previous era of the band unavoidable and expected. Though he opened the record with a comical, almost Roth-like riff on Big Bopper's 1958 hit "Chantilly Lace" by shouting "Hello Baaay-be!" before the squeal of Eddie's guitar on "Good Enough," there were glaring differences between Hagar and his predecessor. The latter was lyrically dexterous, while Sammy was more simplistic, even blunt, in getting his point across—especially when it came to addressing the opposite sex. Both were perfectly suited to the music behind them, though.

It also turned out that the keyboards on "Jump" and "I'll Wait" were merely a precursor of what was down the road. A handful of songs weren't even recognizable as Van Halen until the guitar solo dropped. To that end, it was a wise decision for the band not to do any videos for *5150* and, despite the cliché, let the music do the talking and encourage listeners to come see the live show.

"I think when I joined that band and everybody heard 'Why Can't This Be Love,' they just went, 'Yeah, this is better than we thought,'" Hagar said. "We took a giant step. We didn't just make another Van Halen record; we made a frickin' new Van Halen with songs like 'Love Walks In' and 'Why Can't This Be Love.' There was a 'Good Enough' on there, and songs like that were kind of a 'Panama-ish'—we had some songs. But 'Summer Nights,' that was sophisticated music we started playing, that was frickin' good. 'Best of Both Worlds'? Get outta here. That song still holds up when I play that with my band, and it's still one of the great moments in our set."

The pop injection to Van Halen's music may have been off-putting to fans who wanted the straight-ahead bombast of albums past and fiery guitar-driven songs. But Eddie hadn't abandoned the instrument that made him famous—instead, he leaned heavily into synthesizers to show that when it came to crafting rock songs in the 80s, there was more than one way to skin a cat. Enough ink was spilled about how listeners might react to the lustrous new sounds but, going by the airplay the singles were receiving and the record pace at which fans were snapping up tickets, it didn't appear to be an issue.

"It was a huge change—there's no getting around it, because a lot of the entertainment value they had, a lot of the appeal they had, was Roth and his antics," said William DuVall. "It was the whole package. The humor in the records. Roth's a very underrated lyricist. Even some of the seemingly throwaway lines are kind of genius. He really had a great delivery and a really good stage presence, and he was so compelling as a front person. I was always gonna root for the band as a brand or whatever, but it was a huge difference. You had to accept that it was a very different thing."

"GUESS WHO'S BACK IN CIRCULATION?"

As Van Halen were celebrating, Roth was in damage control. News broke concurrently with the release of the band's first single that the *Crazy from the Heat* film deal had fallen apart as, in the midst of a restructuring, CBS had done away with its movie-production division. The singer was suing the company for $25 million. To offset the downer nature of the report, he rush-released an announcement that a backing band had been found for his full-length solo debut, which he promised would be nothing like the campiness of the *Crazy from the Heat* EP. "More attitude than love songs," he promised in *Rolling Stone*.

Invited to Roth's ongoing party were a trio of hotshot players, headed up by former Frank Zappa band associate Steve Vai, who was making waves in guitar circles with his 1983 experimental and innovative solo debut *Flex-Able*. Also aboard were Talas bassist Billy Sheehan—long courted by Eddie to replace Michael Anthony in Van Halen—and drummer Gregg Bissonette from Detroit, whose playing was rooted in jazz. Roth had been settled on his new band for months, as all the musicians were originally going to be a part of the now-torpedoed movie. He simply shifted the focus from doing songs for a film to making a record and creating an opening to comment on the verbal hostility he was receiving from his former outfit.

"I'm getting a lot of bad-mouthing from those guys," he said, according to the *Palm Beach Post*. "I wasn't aware that the music was rotten and that they put up with me for twelve years. Sure, Big Bad Dave held those guys at bay for over a decade, forced to live a lie. Why would anybody stick around for over a decade? Was it the fame? Was it the money? Probably. I had a great time! I'm still havin' a great time!"

David Lee Roth's *Eat 'Em and Smile* hit record stores on July 7, 1986, entering the *Billboard* 200 at No. 36. Before the summer was out, it would make it to No. 4, proving he was on the competitive track with Van Halen and out to disprove the narrative he had no interest in making music in favor of Hollywood. The cover featured a close-up of the singer's face, colorfully made up with face paint and feathers in his hair, inspired by the indigenous tribesmen he had encountered in Papua New Guinea.

The LP was preceded by the single "Yankee Rose," a slice of hard rock Americana released ahead of the long Fourth of July weekend and doubling as an ode to the Statue of Liberty. The patriotic slant saw the singer crowing at one point, "Here's the national anthem here," perhaps in a bid to get added as a modern question on the United States naturalization test. Speaking of which, Roth looked to appeal to a new audience, specifically the Hispanic population, which in the U.S. jumped nearly 16 percent from 1980 to 1985, by recording a Spanish-language version of the LP, *Sonrisa Salvaje*. The sheer absurdity—and audacity—of Roth deciding to recut his vocals in Spanish shows how over-the-top he could be in his valiant attempt to outdo the Van Halen brothers. Roth had always prided himself on becoming bilingual, and the move gave him a chance to show it off, even if it was more street Spanish than Nino Bravo.

No matter what language it was, the music of *Eat 'Em and Smile* was marked by ferocity—sans synths all over it. The Sheehan-penned "Shyboy" is a bombardment of laser sonics, courtesy of the bassist and Vai. "Ladies' Nite in Buffalo?" has a passionate thump, as does "Big Trouble," which lifted only its name from the Van Halen demo from the '70s. Roth's penchant for covers continued: there are three on the LP, two of them carrying over the "lounge act" persona he so clearly enjoyed embodying. "I'm Easy" was a take on Australian jazz/pop singer Billy Field's "Baby I'm Easy," released in 1981; "That's Life," made famous by Frank Sinatra, closed the record. The former was placed early in the track listing—a risky move, but one emboldened by the praise *Crazy from the Heat* had received the year prior.

Van Halen had gotten the all-important jump on the touring landscape, but Roth provided a visual feast for audiences before setting foot in an arena. The opening vignettes to the "Yankee Rose" and "Goin' Crazy!" clips introduced a series of recurring characters, like the "immigrant grocer" and the Fabulous Picasso Brothers: pompadour-sporting lothario Pete Picasso, played by Pete Angelus; and his obese brother, Buck, played by Roth in a fat suit. The singer dials up the "Hot for Teacher" humor to 11, while the performance components show a band vividly working hard to make their physical presence known, with Vai slinging his guitar about with reckless abandon and Bissonette barely sitting while he played drums. The videos would drive both songs into the Top 100, to No. 16 and No. 66, respectively.

The looming showdown between the two parties wouldn't take place on the charts so much as on the road. But it wasn't a coincidence that Van Halen gave approval to allow one of their new songs, "Dreams," to be used in a video to air on MTV exclusively over the week of Independence Day, right as *Eat 'Em and Smile* was set to arrive. Warner Bros., in conjunction with the channel, got the notion that if the band weren't going to do a traditional clip, they would have to improvise. Inspired by one of the blockbuster films of the year, *Top Gun*, executives reached out to representatives for the naval-demonstration flight squad the Blue Angels, who provided them with archival footage from the '70s of the unit going through its maneuvers in Douglas A-4 Skyhawk II jets.

Van Halen weren't even shown in the "Dreams" video, but it became an unexpected hit, and, due to popular demand, it was added into regular rotation on MTV, if not raining then certainly blocking out the sun on Roth's hopes for a solo parade on the network. Out on the road, though, the venues were covered, and each band would have to create their own atmosphere.

15
SUMMER NIGHTS

The tour to support *Eat 'Em and Smile* began in mid-August 1986, and saw Roth playing many of the same arenas Van Halen had also visited since they launched the *5150* trek the day that record was released in March. The major difference was that the Hagar-led unit were often doing twice the number of nights in any given city. Roth was primarily doing one-night stands, with the occasional two evenings in a town, but Van Halen were drawing three and four shows worth of crowds in places like Philadelphia, St. Louis, and Detroit. "When I joined Van Halen, we couldn't get any bigger in those markets," Hagar said. "We did four Bostons, we did four Philadelphias, we did four New Yorks. It was huge."

Prior to the run kicking off, Roth was already calling foul, telling *Billboard*, "You know they drag around a sign from city to city that says, 'Screw Dave Lee Roth.' It's in orange marker. Look for it. They pull it out every night at a certain point in the show. Initially, sure, you're going to be P.O.'d. But then you think, 'What kind of person is going to force themselves to remember to pack the sign every night?' My exact response? A giggle, and on to the next victim."

The singer may have been setting the stage for the battle to come, but Van Halen weren't going to take the bait, issuing a band statement to *Billboard* that said, "Without making a whole issue out of this, our consciences are clean—we don't play dirty," it read. "Nineteen eighty-six has been a great year for Van Halen, and we couldn't be happier. Dave's just released his album, and we wish him the best."

"IT IS NOW, OFFICIALLY, *5150* TIME!"

It sounded like Van Halen were going to play nice, but of course they didn't—the press wouldn't let them. In interviews to promote *5150*, Alex was fond of making comparisons between the two frontmen using engine-propelled metaphors. Roth was a Piper Cub light aircraft or a Volkswagen, while Hagar assumed the role of a Concorde or a Porsche. In July, the band's first ever *Rolling Stone* cover story contained a plethora of complaints and barbs directed at their old singer, who, they claimed, was "underhanded" in the way he left.

"We were very, very different people," Eddie said, adding that Dave wanted everyone around him to conform to his way of living.

"I would dread having to do a photo session with the guy because I worried about how Roth would think I looked when I got there," Michael Anthony added. "I know Edward and Alex felt the same way, because Roth's saying, 'You gotta dress this way. Go and buy some clothes. Why are you wearing that?'"

Anthony then lampooned their former frontman by saying they weren't a Vegas act any longer and more a band, again making it sound as if Roth was all show and little substance.

The anger and bitterness were omnipresent, but there were other moments in the piece where it looked like Van Halen really did want an armistice between the warring clans. Hagar spoke of initially wanting to reach out and have a conversation with Roth—one he hoped would end with the two of them shaking hands and wishing one another the best in their future endeavors. The band as a whole asked him to dial back his onstage criticisms of their ex-leader. And Eddie admitted he was freaked out by Dave upping and splitting.

"I said a few things in anger, you know, that I should apologize for," the guitarist said, adding bluntly, "I cried, I was bummed. I slagged him in the press because I was pissed, and I was hurt. The thing was Dave is a very creative guy and working with him was no problem. It was living with the guy."

The overall sentiment in the *Rolling Stone* piece, high above everything else, was how much of a lovefest it was between the bandmates. It was destiny, they intoned; none of them had ever felt the way they did now; this was the real Van Halen. Backstage before shows was a minor laugh riot already, full of pranks and jokes, so getting to do it front of people with music was a purely a bonus. Hagar made it a point to say the group were still the same old party band the fans fell in love with in the first place, maybe even more so, because they were a tighter unit with him at the helm.

Audiences were locked in for the ride—rambunctious, rowdy, and ready to revel in Van Halen's success at all the stops along the way. They brought signs of support, expressed anti-Roth invective, and confirmed via their enthusiasm for the new material that the band had made the right move. Each gig being a packed house represented a challenge too, though, because the naysayers wanted to see if the group could pull it off.

The concerts began with a smartly planned one-two punch. Opening every gig with their first single, "You Really Got Me," showed they wouldn't be forgetting about the past. Following it with Hagar's own "There's Only One Way to Rock" was a tip of the hat to their new frontman, acknowledging he too had a history in music—and that it would be a part of the Van Halen future. Additionally, "I Can't Drive 55" was a set staple. Still, Hagar felt the pressure of the band's existing legacy and the need to escape the shadow of Roth—something that didn't come quickly or easily.

"I gotta admit . . . it took me a while," he said. "It made me—boy, I mean, I came out with a fire in my belly and frickin' . . . I came out to prove something for a long time. I don't think I ever settled down without trying to prove something in that damn band until the reunion in '04, and by then it was too late."

A SPLIT IN SETS

Van Halen tore through nine of the ten songs from *5150* nearly every night of the tour. The only exception was the album's oddity, "Inside," an off-the-wall piece that was more a stab at humor than anything else. A cover of Led Zeppelin's "Rock and Roll," a throwback to Sammy and Eddie's Farm Aid appearance, would close out the encore, with an occasional "Wild Thing" by the Troggs or a random Montrose track getting tossed into the set.

Longtime fans were left disappointed, however, as—other than "You Really Got Me," a Kinks cover—there were just two compositions culled from the first six Van Halen records, "Panama" and "Ain't Talkin' 'Bout Love." Conspicuously absent at most shows was their sole No. 1 single, "Jump," which, when it *was* played, saw Hagar pull a fan out of the crowd to do the vocals.

"I didn't feel comfortable singing those songs, and I felt like I always had to prove myself to sing them different," Hagar said. "Once I got over that, it was like, 'No, sing the songs like they are, for God's sake; you didn't write them, but do them right, do them justice or don't do them.' It took me a while to get that much confidence to be able to stand up there and sing a great song like fuckin' 'Jump' or 'Panama.' Those songs are kickin' ass. 'Unchained'? Shit, come on, that's just rockin'."

Despite his insistence that he had come to terms with Van Halen's back catalogue, though, Hagar would only take lead vocals on a total of six tracks penned by Roth throughout his entire, combined tenures with the band.

Roth had a cakewalk, comparatively, in the live setting. No one was coming to shows to hear him tackle "Why Can't This Be Love." They wanted the old stuff, and he was more than willing to oblige, putting "Panama," "Jump," "Unchained," "On Fire," "Ain't Talkin' 'Bout Love," "Pretty Woman," "Everybody Wants Some!!," and "Ice Cream Man" into the mix. Fans ate it up.

Some critics were on the fence for the *5150* tour, many of them taking a wait-and-see attitude until they could stack the shows up against Roth's. "New Van Halen Band Still Finding Its Feet" read a headline in the *Boston Globe* after the first of four sold-out shows at the Worcester Centrum. But, for the majority, the reports were positive, evident in the *Austin American-Statesman* proclaiming, "Van Halen Steamroller Flattens Erwin Center."

In mid-October, as Van Halen's tour wound down, they released live clips to MTV of the songs "Best of Both Worlds," "Love Walks In," "Summer Nights," and "There's Only One Way to Rock." The tracks were recorded at New Haven's Veterans Memorial Coliseum in late August, and, with an audience starved for videos featuring the band, they went into heavy rotation. The majority of the show would be packaged as *Live Without a Net* for a home video release in late November, but missing a handful of songs, including opener "You Really Got Me" and the popular "Dreams" from *5150* among them, mainly due to the time and quality limitations of putting it on a single VHS tape. Even so, it proved frustrating for fans of the original era of the band who went six records and numerous tours without a concert video, and here was the Hagar version dropping one a couple weeks after the first tour ended.

Meanwhile, the *Eat 'Em and Smile* tour was garnering hesitant yet complimentary coverage. The *Asbury Park Press*, for example, ran the headline,

"David Lee Roth Show Proves There Is Life After Van Halen." But the trek wasn't doing great everywhere. "Roth's Rocky Road," went a brief in the *Chicago Tribune*, which noted that in the Midwest the singer was drawing half-filled halls in spots. Roth ramped up the promotion and talked up getting ready to bring the band to South America, Great Britain, Australia, and Japan, but the outing ran out of steam. Not only was a third video idea shelved, but plans to film his February 1987 tour closer in Lakeland, Florida, were scuttled at the last minute as Warner Bros. were done putting any additional money behind the record.

BOILING OVER

Roth was adamant he had done everything in his power to keep Van Halen intact for six months before giving up and departing, having waited on them to get it together and get serious about making a new album. But as the band began their promotional blitz, the bashing of their former frontman went to another level, where every comment seemingly circled back to what a bad person Roth was and how much better off they were without him, even when Van Halen would intimate—sometimes in the same conversation—that they wished him the best. Roth was deft at deflection, and he did his best to joke his way out of a back-and-forth, but when Hagar started to poke at him—saying Roth should be happy he was in Van Halen at all, as he was able to use it as a springboard to his solo career—the gloves started to come off. "David Lee Roth Lets Loose His Anger," rang out one headline, while another read, "'Bitter' David Lee Roth Striking Back Against Former Bandmates."

Three months into the *Eat 'Em and Smile* tour, the singer sounded the worse for wear as he gathered in front of the assembled media in Toronto for a press conference. His voice was breaking due to overuse as he laid out what had happened with the breakup in a startling display of transparency. Absent this time were the slapstick routine and rat-a-tat one-liners; the split was a hard decision on everyone, he said, and he and Eddie had had an emotional parting of ways.

"Two weeks later, I'm reading in *Rolling Stone* what an asshole I am, and how poor little Eddie was forced to spend the last twelve years of his life living a lie, like the fuckin' *National Enquirer* or something," he said. "And here comes his wife, you know, to back it up. . . . So, I stayed quiet for six months, seven months. And I'm just reading diatribe after harangue, after this, after that, you know, again and again and again."

He went on to say it was clear that after the music and the stage production, Van Halen had nothing better to talk about, so they directed their attention his way at their live shows. They were making him a "scapegoat," and not once did Roth talk about them during his concerts. It wasn't necessary to make a comparison, he added, nor did fans have to make pick between the two musical entities. "But Van Halen demands it. Van Halen is demanding—for some bizarre, retarded reason—for the audience to make a choice," he said, as he slowly regained his composure. "'You have to either love us and hate him,' or vice-versa. They demand it, they demand it. Well, I'll rise to the challenge. If we *have* to have a comparison, fine. I eat you for breakfast, pal. I eat you and smile."

Seeing Roth let his guard down was a testament to how much things had deteriorated between him and Van Halen, and especially Eddie. He was known to talk in circles in interviews and dodge pointed questions with adroit wordsmithing and an uncanny ability to shift the subject. This wasn't for show anymore—the feelings were raw, the emotions coming on like festering open wounds.

One has to wonder how it all might have transpired if Roth had been the one to put out an album and tour first. Facing down the press in that scenario, he would probably avoid and redirect and find a new catchphrase to address his time in the band and the split. As to why his ex-bandmates were so vindictive—seemingly from the outset—there was most likely some actual pain at being left behind.

"You don't fight in public," said former manager Noel Monk. "You don't make a show of yourself being, 'Oh, he's an asshole.' You don't do that. It's not only immature, it's in bad taste. Leave the fans at least a little bit of dignity."

"From the Van Halen brothers' perspective, there was a lot of anger and hurt feelings that they'd let this guy in the group and took him on when no one else would around Pasadena," said Greg Renoff. "They defended him, and then he turns around and burns them. I presume that's probably what fueled that intense need to put him down: 'This guy used us for six months,' while they, for lack of a better term, 'created' David Lee Roth."

Early 1987 saw Roth's tour conclude, and both his and his former band's respective campaigns went into the books. It appeared as if Van Halen had won the first round of the battle, but a bitter war of words was just beginning to rage, not only with Roth but between the fans, too.

16

THE BEST OF
BOTH WORLDS

Everyone between a certain age range, one that crosses generations, has an opinion on the Dave versus Sammy debate. No one is completely down the middle, no matter what they say. If they do profess to be neutral, dig down and ask their favorite songs, albums, and shows, and the choice is there. From fellow musicians to comedians to former employees, they all have a preference.

"When I heard that Dave was out and that Sammy was in ... I was definitely not feeling it," said Michael Sweet. "There are people that say they like the Sammy era better. I think those people—most of the time—that say that didn't live as a fan through the first era. They weren't old enough to experience early Van Halen. If you took all those people and put them in a time machine and took them back to early Van Halen? I guarantee you, most of them would say, 'Oh yeah—early Van Halen is my favorite form of Van Halen.' Because that was unmatched; that energy and that fire was unmatched—it wasn't even close—with Sammy. David brought such a unique quality to Van Halen in his personality and his delivery ... he had such a charisma as a frontman and as a singer that Sammy just doesn't have. Van Halen with Sammy just didn't do it for me."

"I didn't give a shit. Van Halen was over," former band manager Noel Monk said, recalling the moment he heard of Hagar's arrival. "[Then] they brought [Gary] Cherone in ... what did I think? Nothing. This is not Van Halen; this is Van Cherone! This is Van Hagar. This is Van who? But without Edward and David, and I gotta press this point, there is no Van Halen! You cannot take the two seminal people who created that band and take one of them away. With all due respect, Van Halen is Edward and David. That's it. There's no 'Van Cherone'—there's no 'Van' anybody. I'd like to see any of those other 'Vans' jump off a drum riser fifteen feet in the air, do a split, and when they landed, we'd take 'em to the hospital. No one could do what David could do."

"I think you gotta go with Roth because you got, like, 'Ain't Talkin' 'Bout Love' and songs like that are just old-school good Van Halen," said comedian and actor Adam Carolla. "Plus you've got all the crazy spinning kicks onstage and chaps and everything, so you gotta go Diamond Dave on that one."

"I gotta go with Diamond Dave," said Jon Taffer, nightlife impresario and host of *Bar Rescue*. When I used to run [West Hollywood nightclub] the Troubadour, Diamond Dave used to come hang out, and I remember a lot of wild Diamond Dave nights . . . there were some amazing stories at the Troubadour, and he was involved in quite a few of them, actually [*laughs*]."

"I think Sammy's got the vocal chops," said Nina Blackwood. "Sammy's like a musician's singer. David really is the clown prince of rock and roll. Between his gymnastics—I mean, there's nobody like David Lee Roth—that personality, that mouth of his, and his unique songwriting. He's a very clever guy—he really is! I don't think they would've been as big as they initially were without Dave."

"I just think it's human nature," said William DuVall of people wanting to choose sides. He faced circumstances not dissimilar when he took on vocals for Alice in Chains some years after Layne Staley died. "Especially anything that achieves a certain level of popularity and finds a home in people's hearts, they really take it personally. You see it with sports teams all the time and it's like that. You have a certain segment of the population that falls on one side or the other. They're going to pick their camp and they're gonna stick with it. Whenever you get that level of popularity, you're going to have some fierce emotion around it."

"It was never fun as a fan to listen to the bickering and the back and forth and the insults, whether it be David Lee Roth dogging out the brothers or vice versa," said Phil Anselmo, whose first song when he jammed with Pantera when trying out was "Outta Love Again" off *Van Halen II*. "You don't wanna take sides with your favorite players. Even if you wanna look at a band like KISS;

when Ace was on the outs or Peter Criss was on the outs, you always heard little reasons why and … it just sucked. And back to Van Halen, for sure, I don't want to have to pick between my guys. I love Van Halen—and that's that."

A FAMILIAR SITUATION WITH A TWIST

Bands switching vocalists is nothing new these days, and even in 1985, it wasn't a novel event. Pink Floyd ousted Syd Barrett in 1968, and David Gilmour took on a greater vocal role. Steve Marriott quit the Small Faces in 1968, his place soon taken over by Rod Stewart and the "Small" dropped from their name. Peter Gabriel left Genesis in 1975, with drummer Phil Collins moving to the microphone. Yet you don't typically see drunken arguments occurring between the staunchest enthusiasts of the prog-rock Gabriel era in Genesis and the more pop leanings of the Collins-led edition. Maybe hard rock fans are more passionate about this sort of thing?

Deep Purple with Ian Gillan singing their early hits ended when he quit in 1973 and David Coverdale stepped in, joining Glenn Hughes as co-vocalist. There wasn't really enough time to compare them, though, as the group had imploded by the summer of 1976; and, when they reunited in 1984, it was with Gillan. Sort of similar was Ronnie James Dio coming into Black Sabbath after Ozzy Osbourne was fired in 1979. The former left in 1982, before the group descended into self-parody, leaving only a small window to examine each period.

The closest comparison at the time was AC/DC. The Australia-based outfit had achieved overseas notoriety with singer Bon Scott and broke through in the United States with the 1979 LP *Highway to Hell*. Tragically, Scott died in early 1980, and he was swiftly replaced by Brian Johnson. The group released *Back in Black* that summer, which went on to become the biggest-selling hard rock album of all time. By 1985, they had since long peaked and were on the decline, and the fans started to deliberate between one another as to who was better, Bon or Brian?

Other than hackles getting raised by the rumors that, lyrically, *Back in Black* was a product of Scott's notebooks, and the reason sales and popularity dipped in the mid-'80s was because that well ran dry, the point was moot. Scott was never coming back, no matter how much one preferred *Powerage* over *Flick of the Switch*.

The difference with Van Halen was that both lead singers were readily available, willing to compete in the press and talk smack about the other with little prodding. Roth said the group was nothing without him. The hits and sold-out tours with Hagar told another story. And, unlike AC/DC, the sales didn't drop off . . . or did they?

THE SALE OF THE TAPE

"God bless Dave, but he refuses to acknowledge that Van Halen with me was even more successful than Van Halen with him, and that's very stupid of him," Hagar told *Planet Rock* in 2019. "That'd be like me not acknowledging what he did for the band before I joined: that would be stupid, wouldn't it?"

The narrative perpetuated by Hagar—that Van Halen sold exponentially more albums and drew more audiences with him in the band—is one of the main assertions his followers love to latch onto, but it also makes Roth fans grind their teeth. The way that version goes, Hagar was already "as big as Van Halen"—as he told Dan Rather in 2016—and, when he joined the group, everything essentially doubled. And while it can't be denied that, on the *5150* tour, they were indeed doing three and four nights in major cities, that didn't last; by 1991, the next time there was a proper VH headlining run, there were only a handful of even two-night stands.

Even factoring in inflation, comparing box-office numbers is always dicey, and with tours between Van Halen's lead singers it's virtually impossible. Where do you even begin to tabulate? Does the first tour with Roth get excluded because they were openers, whereas with Hagar that was a rarity? What about the 1988 Monsters of Rock tour, where they headlined stadiums but were packaged with the up-and-coming Metallica? Finally, there's the number of shows fronted by each singer; Roth did so for more than a thousand, while Hagar was there for barely over half that amount.

Absolutely not up for discussion is that Sammy Hagar in Van Halen delivered four No. 1 albums—in a row—and with David Lee Roth that didn't happen once. The usual excuse for the latter is the juggernaut that was Michael Jackson's *Thriller* kept *1984* off the top spot. Eddie Van Halen gave credence to that rationale in a 2012 interview with CNN when he said *1984* was just about to hit No. 1 when Jackson had the accident filming a Pepsi commercial that left him with second-degree burns and *Thriller* leapt back to the top spot.

In reality, Jackson's accident took place on January 27, 1984, and *Thriller* was already locked into the pole position through all of that month, on the heels of the epic video for the title track premiering on MTV the previous month and then playing in nonstop rotation. At that point, *1984* was just entering the charts, first at No. 18; by the week the burning of the pop star was reflected on *Billboard*, it had only reached No. 4. When Van Halen's LP peaked on March 17, Jackson's grip hadn't loosened yet: *Thriller* held on for three weeks before it fell to No. 3 after being overtaken by the soundtrack to the film *Footloose*. The April 21 charts saw *1984* back at No. 2, behind the compilation for the Kevin Bacon vehicle—which ironically contained a Hagar song—where it languished for two weeks before slipping down for good.

When a Roth-fronted Van Halen got their next opportunity, with *A Different Kind of Truth*, in February 2012, the timing was incredibly unfortunate. The day it was released was also the day of the Grammys, and that night's telecast saw Adele give a stunning performance of her single "Rolling in the Deep" and take home awards in all six of the categories she was nominated in, including Album of the Year and Song of the Year. Had the late Michael Jackson himself moonwalked onto the stage drinking a Pepsi that night, it's doubtful that even he would have outshone the U.K. songstress. The week the awards show was reflected on the charts, VH with Roth peaked at No. 2 once again.

Calculating which iteration of Van Halen sold more albums is what a large contingent boil it down to, doing the equivalent of a "scoreboard" point and looking at how many times platinum-sellers exist on each end. Both the band's self-titled debut and *1984* have been certified by the Recording Industry Association of America as going diamond, which means they have sold in excess of ten million copies in the States. The closest a Hagar LP has come to that is the six million sales of *5150*.

The problem with this, though, is that the RIAA stats aren't regularly updated. To get an album—or single—recertified costs $350 per title, with an independent audit then conducted. The only way that can occur is if the label on which the record was released, or the artist, or the band's proxy, requests it. Even though it's a nominal fee, most catalogue bands don't do it. Partly this is because there's no benefit to doing so on a regular basis, while others likely don't want the actual numbers to go against what they put forth publicly as fact.

Take, for example, Gene Simmons, who is on record as saying KISS have outsold the Beatles and Elvis *combined*. While he's referring to the entirety of the KISS brand, it's also been widely published that the band have sold one hundred million albums worldwide—with an alleged forty million in the U.S.—which is apocryphal at best. Save for *Destroyer*, none of the band's records with the original 1970s lineup has been recertified since that time period. And to do so would ruin the myth, so it's better to keep the charade going.

Van Halen don't fall into that category. The only ones who care about such statistics are those who stand firmly on one side of the "Sammy versus Dave" debate and want to back it up with hard numbers. The last time the band did an RIAA recertification across the board was in the summer of 1994. It was around then that management began to kick the tires on a greatest hits package, and those numbers would assist the campaign in a variety of ways, both in and outside of the meeting rooms. Ahead of the 2004 reunion tour with Hagar and the release of a two-disc best-of compilation, all the titles from that era of the band were recertified for marketing purposes, with the exception of 1991's *For Unlawful Carnal Knowledge*. Even then, up against the 1994 Roth numbers, it was no contest.

Equality being what it is, Roth recorded seven studio albums—six with reported sales data—in his time with the group, while Hagar did just four. At the time of this writing, the former has thirty-four million records under his belt with Van Halen, according to the RIAA, while Hagar checks in with sixteen million. If one were to take the four lowest-selling Roth records and put them against Hagar's four, the Roth era would trail by Hagar just two million copies. And what if Hagar did two more LPs with the band to even it up? It's conjecture to say whether they would or wouldn't have together moved eighteen million copies.

Also, there's the issue of not just two separate singers but two different ways in which sales were tabulated during their respective tenures. Bringing KISS back into the conversation, when the band decided to do their solo records in 1978, the LPs were advertised as having "shipped platinum," meaning at least a million copies of each album went out to stores. The RIAA counts the albums that are shipped, and therefore the band could—without technically lying—

boast in marketing they were all solo stars who went platinum. But what the RIAA then does is subtract what is returned. That's why, to this day, the KISS solo albums are still reported in many places to be platinum *sellers*, when in reality they were platinum *shippers*, with none of the four getting near the one million *sold* mark.

There was a drastic shift in early 1991, when *Billboard* adopted Nielsen SoundScan as the preferred way to track sales. This method, which uses computer data to accurately report actual sales of albums in real time, makes certification a more exact process, and it soon became the industry standard. Had sales for the first six Van Halen albums been counted in that manner, would the numbers hold up? And what about the stores that don't use SoundScan to report sales?

Chartmasters bills itself as the "most accurate chart-related place you will ever find." It may have the final answer in this case. One of the things the site does is collect raw data from album sales and interpret the numbers collected to better inform those who are interested in how to better assess the perceived numbers. And while Van Halen have never had a strong foreign audience, they also dig up the figures from countries outside the U.S., ultimately giving a more rounded representation.

What Chartmasters did was further confirm that the Roth era was the top seller. Globally, the David Lee Roth albums have sold a total of approximately fifty million units; with Sammy Hagar, the figure is 24.5 million. Overall, with live records and compilations factored in, the Van Halen catalogue has sold in excess of one hundred million units worldwide. Perhaps most surprisingly—and leaving little question as to just how popular they are—beginning with their self-titled debut in 1978 and through *Balance*, Van Halen are one of only five artists to have ten consecutive multi-platinum albums. The other four are the Beatles, Queen, U2, and Madonna.

Of course, whether questionable or fact-checked, the numbers only tell part of the story when it comes to pitting the two frontmen against each other. To some, it doesn't matter at all: they've already chosen one to side with while spitting venom at the other.

17

FEELS SO GOOD

The year 1986 couldn't have gone much better for Van Halen, looking at all that was accomplished. The band's label was elated at the sales of *5150*, and the fans looked to be growing in numbers, with a four-night run at the Cow Palace in San Francisco putting an exclamation point on the tour. There was major misfortune to follow in early December, though, with the passing of Jan Van Halen, the family patriarch. He had suffered a severe heart attack several months prior and never quite recovered.

Jan's passing at sixty-six years old sent Eddie into a drunken spiral. Both he and Alex would end up facing interventions that sent them off to rehab in the months that followed. The latter stopped drinking completely in 1987, and a large part of that decision had to do with his father's passing. Alex was just about thirty-four when he made the momentous change in his life, and in 2020 he told *Modern Drummer* it had reached the point where he felt the need to see clearly.

"We spent the first thirty years of our lives, trying to cloud what reality was, and you have a different interpretation of it," he said, laughing before adding that when you reach a certain age, "You'd better change your ways or you ain't gonna make it any further. . . . We're very lucky, so don't fuck it up. That's the message. When our dad passed away, after our long life of touring and making music—and yeah there was alcohol involved—but I looked at him and, unspoken, I said, 'I'll try to make it better.' So, I quit. You do have an obligation and responsibility to [work] without artificial inspiration."

Eddie would go into rehab for alcohol abuse later that year, but it wouldn't take, and he was even charged with a DUI on his motorcycle in September after getting out of Betty Ford and going on a drinking binge, setting a pattern that would repeat itself throughout his life. Alex was a much harder and heavier drinker than his brother, pounding untold amounts that would amaze—and shock—his bandmates. But when he was done with the bottle, he was done. Eddie struggled, and the longer it went on, the more painful it got for his friends, family, and eventually his fans to watch.

The Van Halen brothers were introduced to alcohol at an early age. Eddie said he was drinking and smoking by the time he was twelve years old and would show up to high school drunk; Alex was fond of shot-gunning multiple cans of malt liquor just to get the night—or day—started. It was a combustible combination, but at least with one of them on the wagon, things weren't as bad as they could've been; Alex would be able to keep a clear eye on his younger sibling.

SAMMY GOES SOLO

As part of the negotiations to join Van Halen, Sammy Hagar still owed one studio album to his former label, Geffen Records. He'd already started off 1987 with a solo hit, "Winner Takes It All," the theme to the Sylvester Stallone film flop *Over the Top* that had a plot centered on an arm-wrestling competition. Eddie played bass on the song, and Hagar had him do the same on the upcoming full-length, as well as having him co-produce it.

The self-titled Hagar record was released on June 23 and became his highest-charting solo effort, making it to No. 14 on *Billboard*, no doubt assisted by word of Eddie's involvement. There was also a contest held by MTV to name the record, and by mid-August it was rechristened *I Never Said Goodbye*. Hagar didn't do any live dates, and promotion was minimal, other than a few appearances on television shows like *Good Morning America* and *Late Night with David Letterman*, as well as a turn as guest VJ on MTV.

Eddie didn't play with Hagar on *Letterman*, but the two appeared together on a July edition of *Rockline*. The singer declared the war with Roth to be over, saying there was no more animosity: Van Halen just wanted to "get on with it." A funny moment occurred during the show when "Claudio" from Los Angeles called in, and Hagar began talking him up as the one responsible for bringing him and Eddie together, thinking it was the Italian car dealer and mechanic Claudio Zampolli. In fact, it was bassist Michael Anthony pranking them.

Other than "Give to Live," which peaked at No. 23 on the *Billboard* Hot 100, there was no breakout single from *I Never Said Goodbye*, but the video for the song "Hands and Knees" was notable as it included the rest of Van Halen in a guest spot. The clip sees Hagar on the deck at his beach house, reaching out to Eddie, Alex, and Michael to come jam, but none of them is available, so he uses a computer "cybernetic program" to create a backing band. The two robotic models blow up by the end of the song, throwing Hagar to the ground just as the rest of VH arrive to play.

"Hands and Knees" wasn't the first video—other than the *Live Without a Net* performances—to feature Van Halen with Hagar. Late in 1986, all four members took on the role of the backing band in the Hank Williams Jr. clip for "My Name Is Bocephus." In it, the singer walks into a country bar where everyone is wearing sunglasses—one of his trademarks—and roots out the imposters before taking the stage, with Hagar and a short-haired Eddie on guitar, Michael on bass, and a bald Alex on drums. Williams had gotten word that the guys were using his nickname as a call to party: "Bocephus mode." The track ended up becoming one of the few country videos to receive airplay on MTV.

Late February of 1987 saw Valerie Bertinelli host *Saturday Night Live*, with Eddie sitting in and jamming with G. E. Smith and the Saturday Night Live Band on a song called "Stompin' 8H." He also appeared in a throwaway sketch titled "Dinner at the Van Halens'," where overattentive roadies—played by Kevin Nealon, Dana Carvey, and Dennis Miller—set the lighting, table, and chairs for a meal between the guitarist, his wife, and another couple played by cast members Phil Hartman and Victoria Jackson.

THE WAR CONTINUES?

Just as Van Halen were gearing up to head back into the studio to work on the follow-up to *5150*, seemingly out of nowhere came a scathing condemnation from David Lee Roth in an August 1987 interview with *Playboy*. The talk was apparently going fine, but when the singer was asked what he most regretted about the breakup with his former band, he gave a "tight-lipped stare."

"I regret most that Van Halen saw fit to kick me when I was down and they were on their way up," he said. "It was unnecessary and particularly vicious, and I think they are a bunch of sick little morons for doing it. I'm angry."

At that point, Roth paused before retelling the familiar story of how he and Eddie had ended things with a handshake and tears, but later he read about how bad things were in their decade together. He said Van Halen then tried to say he'd left to be a movie star, but when nobody bought it, the story changed to them wanting a better singer. "Now, after months of this, I'm bitter. They're little-time people, in a little-time band, making little-time music because of it," Roth continued, adding that the reason Van Halen didn't do a proper video for *5150* was because the above would be laid out for all to see.

Asked if he thought the press blew the split out of proportion, the singer was steadfast in pressing all the blame squarely on the band, saying they were the ones who kept it going. And to the point about Van Halen doing better without him because they finally had a record to make it to No. 1 on the charts, Roth said the majority of people don't know how the music industry works, so it was a moot point.

"Besides," he added, "Van Halen still sold millions less than the last time I was in the band . . . so fuck you, pal."

Harsh as the words were, they were all the more surprising because Dave had apparently telephoned Eddie to express condolences in the wake of his father's passing. It turned out the interview predated the call, having been conducted while the singer was on the road in late 1986. For whatever reason, *Playboy* held onto the piece and didn't run the interview until the next summer.

OH . . . YOU ATE ONE TOO

Van Halen were firing on all cylinders, getting along personally and professionally, and excited about the music they were making together. *OU812* was released on May 24, 1988, and was the first not to have a production credit. The band considered it to be self-produced, but they included a nod to their longtime engineer on the back cover, which states, "Recorded by Donn Landee." There was also a dedication to Jan Van Halen in the liner notes: "This one's for you, Pa." The album debuted at No. 5 on the *Billboard* 200 and hit the top spot the next week.

The name of the album was a pun on the phrase "Oh, you ate one too," but many saw it as a none-too-subtle response to the title of Roth's full-length solo effort *Eat 'Em and Smile*. *OU812* has mature and subdued black-and-white cover art, with the faces of each member lit from one side—an obvious take on the second LP by the Beatles, *With the Beatles*, but flipped. The back cover shows a variation of the 1893 piece *Affe mit Schädel*, or *Ape with Skull*, by the German sculptor Hugo Rheinhold, a work inspired by Rodin's *The Thinker*. Provided by Austin Productions, who produced it in 1962, the sculpture was done by the Spanish artist Francisco Ramo, who titled it *Darwin Ape*.

Reviews for *OU812* skewed toward the negative. Though the group continued to expand their sonic palette with the freedom Hagar gave them to delve into ballads and basic pop, that meant less in-your-face rock and roll for longtime fans. This was where the Van Hagar–era band came into their own, fully breaking free of the past and establishing their own identity. It may be their most musically diverse album, but it's also became heavily dated for its over-embracing of some of the sounds of the period. Hagar would later say that after getting sober, Alex's drumming suffered and wasn't as adventurous, while the production on the LP buried the bass guitar.

Another issue was the lyrics. Hagar had never been known for putting his love of women and sex elegantly, but *OU812* has some of his most ham-fisted odes yet—something he readily admitted. Lead single "Black and Blue," with its sleazy, bluesy feel, could have been one of the greats in the VH catalogue, were it not for the words. The opening verse spoke frankly about slipping and sliding and sticking it in before the singer punctuated it with the unfortunate sound of what Hagar must sound like when thrusting. There's no way to parse his lyrics other than calling them god-awful.

In stark contrast was the opener, "Mine All Mine." It was unlike anything Van Halen had done at that point, both lyrically and musically, and showed both their growth in those two respects and also how they were still able to call back to some of the things that turned fans on in the first place—in this case, the scorching guitar work by Eddie. It was still taking some digging to find his fretwork, given his continued fascination with keyboards, which drove almost every track.

"I'm not saying I've mastered the guitar, and I'm not saying guitar isn't fun. But keyboards are more fun to dick around with, because I make more mistakes on them and making mistakes is fun," Eddie told *Rolling Stone*. "And then our manager or somebody will say, 'Not too many keyboard songs on the record, okay? Come on, Ed. You're a guitarist.' And I go, 'Yeah, okay, I forgot.'"

REACHING FOR THE TOP

Also embracing keyboards this time around was Roth, who, four months earlier, had released *Skyscraper*, his second and final record with the *Eat 'Em and Smile* band backing him. His goal for the LP was to make it more dance-oriented, which led him to bring in touring keyboardist Brett Tuggle for a more central role in the composition and recording process. The change is felt immediately on the unabashed pop cheese of lead single "Just Like Paradise," a track so mainstream that the producers of the teen drama *Beverly Hills 90210* wanted to use it as the show's theme song. (The message never made it to Roth.)

"Experimental" is the best word to describe much of *Skyscraper*—the rest was a transition into an arena that was quickly becoming old hat—but it still made it to No. 6 on the *Billboard* 200. However, fans who stuck with the singer for the loud guitars and attitude were now hearing synthesized leads and programmed bass; the confusion and betrayal those same fans had felt about *5150* came rushing back, and Roth lost much of his core audience—along with his band. Bassist Billy Sheehan said the situation was no longer fun and left before the tour began, replaced by drummer Gregg Bissonette's brother, Matt. Guitarist Steve Vai, who was getting more abstract in his own musical leanings, departed when the lengthy trek wrapped up its wind through Europe, Japan, and Australia.

As with *5150*, Van Halen initially decided not to make any videos for *OU812*, but they ultimately succumbed to pressure from Warner Bros., which wasn't seeing the sort of sales numbers it was used to. The band ended up filming two performance clips, paid for by the label, which went into heavy rotation on MTV.

The video for "When It's Love" has the group playing in a darkened bar to a couple swaying back and forth on the dancefloor who ostensibly leave mid-ballad, leaving no audience but a female bartender and a dishwasher, who end up making out by the end of the clip. "When It's Love"—a readymade prom theme cum wedding song—would be one of the band's highest-charting singles with Hagar: it peaked at No. 5, second only to "Why Can't This Be Love," which topped out at No. 3.

Brighter in every way, the black-and-white "Finish What Ya Started" clip was filmed against a plain white background and intercut footage of dancing women pulled from the pages of a male cowboy fantasy pictorial with shots of the bandmembers miming their own individual performances. The song made it to No. 13, and, with "Black and Blue" and "Feels So Good" going to No. 34 and 35, respectively—without video assistance—marked the only time in the Hagar era that all of the singles from one album cracked the *Billboard* Hot 100. (It had happened previously, during the Roth era, with *1984*.)

MONSTERS OF ROCK

Over Memorial Day weekend, and three days after *OU812* arrived in the hands of fans, Van Halen kicked off their first ever stadium tour of the United States. Dubbed "Monsters of Rock"—ripping off the name of a long-running heavy metal festival at Castle Donington, England—the bill featured German rock legends Scorpions, a close-to-splitting-up Dokken, ready-to-break-big Metallica, and Led Zeppelin clones Kingdom Come. The jaunt played to upward of a hundred thousand people per night for almost thirty shows throughout the summer. It was something the band had talked about doing for some time, but that Roth had long said he wanted to avoid: playing fewer shows for more people. Though sales were soft in many markets, it turned a profit.

Behind the scenes, while Alex had succeeded in swearing off alcohol, Eddie was having a much more difficult time. "You know, my dad died a year ago December, from drinking, and he asked if we'd stop drinking and shit, and partying, and I tried to do it for him," he told *Rolling Stone*. "I tried to do it for my wife. I tried to do it for my brother. And I didn't do any good for me."

Hagar was having his own issues, dealing with a broken tailbone from a stage accident on Monsters of Rock's opening night and battling various upper-respiratory ailments all through the tour. He was looking forward to a rest when the run ended, but the newly sober Alex was bored at home and having financial issues—one of the reasons they decided to go back out in the fall, risking overexposure in some regions. At the same time, the singer's marriage to his longtime wife Betsy was crumbling, and he wasn't helping matters by cheating nonstop on the road.

"It didn't feel good . . . cheatin' on your wife," he said. "I don't care what anyone says: rock star, get a little buzz on and start messin' around and have four or five girls in a room and doin' all those things that everyone dreams of. Single man? I probably would've killed myself. But as a married man, you do it and the next day you'd wake up feelin' like shit. I'd feel like a dirty dog. And even when my marriage was over, I just couldn't live with myself. That's why I had to get divorced, because I said, 'I just can't go home and face my wife after doin' this so much. I can't lie to her anymore. I can't be that person.' We had to split up. I don't recommend it. You don't feel good about yourself after a while."

Shortly after the *OU812* tour, which finally ended with two nights in Honolulu after an early 1989 trip to Japan, Betsy had a nervous breakdown. While Sammy had received pushback from Alex and Eddie about his commitment to the group when he requested the band take time off after Monsters of Rock, now he was demanding it. There would be no Van Halen for the rest of the year.

18

TOP OF THE WORLD

Though recording didn't officially get underway for the next Van Halen album until the early spring of 1990, Alex and Eddie had been coming up with fresh material, as always. This time, though, it was at the newly renovated 5150 Studios, which had doubled in size, with a drum room added. It also recently received a long-overdue zoning clearance from Los Angeles County officials. No longer was it on the books under the guise of a racquetball court.

Producing the LP would be Andy Johns, who had worked as an engineer on the first six Led Zeppelin recordings, and on classics like the Stones' *Exile on Main St.* and Eric Clapton's self-titled debut. As a producer, he'd recently done work with Cinderella and hair metal also-rans House of Lords and Tangier. Alex especially wanted Johns: he'd been chasing that big, John Bonham–esque drum sound for his whole career, and now he had the opportunity to work with the guy who made it happen.

Taking a break at the outset of the sessions, the band headed down to Cabo San Lucas, Mexico, to play a pair of shows at a bar and restaurant they had financed with their manager, Ed Leffler, and a local investor. Hagar had long ago fallen in love with the region, which inspired him to write the lyrics to "Cabo Wabo" on *OU812*. When he and Leffler decided to go in on the building, Hagar asked the other three members of the group if they wanted a part of it, telling them it would be a great opportunity. It was a bit of a sell, but the singer was convinced that the area was going to blow up and that the venue would become a hot property.

The grand opening weekend of the Cabo Wabo Cantina in April 1990 was covered by MTV in a special called *Viva Van Halen Saturday*. Most importantly, it kept the band in the public eye in an ever-changing music scene where Sunset Strip glam had been ruling the day. Groups like Poison, Warrant, and White Lion took their image and musical cues from early Van Halen but added a dose of glam and theater. Guns N' Roses had recently broken through, and an even bigger change was on the way.

Sequestered away from all of that were Eddie, Alex, Michael, and Sammy, as their latest release would take over a year to put together, from March 1990 to April 1991. Hagar, in particular, was out of sorts; his wife's mental health issues required constant attention, precluding him from making the recording process communal for the duration, as it had been in the past, where decampment to the studio together was all that mattered. Now, he was being torn in different directions.

"The songwriting was drawn out," the singer said in 2015, in a video posted to his official YouTube channel to mark the twenty-fourth anniversary of the record. "I would get behind on the lyrics, because I wouldn't have time to focus on it."

Additionally, Hagar was experiencing tension with Johns, who had become Eddie's new drinking buddy in the studio. One day in early 1991, the producer accidentally erased a strong vocal take the singer had done, causing him to lose his patience and refuse to work with the Englishman anymore. In a move that, on paper, seemed like an odd one, the band reached out to Ted Templeman to help in finishing Hagar's vocals.

The reality was, Templeman had remained in the Van Halen orbit since the departure of David Lee Roth. Eddie and Donn Landee had visited his office at Warner Bros. in early 1986 and asked for help with the song sequencing for *5150*. Eddie also brought him in to co-produce the 1990 sophomore record for the radio-friendly Los Angeles rock outfit Private Life. In a less constructive set of circumstances, it was Templeman who Valerie called to help get Eddie to the emergency room after her father cold-cocked the guitarist on New Year's Eve, 1989, breaking his cheekbone in an attempt to stop the couple physically struggling over their car keys.

Templeman was Hagar's choice, too—their union had worked well before, both on the first two Montrose albums and the singer's last solo effort before joining Van Halen, the hit *VOA*. Johns wasn't thrilled with the turn of events, to say the least, so Templeman did his best to stay out of the way, except for when doing Hagar's vocals. When the two producers set about to collaborate on the final mix, it became more challenging: they routinely clashed, especially when Johns was drinking, but somehow they made it work, and the record finally wrapped up.

FUCK CENSORSHIP

Hagar wanted to call the record *Fuck Censorship*, in an unsubtle rebuttal to the Parents Music Resource Center, his idea being to wrap the album in brown paper to get it past the retail uproar. Everyone at the label was against the idea, but another one presented itself when the singer was training one day with boxer Ray "Boom Boom" Mancini, who told him the word "fuck" was actually an acronym and really meant "for unlawful carnal knowledge." This etymology has since been disproved, but at the time the rest of the band thought it was a great idea.

For Unlawful Carnal Knowledge landed in stores on June 17, 1991, making it a rare Monday release instead of a Tuesday, and debuted at No. 1 on the *Billboard* 200—a first for Van Halen and their inaugural entry into the era of Nielsen SoundScan, which the publication had begun relying on to track sales beginning the previous month. It spent three weeks in the spot and was certified platinum by August. Three years between albums certainly hadn't dulled interest in the group. The title was a stroke of genius: it became a beacon for attention from the media, and it was blasted by conservatives, who bristled at anything remotely obscene. Fans required little prodding to refer to it as "*FUCK*" or "*F.U.C.K.*," and they could tell anyone who was offended, "What—it's the name of the record!"

The cover art for the record wasn't as understated as *OU812*, but it was still fairly simple, with the ringed VH logo overlaid on a red background made to look like dyed leather, and *For Unlawful Carnal Knowledge* in thin, silver type along the bottom. Far more interesting were the interior shots, one of which shows a chalkboard from 5150 Studios that had a series of phone numbers scribbled on it. Van Halen fans being the inquisitive types, they began dialing what turned out to be a variety of residences and businesses.

It went beyond crank calls in one case: some fans misread a set of numbers and began ringing up a family in Tulsa, who saw the harassment escalate when they went to the media to gripe. Their garage was firebombed, their car and driveway spray-painted with obscenities, and their tires slashed. Supposedly they needed to hire a guard service and ultimately relocate. Van Halen were sued to the tune of $2 million for invasion of privacy; they agreed to remove the photo from subsequent pressings. Other than that, the terms of any settlement were not disclosed publicly.

The lead-up for the album was the single "Poundcake," which features Eddie using a Makita 6012HD power drill he'd picked up in the studio and found was in the same key as the composition. He placed it over his guitar strings to start the song, peppering the move throughout the rest of the track. As cool as the idea was, though, it wasn't another Eddie Van Halen innovation. Much like tapping, he popularized the technique but wasn't the first to do it—not even in 1991. "Daddy, Brother, Lover, Little Boy (The Electric Drill Song)," the opening track on Mr. Big's *Lean Into It*, which came out that March, features guitarist Paul Gilbert and bassist Billy Sheehan dueling with one another using an electric drill on their respective instruments.

One of the most delicate moments in the Van Halen catalogue is the minute-and-a-half-long guitar piece "316." Eddie had incorporated part of it into his live solos in 1986, but, more meaningfully, he would also play it on an acoustic to Valerie's belly while she was pregnant with their unborn child in the months leading up to the release of *For Unlawful Carnal Knowledge*. Wolfgang William Van Halen was born March 16, 1991, his birthdate giving Eddie the perfect name for the instrumental.

RIGHT NOW...

Reviews for the new record were mixed. Most critics applauded the music, citing the production and thick bottom end courtesy of Andy Johns, but there were the usual knocks on Hagar's lyrics, which continued to veer toward locker-room humor at times. *Rolling Stone* savaged the album in a two-star review, describing it as "so stuffed with zigzagging guitars and blustery vocals that it almost forgets to rock." That criticism was particularly surprising and unfounded, as *For Unlawful Carnal Knowledge* was the most guitar-heavy LP Van Halen had made in years, contrasting greatly with the excessive keyboard on their prior two recordings with Hagar.

The one keyboard-driven track would become one of the band's biggest hits. The main piano riff of "Right Now" had its origins in 1983, when it was mothballed due to lack of interest from the rest of the band, and it had met the same fate during the *OU812* sessions. But Hagar had been toying with the lyrics, which he considered his most serious to date, and now Eddie's melody suddenly clicked.

"I think the cool thing about 'Right Now' is that it was the last song we wrote on the record," Hagar said in 2015. "It was kind of like 'Dreams' from *5150*—we thought we were done. Eddie kept playing the piano part, I kept singing these lyrics, [*sings*] 'Right now, it's your tomorrow,' and finally the two came together."

Less serendipitous was the idea director Mark Fenske had for the video, which involved overlaying various scenes with text ranging from social justice slogans to goofy phrases with the song title preceding them, which Hagar hated.

"'Right Now' was the best lyric I'd ever written for Van Halen," Hagar recalls in the book *I Want My MTV*. "But the treatment for the video was bullshit: 'Right now, Sammy's looking in the mirror and licking the milk off his mustache,' or something. I told the director, 'Fuck you, man. People won't even be listening to what I'm singing because they'll be reading these subtitles.' I thought, 'How dare they?' People probably don't know this: I refused to do the video."

The singer stalked off and retreated to the sea island of Kiawah in South Carolina with his then girlfriend, Kari. No one knew how to contact him; Warner Bros. head Mo Ostin eventually had to talk Hagar down and convince him to go along with the clip, which he begrudgingly did. Yet even when it took home three MTV VMAs—including one for Video of the Year—the frontman wasn't sold. He stated while he understands it was groundbreaking, it still didn't do much for him as it wasn't focused enough on Van Halen, and he wasn't a fan of the look or the feel to it.

More frustration followed when Pepsi asked to use the song—and the video concept—to push its Crystal Pepsi brand, beginning with a high-profile advertisement that would premiere during the 1993 Super Bowl. The band turned it down at first, not wanting to look like sell-outs, but eventually felt their hand was forced.

"The only reason we gave Pepsi the music was because they were going to use the song anyway," Eddie would later tell *Guitar World*. "They would have just recut it with studio musicians, like they do for some TV movies because they can't use the original. If they use the original recording, they've got to pay, but if they don't, all they do is give credit to the artist and then pay the studio cats. Pepsi told us they were going to do that, so we said, 'Hey wait a minute, we might as well get the money.' I ain't that proud, you know. I'm not going to say, 'No, go ahead, rip us off. And keep the money, too!'"

SLIPPED A LITTLE OFF YOUR PACE

A shelved part in the "Right Now" video would have had Hagar looking at a poster of the previous lineup of Van Halen, with the text reading, "Right now, Dave wishes he was Sammy." It was a cruel dig at Roth, mainly because it probably wasn't far off the mark.

The former singer for the group released *A Little Ain't Enough* in January 1991, and though the album flirted briefly with the Top 20, it quickly nosedived off the charts. He had picked up yet another guitar whiz in Jason Becker, who during the recording of the album tragically became afflicted with ALS, also known as Lou Gehrig's disease. Today, he is confined to a wheelchair and cannot speak or move, but he is still able to create music and communicate via a unique system using his eyes.

Roth admits in his autobiography that it was around this period that he started to lose passion for the whole idea of rock and roll, putting together a band, and trying to make something happen. "You run into so many wanna-bes, never ever gonna-bes. Spotlight junkies, folks who would play an Edward Van Halen riff and watch my face to see if I was impressed."

Seeing many of his concert dates on the *A Little Ain't Enough* jaunt canceled due to low ticket sales may have provided a wake-up call for the diamond one. He'd even made peace with the aftermath of the split with Van Halen, telling one interviewer in 1991 that he wasn't bitter anymore and was hopeful for what the future might hold with his ex-bandmates.

"I still think I left Van Halen for all the right reasons, and that I made the right decision. But that was some years ago—people change; times change," Roth said, adding that he hadn't spoken to anyone in the group in six years. "But I think that should anything transpire between us in the future, it would be positive."

...RIGHT HERE

The North American tour in support of *For Unlawful Carnal Knowledge* began in August 1991 and continued through May 1992. The break from the road had ramped up demand, and once again the band were doing two nights in markets like Philadelphia, New York, and Fresno. They were also asked to open up the 1991 MTV Video Music Awards by performing "Poundcake."

Opening the first leg of the run were Seattle rockers Alice in Chains, who were considered a heavy metal outfit following the release of their single "Man in the Box." When the grunge explosion took off later in the year, they were belatedly lumped in with the rest of Pacific Northwest acts who made up the burgeoning movement.

Following a break in the summer of 1992, Van Halen saw just how different the musical landscape had become when they arrived at the MTV Video Music Awards in September. Though "Right Now" was a big winner, the band seemed woefully out of place—especially Hagar, whose checkered suit looked as if it was nicked from the décor of Louis Restaurant in *The Godfather*. Performances that night by Nirvana, Pearl Jam, and Red Hot Chili Peppers were representative of what young audiences were leaning toward, while Guns N' Roses and U2—the latter's spot beamed in from the Pontiac Silverdome in Michigan—showed acts who were at another level.

Where Van Halen fit in all of that remained to be seen, but juvenile lyrics and flashy, over-the-top wardrobe choices weren't going to work for a rock and roll band going forward. It was time to move in a more sophisticated direction—at least slightly—or run the risk of becoming a caricature of themselves. Or, worse, go the way of hair metal, which in a few short months had been nearly excised by an unforgiving industry all of a sudden hot on substance over style.

Van Halen seemed to be riding a wave of resurgence with the release of a concert album and video, *Live: Right Here, Right Now*, culled from a pair of shows late in the *For Unlawful Carnal Knowledge* tour at the Selland Arena in

Fresno. The home video was released on January 26; the two-disc audio version came out February 23 and entered the charts at No. 5, which ended up as its highest placing.

Essentially, the set was nothing more than a political move to stave off Warner Bros. from putting out a greatest hits compilation focused on the Roth era of the band. The label even asked if Hagar would re-record some of the old songs from the catalogue—an absolutely ridiculous idea. Van Halen thought that would stymie the path they were on with Hagar and unnecessarily bring comparisons between the two singers to the forefront—resurrecting an endless debate that was then on the backburner with the recent stalling of their former singer's career.

Overall, *Live: Right Here, Right Now* was disappointing. The summer before it was released, the concert had been broadcast as the "Cabo Wabo Rock Radio Festival" on Westwood One via radio stations across the country. Fans who had taped it would notice quite a difference when they compared it with the polished-up product they purchased in 1993. Hagar claims in his book *Red* that Alex and Eddie re-recorded the majority of the music at 5150 Studios. He said he recut vocals there as well, singing along to a video of the concert.

As expected, the live record was tilted toward more recent material. But including ten of the eleven songs from *For Unlawful Carnal Knowledge* was a bit much, given there were just four songs from Roth's time in the band, one of them being "You Really Got Me" by the Kinks. The mix isn't the best, either, with some complaining that the crowd noise is positioned way too high in it.

Live: Right Here, Right Now did give justification for embarking on another tour, with this one launching at the Whisky a Go Go in Los Angeles on March 3, 1993. The thinking behind the event was to kick off the trek at the spot where it all started, but that didn't make sense, as Hagar wasn't in the group when Van Halen were signed to a record deal at the Sunset Strip nightclub back in the day. That didn't matter to the three thousand fans who showed up on the day of the show in hopes of snagging one of the two hundred tickets that were made available. There were no arrests, and nobody was injured, but the band picked up the $10,000 tab for the extra police patrol.

The proper promotional tour started in Europe—the band's first shows there with Hagar in the group. Back in the States, the summer gigs were held mostly in amphitheaters, which were growing in popularity as the venue of choice for acts to play in warmer weather. Vince Neil, estranged from Mötley Crüe and touring solo for the first time, was the opener for the entirety of the run until its end in late August.

Privately, relationships were being tested by the time the tour was finished. Manager Ed Leffler was diagnosed with thyroid cancer and died just a couple of months later, in October 1993, at the age of fifty-seven. This came in the midst of Hagar negotiating with Geffen Records to put out a solo best-of collection with two new tracks as a way to pay for his upcoming divorce—a maneuver that made Alex and Eddie furious.

Leffler's death had further adverse effects. Eddie's grief over the loss drove his drinking into more problematic territories than before. He showed up backstage at a Nirvana concert at the Forum in Los Angeles on December 30 and by all accounts was obscenely drunk, petitioning the band to let him come onstage and jam with them. Seeing the shape he was in, they tried to blow him off by saying there weren't any spare guitars, leading Eddie to reportedly plead, "C'mon, let me play the Mexican's guitar," referring to Nirvana's multiracial guitarist, Pat Smear. Kurt Cobain, equal parts horrified and offended, apparently told Eddie he was welcome to come out and jam—after their encore was over.

Heading into 1994, the lovefest in Van Halen with Hagar had run its course. Arguments were growing more frequent; they couldn't agree on who would be a good fit as manager; and a clear breakdown in communication was occurring. It was the onset of a slow, painful deterioration in yet another era of the band.

19

NOT ENOUGH

Sammy Hagar began 1994 in promotion mode for *Unboxed*, his new collection on Geffen Records. It wasn't an easy media barrage: he had to straddle the line between trying to garner interest in the album and assuring fans—and his own bandmates—that he wasn't leaving Van Halen. It got to the stage where he had to categorically state in a press release that it was "the end of the book for my solo career . . . I can't go out and support my solo albums the way I should anymore, so I'm going to make Van Halen my full-time job."

The declaration did little to quell the growing dissent in the band as they entered the studio to record the follow-up to *For Unlawful Carnal Knowledge*. Production duties were handled by Bruce Fairbairn, whose recent track record included Bon Jovi's *Slippery When Wet* and reviving Aerosmith's career with *Permanent Vacation* and *Pump*. To an outside observer, Van Halen fell somewhere in the middle of those two: sales were slipping, but not so much that they needed a savior, though some new blood behind the board couldn't hurt.

Months prior, as a by-product of trying to get sober again, Eddie had shaved his head. He told *Rolling Stone* he had done it in a fit of despair and frustration over manager Ed Leffler's passing and his singer going "off doing his loony fucking solo career." He later explained to *Guitar World* that although he played the majority of the sessions sober, if he heard something that sounded a little "stiff," he would redo it with some liquid assistance to loosen him up.

Hagar would say the guitarist was far from on the wagon, accusing him of hiding a stash of vodka and cocaine in the bathroom of 5150 Studios. He was positive Eddie was trying to make him quit the band by criticizing the lyrics he was writing—for the first time in their working history—and making suggestions about how he should sing. It led to the frontman and Fairbairn retreating to Vancouver's Little Mountain Sound Studios to finish the vocals away from the distractions.

They'd also gotten a new manager—or at least three-quarters of the band had. After mulling over it for months, Alex and Eddie elected to go with SRO Management, which also handled the careers of Rush and Extreme. The company—SRO stands for "Standing Room Only"—was founded by Ray Danniels, who happened to be Alex's brother-in-law at the time. Hagar was having none of it. He didn't like or trust Danniels from the outset, so he went with his own representation, though SRO still handled the affairs of the band as a whole.

One thing Danniels did assist the singer with was getting the brothers off the hook for the Cabo Wabo Cantina. The investment was losing money hand over fist and owed a significant sum in back taxes, and they wanted out. The agreement the manager came up with said that Alex and Eddie would have first right of refusal if another restaurant were to be built, and, if it was sold within five years, they'd get some degree of compensation. They also wouldn't be liable for any future debts or legal issues.

STRUNG OUT

Balance was released on January 24, 1995. Like every studio album of the Hagar era, it went to No. 1 on the *Billboard* 200, although it had dipped out of the Top 10 by late March, the same month it went platinum. Generally speaking, it was a wildly inconsistent work, from the jarring sequencing of the songs to the number of seemingly unfinished ideas it included, which made it an absolute mess in parts.

The record came after another long wait between Van Halen studio efforts—three and a half years. Though it was still hotly anticipated by fans, if the shift in mainstream tastes had been just getting underway when their last album came out, it had now become seismic.

Wisely, the band tried changing things up a bit while retaining their core sound to stay relevant. Opener "The Seventh Seal" was sent to radio in late 1994, when the LP was being marketed with that name as the title. It begins with twenty seconds of chanting by monks from the Gyuto Tantric University. There's a more serious tone throughout, both musically and lyrically, as is evident in the lead single, "Don't Tell Me (What Love Can Do)," which took inspiration from Nirvana frontman Kurt Cobain's suicide. Another highlight is "Aftershock," a deeper cut full of anxious guitar accents and Hagar's fierce vocals.

Concerned by the menace of the music in parts, Fairbairn had asked Eddie if he had any "pop ditties" lying about that he could offer the record company when they came calling looking for a track to push out to radio. The guitarist quickly tired of digging through the extensive 5150 Studios library and figured it would be easier to write a new song from scratch, resulting in "Can't Stop Lovin' You," unquestionably the most pop-oriented track recorded during Hagar's tenure with the group.

The song's glossy acoustic guitar tones and mawkish "oooh, oooh, oooh" backing vocals made it one of the less popular numbers among hardcore fans. Casual listeners were the exact opposite, however, as the number became the biggest hit from *Balance*. It was the only single to crack the Top 40, peaking at No. 30 in early June.

"Can't Stop Lovin' You" joined the ranks of "Every Breath You Take" by the Police and "The One I Love" by R.E.M. among songs that sound like odes to deep affection on the surface yet are anything but. Hagar wrote it from his ex-wife Betsy's point of view, exploring their protracted divorce proceedings and how he was trying to move on with his new girlfriend, Kari, but she wouldn't let him go. The video for the track belies the meaning behind it, though, with footage of Van Halen performing in a nondescript living room intercut with a montage of scenes related to love.

"Can't Stop Lovin' You" was featured on MTV's *Beavis and Butt-Head*, with the cartoon metalheads not quite savaging the clip but expressing suspicion. After starting off with the obligatory "Van Halen kicks ass!" they quickly shift to, "Uh…uhh…uh—oh boy."

There are three instrumentals on *Balance*, none of them memorable in the slightest. And while Hagar's lyrical misdeeds were largely kept at bay, when they did show up, they were dreadful. "Big Fat Money" features a number of regrettable lines, including one that rhymes "space station" with "premature ejaculation," and the fact that the main focus of "Amsterdam" was getting high infuriated Alex and Eddie as the city was their homeland, and they thought its lyrics deserved some imagination. "At least be a little more metaphorical," the latter told *Guitar World*.

CROSSING OVERSEAS

For the only time in the Van Halen catalogue, there was a non-album B-side for *Balance*: "Crossing Over," a fascinating piece of experimentation with a storied history. The roots of the song stretch back to 1983, when Eddie demoed the track on his own, titling it "David's Tune" for a friend who had taken his own life. The guitarist handled all the instruments in the studio, including drums and bass, and laid down some scratch vocals.

When Hagar joined the band in 1985, he was eager to flesh out the song, but Eddie rejected his overtures and it sat on the shelf for another decade. Following the death of Leffler, and thinking about the passing of his own father, the singer contemplated the idea of what happens when a person dies and "crosses over" to the other side. Eddie finally caved and let the frontman use the long-gestating music. Rather than redo it entirely, though, he retained the original track with all of his instrumentation and minimal vocals, but only in the left channel. New music, with Alex on drums and Sammy singing, was panned across the music in stereo.

Interesting and unique as the song may have been, it was left off the album in North America. In Japan, though, it was a different story, as one of the methods the country used to move units of its homegrown product was to include some sort of bonus for music fans. In the case of *Balance*, this meant tacking on "Crossing Over" at the end of the album, although it wasn't indicated anywhere on the jacket or physical CD. Fans were clued in only by a sticker on the front, and a Japanese insert included within the packaging.

There was already a budding controversy about the album artwork for *Balance* in Japan, because of its depiction of Siamese twin children on a seesaw, though in reality it was a composite picture of the same child. The cover was a stark reminder to residents of the country of the conjoined Vietnamese twins Viet and Duc Nguyen, who were said to have experienced their birth deformity due to the usage of Agent Orange by the United States in the Vietnam War. The pair were separated with the assistance of the Japanese Red Cross in 1988.

"Retailers have called us to tell us that people have come into their stores and said it's just gross," Warner Music Japan spokesman Jonny Thompson told *Billboard.*

The Japanese arm of the label anticipated some sort of reaction to the record art and had a backup image ready to go, showing just one child on the seesaw, for the country's pressing of the album. Released one week later than the United States import, the Japanese edition quickly began to sell better than the American pressing, despite a $4 increase. It was one of the rare cases where a domestic edition outsold the import, as Japanese labels typically had difficulty selling compact discs manufactured there because of the inflated price tag.

Van Halen's fan base in the States and elsewhere quickly caught wind of there being a bonus track on the Japanese pressing of *Balance,* leading many to scramble to get a copy—often for two times the cost, or more, of a traditional compact disc. It was then that the band decided to add "Crossing Over" as a B-side to the "Can't Stop Lovin' You" single, touting it as a "non-album track" on various configurations of the release worldwide.

Fans also got their first look at the newly shorn Eddie Van Halen in the liner notes to the record, with the guitarist pictured sporting a close-cropped cut and goatee. And, on the back cover, amid what looked to be an innocuous shot of the band walking down an alley, there is perhaps a small middle finger to Pepsi, which had strong-armed the band into allowing the usage of "Right Now" for its doomed Crystal Pepsi a couple of years before. Close inspection reveals a Coke can sitting by the curb.

THE AMBULANCE TOUR

To celebrate the release of *Balance,* the band played a secret show two days after it came out at the Luxor Theatre in Arnhem, Holland, that was simulcast on Dutch national radio. It was a clear move to play on the Van Halen brothers' connection to their native land, as well as the regionally appealing single "Amsterdam." The audience for the truncated set was made up of eleven hundred people, including three hundred from the group's small but fervent local fan club. A few nights later, they did a similar gig at Factory in Milan, Italy.

March 1995 saw the official start of dates to support the new release, soon dubbed the "Ambulance Tour" due to a string of wellness issues afflicting the band. Hagar was plagued with throat problems during the first leg, which led to some shows being rescheduled. Worse, though, were the medical complications the brothers were dealing with.

Eddie had a bad hip that was diagnosed as an avascular necrosis—the death of bone tissue due to lack of blood supply. It stemmed from excessive alcohol intake, and it wasn't helped by all the leaping around the guitarist had done over the years in concert. His hip needed to be replaced, and, in the meantime, he started walking with a cane. He would sit down during shows and remain in one spot more than normal but was still pushing it with the jumping, and he was on painkillers as a result.

Alex was in his own sort of pain; he had ruptured three vertebrae in his neck and back after aggravating injuries from when he was younger. He had to wear a neck brace for the majority of the tour.

Continuing to focus on raising their profile in Europe, Van Halen did a run of shows in the spring as openers for Bon Jovi. The New Jersey band were on a sharp decline in album sales in the U.S., but they still had a stronghold on the road internationally. For Van Halen, the embarrassment of the situation—having to play support act for the former hair band who were bigger than them outside of North America—didn't do any wonders for group morale.

Toward the end of the *Balance* trek in late 1995, while in Japan, Hagar claims a wasted Eddie called him in his hotel room one night and said he had some ideas for the future and he would let the singer know if they included him. Incensed, Hagar said, "Fuck you," and slammed the phone down. The tour ended a few nights later after a pair of shows in Honolulu.

A TWISTED TURN

Hagar and his brand-new wife, Kari, decided to buy a house in Hawaii after the singer came off the road. She was pregnant with their first child, and the couple couldn't think of a more beautiful place to start their life together. The baby was due in April, and the plan was for Van Halen to take some much needed distance from one another.

"We needed time off from each other after our last tour, because there was a lot of personal stuff we had to take care of," Hagar told *Guitar World* in 1997, adding that there were a variety of reasons for slowing down over the first half of the new year. "Eddie needed hip replacement surgery. Al needed his back worked on. And I was going to have a baby. . . . We needed to regroup and retool ourselves before we hooked up again for a new album."

Alex and Eddie had other ideas, though, and reached out to Sammy in the spring of 1996 about doing a track or two for the soundtrack to the upcoming big-budget disaster film *Twister*. Director Jan de Bont apparently told the brothers—and later the singer—that no matter what, he didn't want any songs about tornadoes.

"And so what does Sammy come back with? 'Sky is turning black, knuckles turning white, headed for the hot zone,'" Eddie told *Guitar World*. "It was total tornado stuff! Not only did Alex tell him not to do that, but the director of the fucking movie told him, 'Do not write about tornadoes.'"

According to Hagar, the opposite was true: de Bont loved the demo of the song, titled "Drop Down," that the singer had sent him. He said the Van Halens were again criticizing his lyrics and subject matter and going back on their word about the intended break. In the end, they cut a different song for the *Twister* soundtrack: "Humans Being," a heavy, dark, and moody number. A second song, the ballad "Between Us Two," wasn't completed, so Alex and Eddie—on piano and guitar respectively—came up with a new piece called "Respect the Wind," which played over the movie's credits. The instrumental would be the only song performed under their own names, attributed to "Edward & Alex Van Halen."

Come that June, on Father's Day, Eddie phoned Hagar to come to the studio to finish up "Between Us Two," as the guitarist still didn't think the track was finished. Along with "Humans Being," it would be one of two new songs on a proposed greatest hits collection—which the singer was adamantly against. He was convinced Danniels was trying to turn the group into a cash machine and whore them out in any way possible, and that acts who were still relevant didn't put out best-of albums unless their career was over. Eddie pleaded with him to be a "team player."

"That's when he was really getting out there . . . it's all to do with somebody's perverted concept of what things should be," Hagar said. "I was totally willing to make a new record and totally willing to be a team player. I didn't want to do a greatest hits record at that stage. For God's sake, we had one of the only bands in history to sell that kind of record and have that many consecutive number one albums. Why do you want to sell the people the same damn record again? I loved those fans. I did not want to do that to them. I still stick by those guns. That's how I got thrown out; they wanted to take some quick, easy money—mainly Ray—by saying, 'I will put out this record with all the old songs on them, and now I'm the manager so I'll make money off the old stuff too!' That's probably how someone was thinkin' . . . I don't know. I hope they wouldn't be that shortsighted."

The frontman stood firm, refusing to work on new music if it was going to end up on a compilation LP. That's when Eddie dropped the bombshell of the century and told Hagar the band had been working on songs for the collection with David Lee Roth and it had been going great, so Hagar should just go back to being what he always was: a solo artist.

"I just got to the point where I said, 'Fuck it. Fuck these guys,'" Hagar said. "And that's a horrible place to be. I just felt like it doesn't matter what I do, what I say, these guys aren't happy with who I am, and Ray Danniels had already poisoned everybody to make the plan to get Roth back for the greatest hits record and me to do a couple songs, tellin' me it was for something else. That's how those other songs got written, by the way, a couple of them, because I was thinkin' it was for something else, and they were trying to put the greatest hits with two Sammy songs and two Roth songs—and that's when I hit the frickin' fan. They'd already made their mind up."

Eleven years went down the drain in one fell swoop. Hagar getting kicked out—or quitting, depending on who was saying what at any given time—was one thing. But Roth being back in Van Halen was inconceivable. What could be more insane than that?

The world was about to find out.

20

CAN'T GET THIS
STUFF NO MORE

For David Lee Roth, the years since his departure from Van Halen had seen a sharp declination musically, and in terms of popularity. He started off strong with *Eat 'Em and Smile* in 1986, assembling a faction of musicians designed to challenge the best his former outfit had to offer. Unfortunately, it wasn't enough—at least not for the mainstream, who took more to a blend of keyboards and blazing guitars, syrupy ballads, and name recognition than to his attempts at rock infused with big band and swing oddities.

Roth floundered, jumping on the synthesizer train just as it was going into a long dark tunnel and losing the bulk of his wildly talented musical assassins in guitarist Steve Vai and bassist Billy Sheehan. He tried to return to the hard rock of old on 1991's *A Little Ain't Enough*, but soon he was a grunge casualty, needing to scrub a third of his shows in the States due to poor ticket sales.

The singer justified his decreasing popularity in the early '90s by saying it all worked out the same for him because he didn't have to split his money equally with his bandmates. Yet he wasn't shy about making overtures to the media suggesting that Van Halen would be more explosive with him in the band, leading Ed Leffler, who Roth derisively referred to as "Sammy Hagar's manager," to call and say it would never happen.

Even after the failure of *A Little Ain't Enough*, the frontman dug in with the notion he was the better candidate for lead singer in Van Halen, going on *The Howard Stern Show* in 1992 and calling Hagar "a mindless little bridge-troll drone . . . everything that comes out of his mouth is word barf . . . it's meant for children."

"Sammy is my boy. He works for me—he's my bitch. And when he says my name, we just sell that many more records. It reminds people of the glorious past even more. He doesn't even know it."

Despite all of his bluster, no one could deny the singer was making missteps. An April 1993 bust for purchasing between $5 and $10 worth of marijuana in Washington Square Park in the Greenwich Village neighborhood of New York City became a metaphor in the press for how far his career had sunk. He joked about it in interviews, telling Stern that, for many years, it was "like buying a pretzel and a soda pop on a Sunday afternoon."

Your Filthy Little Mouth, Roth's 1994 solo effort, registered barely a blip on the radar, fell off the charts in two weeks, and saw the ensuing tour relegated to state fairs and significantly downsized venues. He'd split with creative partner Pete Angelus, who'd long hitched his wagon to up-and-comers the Black Crowes. The onetime fellow Fabulous Picasso Brother no longer felt he and Roth could co-exist in an increasingly distorted vision of the singer's future. His currency had plummeted, his rock and roll ambitions stalled, and he looked to be a step away from being a casino act for high rollers.

That's when Dave decided to beat everyone to the punch and head to Vegas.

Realizing his blossoming irrelevance, Roth picked up a fourteen-piece outfit dubbed the Blues Bustin' Mambo Slammers and packed his bags for a Las Vegas residency. At forty years old, he had gone to the land that was then still considered the last stop on an artist's road to obscurity.

In November 1995, the singer appeared on *The Tonight Show with Jay Leno* wearing a striking all-white suit, his hair cut short and in its natural shade of brown, and trotted out a lounge-flavored version of "California Girls," the Beach Boys song he'd had a hit with ten years prior on *Crazy from the Heat*.

"Las Vegas is what's new, it's what's happening right now, it's very hip," Roth told Leno.

He was, in fact, correct—though about fifteen years too early. In 1995, Vegas was where careers went to die; where Wayne Newton ruled the strip and people were gambling for one last shot at success. Even the hit flick *Swingers* was a year away. That roll of the dice Roth pimped on Leno was taking place at Bally's Celebrity Showroom, a venue that held fewer than fifteen hundred people. What most didn't know is that he'd already been road-testing the routine at off-the-beaten-path spots in Reno, Lake Tahoe, and Connecticut in the summer and fall, and he'd continue to bounce between those regions while doing the Vegas residency.

The show itself was unspectacular if not outright cheesy. Roth would sing just two Van Halen originals in the format—unsurprisingly, "Jump" and "Panama"— eschewing the rest in favor of standards that wouldn't have been out of place on a night when Don Rickles needed a stand-in. Otis Redding's "Hard to Handle" and James Brown's "Living in America" were staples, as was Edgar Winter—on saxophone for the Mambo Slammers—with his hit song "Free Ride." The singer told bad jokes and made even worse double-entendres, marking a sad decline for the onetime superstar who used to boast macho anthems like "Unchained" and "Everybody Wants Some!!" but had now devolved into a persona more akin to that creepy uncle only seen on holidays.

Roth's descent didn't last long. He had finished with the revue show by the end of the 1995, his diamond status having been sufficiently tarnished in the eyes of detractors and critics who couldn't wait to take potshots. It would take something significant to erase the memory of that black eye.

WELCOME BACK

Word was spreading fast that Hagar was out and Roth was back in Van Halen. The band put out a statement on June 26, 1996, to confirm as much, saying they were working with their former singer on a song for an upcoming greatest hits collection, but made a point to add that it was happening while they were "currently considering a replacement." Most media and fans conveniently ignored that last part, eagerly sharing the news of the original frontman's return.

It was something that had been in the works—at least in some form—for quite some time. Around the period of *For Unlawful Carnal Knowledge*, and the winding down of its promotional cycle in 1992, Warner Bros. began looking for a best-of collection from the group that would focus on the early years. Roth would take part in the process of choosing songs and the subsequent publicity, and he wanted some of his solo hits to be included, like "Yankee Rose" and "Just Like Paradise." This was around the point when Roth was indicating in interviews—like with Howard Stern—that he would be open to returning to the band. The singer was well aware of the firestorm a greatest hits package with his presence would invoke among fans old and new, and he was laying the groundwork for battle, tempering his words toward Alex and Eddie while gleefully ripping Hagar.

Band manager Ed Leffler balked at the idea of a new album with Roth involved, which is how *Live: Right Here, Right Now* came into play. The live collection would keep the suits at bay while the band recorded another LP with Hagar. Then Leffler died, and new manager Ray Danniels was more receptive to working with the older catalogue, especially as material from that era didn't benefit him financially—unless it appeared on a new release.

Deep into production around this time was a Howard Stern biopic based on his bestselling book *Private Parts*. The shock jock was personally involved in lining up artists for the soundtrack to the film, and he had his representatives reach out to Van Halen's management, saying he wanted a new song by the band—but with Roth singing. Much to his surprise, they entertained the request but put a price of $2.5 million on a possible track, which was too much for a film with a total budget of less than $30 million to seriously consider.

Warner Bros. was again knocking around for a greatest hits set, and now that the band's management was on board with it, all that remained was logistics. Hagar threw a wrench into the works when he flatly refused to record any new songs for one; though he had signed a contract with the group that included the provision of a compilation, he wasn't required to contribute new material.

Quite fortuitously, since he was unaware of the drama within the Van Halen camp, Roth reached out to Eddie to discuss the upcoming set, concerned about how he was going to be represented. The singer was also putting the final touches to his autobiography, and he wanted to make peace with the guitarist before it came out. They both apologized to one another for things that had been said over the years, and they got on so well that eventually the two were having cigars together at Dave's mansion in Pasadena.

Eddie came up with the idea of inviting the singer to 5150 Studios to maybe sing on a track to be added to the greatest hits, which would drum up interest in the set. He didn't tell the rest of the band, who were as shocked as could be at Dave's presence when they arrived. Alex was apparently so angry that he threatened to punch the singer if he ever said anything bad about his family again. Tensions then relaxed, and Eddie presented almost half a dozen pieces of music from which Dave could choose.

ME WISE TRAGIC

Throughout much of the history of Van Halen, there's a lot of "he said, they said." This reached its apex over a lengthy, swiftly moving period in 1996.

Roth hadn't sung in over six months—not since his New Year's Eve show at the MGM Grand. At 5150 in early summer, he suggested they run through some of the songs from their first six records to help him warm up. According to the singer's *Crazy from the Heat*, Eddie bristled at the idea, categorically rejecting any such thing and becoming furious it was even brought up.

"No goddamn fucking way," Roth claims the guitarist said, adding they weren't going to do anything remotely tied to the past, nothing referencing the music they did prior. In fact, any of the new songs that would be done were compositions that any singer could complete. It could be Dave, Sammy, or whoever.

The frontman toyed with the idea of putting together a band on the fly to warm himself up but then thought better of it, thinking that if the press got ahold of that information, it would blow up. Banished to a vocal booth in the studio with no windows, Roth made a little "Club Dave," replete with potted palm trees and brightly colored lights.

"What the fuck is this fucking goddamn fucking bullshit," the singer claimed Alex said when he saw the décor. "We're motherfucking forty-year-olds. What is this fucking palm tree horseshit? This is fucking work man. This is motherfucking business, okay?"

Glen Ballard, who had co-written and produced Alanis Morissette's smash-hit LP *Jagged Little Pill* the year before, was on hand to work with the band on the new track. Eddie said in resulting interviews that he coaxed a great performance out of Dave over a two-and-a-half-week period, even though the music was completed in less than a half hour. It had gone so well, went the party line, that they asked him to do another song.

The way Dave remembers it, though, there was nothing easy about the process. None of the lyrics he presented were good enough for Alex and Eddie. Then they brought in Desmond Child, writer of hit songs by everyone from Aerosmith to Ricky Martin to Bon Jovi, but the singer put his foot down.

The first track, "Me Wise Magic," was finished in late July. Clocking in at over six minutes, it was by far the longest song the band had ever done with Roth. Musically, it's a stunner, with a chugging riff and forceful drum work from Alex. Vocally, there was a lot of covering up the singer's rusty pipes. He speaks for much of the verses, and his once-patented howls are tempered with noticeable strain.

The second number, "Can't Get This Stuff No More," was finished in early August. It's a much more laid-back piece—one Hagar said was a leftover from the *Balance* sessions, when it was called "The Backdoor Shuffle." A talk box was used on the track, but a guitar tech had to perform the part because Eddie's mouth was too small for the effects unit they had on hand. The song also has an extremely clairvoyant chorus, with Roth singing about the number of times someone will lie, alluding—possibly—to the band; he asks how long will patience last, pledging a true reunion is running its course, before adding that they should all keep as much in mind when goodbye is finally said that no one—not the listeners, the fans, or whomever—can get this stuff no more. It ended up being the final song released by the four original members of Van Halen while they were all still alive.

A TELEVISED CATASTROPHE

Both Eddie and Dave contend that at one point during their brief time together in 1996, the other said a variation of, "No matter what happens, at least we're going to be friends." It was a sentiment tossed out the window on the night of September 4 at the MTV Video Music Awards.

A reconstituted Van Halen had been rumored to be appearing at the awards show in the week leading up to the event at Radio City Music Hall in New York City, but nothing was confirmed. Warner Bros. figured it would be a good way to build up anticipation for *Best Of—Volume I*, which was due on October 22. Management agreed, and initially asked Eddie and Dave to go. The former said he didn't want to do it at all, but, if he had to, Alex and Michael were going to be in tow. Dave said he didn't want to do it either, as any appearance was a surefire way to lead people into thinking they were reunited. The bottom line, they all felt, was that if the known, existing members of Van Halen showed up onstage with David Lee Roth, then everyone in attendance, as well as those viewing, would logically figure the vocalist was back in the band. Against their collective better judgement, they settled on attending together.

At around the two-and-a-half-hour mark of the VMAs, after Oasis performed "Champagne Supernova"—with frontman Liam Gallagher at his most bratty, spitting, swearing, flipping off the audience, and dumping his beer on the stage—host Dennis Miller set the stage as the booing calmed.

"Our next presenters may very well represent three-quarters of one of the greatest rock and roll bands ever," the comedian began, before referencing the late-'60s/early '70s sitcom *Bewitched*, which switched leading men midway through its run. "Here, having now officially survived their own rock and roll version of the Dick York/Dick Sargent debacle—it's . . . Van Halen."

"Runnin' with the Devil" kicked in, and out walked Eddie, Alex, and Michael—the first two clad in sunglasses—followed a carefully orchestrated few steps behind by Dave. Once the crowd in attendance realized who the fourth person was, they went completely berserk. Celebrities from all walks of life and levels of popularity were immediately standing, screaming and pumping their fists. A beaming Roth stood at the lip of the stage and tapped the wrist on one arm with the fingers of his other, nodding. The message was clear: "It's time."

Eddie, meanwhile, glanced around nervously, like a mouse in a four-walled maze, desperately trying to find a way out. Looking annoyed, he stepped to the podium and admonished the audience with a motion as if to say, "Okay . . . that's enough." They were there to give out the award for Best Male Video, but as much as the guitarist implored Dave to begin reading off the teleprompter, the singer was more intent to soak in the spotlight.

"No, no, no—instead of the 'best award' thing, we have to make an announcement, we have to address a subject here," he said, as Eddie stepped back, fumbled with his now-removed sunglasses, and scanned the room nervously. "This is the first time that we've actually stood onstage together in over a decade."

Alex then reached out his hand to shake the singer's, and then Dave turned to Eddie and the two embraced—awkwardly on the guitarist's end, yet drawing another round of wild applause. The frontman interjected a joke about how much things had changed in the years since they last were on the channel, before Eddie physically moved him away from the microphone. After handing out the award to Beck, an uncontained Roth danced behind the "Where It's At" singer as he gave his acceptance speech.

After the formal show ended, there was an ancillary series of interviews, part of which saw esteemed writer and *MTV News* host Kurt Loder corral Van Halen. The first thing he asked was what they thought the audience was trying to tell them with the standing ovation. Alex was the unlikely member to give an answer—one that, in retrospect, was almost cruel.

"I think there's a lot of history, with the past of this band," the drummer said. "I think since the very beginning, the whole idea was for the band to establish a special relationship with an audience, and I think the people can sense when you're BS-ing them and when you're not."

It was then off to the press tent, where the band were bombarded with questions. Roth said later that the guitarist was in a miserable mood in the limo on the way to the show, telling the others that all he was going to do was address the two songs they did together and nothing else. The singer told him to be prepared for questions about everything *but* the new music, and that's precisely what happened. The media wanted to know about a tour, what went down with Hagar, and why the Van Halens claimed not to be looking for a new singer when the *Boston Herald* had just reported that Extreme frontman Gary Cherone was at that very moment in Los Angeles to audition with the group.

Eddie tried to quash the growing intensity by maintaining that nothing was happening in the near future. He needed to get a hip replacement. There wouldn't be a tour without a new record—that would be cheating the fans. They were taking it "step by step." He wasn't going to commit to moving forward with Roth.

Feeling his own level of frustration, Dave says in his book that he took Eddie aside and said now wasn't the time to start talking about personal issues—especially ones he wasn't even aware of until they were brought up in front of the press. Talking about his hip was bringing the mood down, and that wasn't fair to people celebrating the occasion—it was "bad manners." The guitarist rebuked him and said it was his life, and, if the singer ever talked to him like that, he was going to "kick you in your fucking balls."

The stance Eddie took on what occurred was similar, with a key tweak. In an interview with MTV weeks later, he said that when he asked Roth what was wrong, the singer told him, "Well, hey . . . tonight's about me, man—not your fucking hip." The guitarist claimed he had acquiesced and said he would not mention his hip, to which the singer replied, "You fuckin' better not." That's when he said he told Dave, "You ever speak to me like that again, you better be wearing a cup."

UNFULFILLED PROMISE

The next Monday, Roth went on *The Howard Stern Show*. He'd have gone on sooner, but the program was on a vacation break the week prior. The singer gave no indication that anything had been amiss since the VMAs but deferred to the band when the shock jock asked when a tour could be expected, saying a video was the next step.

It was Stern who premiered "Me Wise Magic" a couple of weeks before the song was officially released, but by the end of September word was getting around that a video wasn't going to be made after all, as Roth was unhappy with the proposed treatment for the clip, which was supposedly going to feature him singing on a screen while the band performed in front of it. Not only that, but reports were coming in that Cherone had been officially offered the position of lead singer in Van Halen.

October 2 saw a press release from Roth hit media outlets. "You've probably heard rumors that Van Halen and I will not be consummating our highly publicized reunion," it read. "And since neither Edward, Alex, nor Michael have corroborated or denied the gossip, I would like to go on record with the following: Eddie did it."

He further claimed to be "an unwitting participant in this deception," and confirmed the hardcore fans' biggest letdown fears: a reunion wasn't going to happen. Chalking it up to a publicity stunt, Roth said the band had hired another singer as much as three months earlier; he didn't give a name, though everyone and their grandmother knew it to be Cherone. Somewhat calculatedly, Extreme revealed that day that they were disbanding.

On October 3, Van Halen served up their own statement of cattiness that read, "We parted company with David Lee Roth eleven years ago for many reasons. In his open letter of October 2nd, we were reminded of some of them. Dave was never an 'unwitting participant.' We appeared in public just as we do before releasing any other Van Halen record."

The band copped to have been working with another singer, but only for two weeks, and they couldn't name him due to "contractual considerations." They assured fans that the group "will go forward and create the best possible music that we can."

Gary Cherone was officially announced as the new frontman of Van Halen the next day, October 4, adding another ingredient to a sloppy Pasadena jambalaya that was brewed in a cauldron of firings, hirings, behind-the-back dramatics, and, as Dave intimated, somebody's lying.

FACING THE MUSIC

Van Halen's *Best Of—Volume I* came out on October 22, 1996, and went straight to No. 1 on the *Billboard* 200, spending one week there. Interestingly, when it was released, neither of the singers featured on the album were in the band anymore.

Backward as that was, it then seems only appropriate that the record itself would feature an error: the wrong mix of "Runnin' with the Devil" was inserted on the first pressings, with the second and third verses flipped. This mistake would be repeated three years later, when the song was included as part of the *Detroit Rock City* soundtrack.

Soon after the album came *Video Hits—Volume I*, which contains only three clips from the David Lee Roth era, all from the *1984* album. Both collections have the same artwork, with a gold "rings" VH logo centered over a black background, the same color type, and the title at the bottom and the top. An extensive fold-out features the covers and track listing of the band's entire catalogue, with the only new pictures black-and-white shots of Eddie's then new Wolfgang model guitar and the empty drum room at 5150 Studios.

There were seventeen tracks on the album: ten from the Roth era and seven from Hagar's tenure. These included the three most recent songs Van Halen had recorded, "Humans Being," "Can't Get This Stuff No More," and "Me Wise

Magic." The Japanese pressing of the LP had one extra track, "Hot for Teacher," which required the radio edit of "Can't Get This Stuff No More" be used. There was also a sticker of the flaming, multicolored VH rings logo. The liner notes concluded with the words, "Dedicated to the Memory of Ed Leffler."

Eddie Van Halen did minimal press for the compilation, as he knew it would be the same questions over and over, all focused on the recent drama. When he did talk, he stuck to the same story: Sammy quit; Dave was never told he was in the band. Both former frontmen were lying. Gary Cherone was the new vocalist, and he could sing like an angel. The best part about Cherone? He didn't have LSD, Eddie's favorite new catchphrase for his previous singers: "Lead Singer Disease." Oh, and there was no truth to the rumors that Cherone had been auditioning for (or in) the group before the mess of the past few weeks took place.

"If we had already hired Gary, then we would have used him instead of Dave," Eddie told the *Los Angeles Times*. "But Gary and I have been writing together, and we've come up with seven songs in the last two weeks. He's quick, he's deep, and he's got a good sense of humor. I can't wait to record with him."

Roth kept quiet publicly after he issued his press release, but he did record a song called "Private Parts" that he hoped would get slotted in as the title track to the Howard Stern film. Unfortunately, it wasn't that good, mainly because the lyrics were way too literal—the antithesis of what the singer was known for writing. Stern declined to use it, with the justification that there was enough Van Halen on the soundtrack and in the movie, with three pieces of music already incorporated. Roth later rewrote the song and turned it into "Tight" on his 1998 solo album *DLR Band*.

THE REAL EDDIE

Amazingly, right in the midst of the outcry and nonstop headlines surrounding his band as 1996 drew near a close, Eddie made an appearance in Chicago, at the Riviera Theatre, to play at a benefit show. The concert—a nearly eight-hour affair with local and national guitarists—was for onetime Roth guitarist Jason Becker, who by then had been totally crippled by ALS, losing all ability to speak and communicating only by eye movements.

Speculation abounded that the new Van Halen would give fans their first look that night, but a once-in-a-lifetime band showed up as a worthy alternative. Playing under the moniker the Lou Brutus Experience after a local disc jockey, Eddie was joined onstage by Toto guitarist Steve Lukather and the rhythm section from Mr. Big, drummer Pat Torpey and Billy Sheehan. They ripped through a bunch of covers that included "Wipe Out" (The Surfaris), "Good Times Bad Times" (Led Zeppelin), "Little Wing" (Jimi Hendrix), "Ain't Talkin' 'Bout Love" (Van Halen), and "I Want You (She's So Heavy)" (The Beatles), closing with Hendrix's "Fire."

It really said something in terms of what Eddie is all about to see him fly halfway across the country to perform at the gig. What no one knew publicly is that he had committed to it in late August, when he went to Becker's house in California to film an ALS awareness video. It had been a particularly tough time for Jason, as he was very weak and had not yet gotten a trachea or stomach tube put in. Eddie spent the day with him, playing music, telling stories, and just being a caring human being.

"Eddie was such a beautiful person," Becker said in late 2020, when he released a video from the day. "He was incredibly kind to me and my family. Not only was he my biggest influence, he had such a huge heart. He honestly saved my life."

ABOVE Van Halen at the MTV Video Music Awards at Radio City Music Hall in New York City, September 13, 1985—the band's first appearance in public with Sammy Hagar. *Ebet Roberts.*

LEFT Eddie and Sammy at Colorado Sun Day at Folsom Field in Boulder, Colorado, July 12, 1986. *Chris Deutsch.*

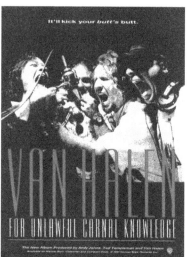

TOP LEFT Van Halen in 1993. *Photofest.*

TOP RIGHT A magazine ad promoting the 1991 release *For Unlawful Carnal Knowledge. Author's collection.*

BELOW LEFT Eddie with his red, white, and black striped drill playing "Poundcake" live in 1991. *Rick Gould.*

BELOW RIGHT Eddie Van Halen onstage at Jones Beach Theater, Wantagh, New York, August 1995. *Eddie Malluk.*

OPPOSITE PAGE, TOP A "reunited" Van Halen field questions from the assembled press at the MTV Video Music Awards in 1996. *Media Punch Inc/Alamy Stock Photo.*

OPPOSITE PAGE, BOTTOM Gary Cherone and Eddie Van Halen onstage in 1998, during the only tour with the Extreme frontman. *Photofest.*

ABOVE The 2004 reunion tour with Sammy Hagar at the Staples Center in Los Angeles. *Pictorial Press Ltd/Jeffrey Mayer/Alamy Stock Photo.*

RIGHT Sammy Hagar and Michael Anthony at the Rock and Roll Hall of Fame induction on March 12, 2007. Neither was in the band at the time. *REUTERS/Lucas Jackson/Alamy Stock Photo.*

TOP The Van Halen reunion with David Lee Roth is announced at the Four Seasons Hotel in Los Angeles on August 13, 2007. *UPI Photo/Jim Ruymen/Alamy Stock Photo.*

BOTTOM Van Halen take a bow at the end of the Boston show on their 2007 reunion tour. Note the red sock hanging off Wolfgang's bass—a nod to the Boston Red Sox, who held their World Series victory parade that same day. *Author's collection.*

ABOVE David Lee Roth onstage at Café Wha?, where the band performed in front of select media and friends to promote the release of *A Different Kind of Truth*, January 5, 2012. *Author's collection.*

RIGHT A Japanese advertisement for the show in Tokyo on June 21, 2013, subsequently released as the two-LP set *Tokyo Dome Live in Concert. Alamy.*

OPPOSITE PAGE, TOP David Lee Roth and Eddie Van Halen share a laugh onstage in 2015. *Author's collection.*

OPPOSITE PAGE, BOTTOM Wolfgang and Eddie having fun onstage in 2015. *Author's collection.*

TOP Eddie Van Halen, 1955–2020. *Author's collection.*

ABOVE LEFT The iconic Van Halen logo has been co-opted in numerous ways over the years, like during the COVID-19 pandemic, which inspired illustrator Rick Pinchera to create a "Working from Home" T-shirt. *Courtesy of Rick Pinchera.*

ABOVE RIGHT Another recent re-interpretation of the logo occurred during the 2020 presidential race in the United States. "Runnin' Against the Devil" was a slight directed at the incumbent, Donald Trump. *Helen Stickler.*

21

HUMANS BEING

The news that Sammy Hagar was out and David Lee Roth was back in—but almost immediately sent packing—and that Gary Cherone would be the new Van Halen singer whenever the next album was going to be released was being digested. Like clockwork, an old argument among fans returned to the forefront: Dave versus Sammy.

The advent and increased availability of the internet provided a brand new forum to debate, coincidentally around the same time *Best Of—Volume I* split the vocalists almost down the middle in terms of song selection. And with the band buried in 5150 Studios for the foreseeable future, it was as good a time as any to dig into what the two established singers in the immediate rearview had contributed to the legacy so far.

At the end of the day, it's all about the fans. The ones who come to the shows, buy the records, seek out the bootlegs, hung the band's poster on their walls and stuck with them through all the theater. They're the ones who have not only a financial but emotional investment in what happens with Van Halen.

Van Halen created a markedly divergent sound on *5150*, and it wasn't what all their devotees wanted—especially those who had grown up with the band, had certain expectations, and who were accustomed to David Lee Roth's vocals and his unique way of playing off the music. Many others were on board with Sammy Hagar's singing style, though, the crowds got bigger, and new supporters replaced those who pledged allegiance to the Roth Army. Immediately, this created a fissure in the fanbase, and the greatest "singer versus singer" debate in music history.

At the height of the battle between Roth and Van Halen, nobody knew who was going to win out. The band had soldiered on with a new frontman, continued an immersion into pop only hinted at on hits like "Dance the Night Away" and "Jump," and were awarded with their most successful tour and first chart-topping album in *5150*. That trajectory may have happened anyway, had there not been a split with their previous singer—who, on his own, was sticking more toward tried-and-true rock and roll with a cadre of virtuoso musicians behind him, peppering it with variations of big band and swing that most saw as humorous.

As time wore on, Roth was the clear loser in terms of popularity. His solo material sold less and less well, while each ensuing tour became more about looking back on his glory days in his prior outfit than drawing listeners in with whatever sonic detour he'd decided to take. He couldn't win; was castigated for a run of shows in Las Vegas tailormade for his sensibilities in 1996, yet ignored two years later, when he released *DLR Band*, his hardest-rocking effort since the first few Van Halen LPs.

Obviously, there were those in the majority who may have preferred one vocalist to another but were going to support Van Halen as a group no matter what. But the lines had been drawn by the scores of fans who always seemed to be the most vocal: they wanted either the unimpeachable "classic six-pack" of Roth or the radio-friendly leanings of Sammy Hagar.

"THE MUSIC LACKED DANGER"

"I thought David Lee Roth was the epitome of cool," Matthew Schaffer said. "He was shockingly articulate, and his interviews were riddled with jokes. Very witty. Plus, when he performed in music videos or live, he did karate kicks. I liked that because I was taking karate at the time."

Schaffer, a native of Venice, California, first got into Van Halen when he saw the video for "Jump" in 1984. He didn't get to see the band that tour, though, and when he heard Roth was out, he felt like he was "robbed of seeing the Eighth Wonder of the World." Still, he wasn't automatically against Hagar.

"I liked his solo work . . . his contribution to the *Heavy Metal* soundtrack [Hagar provided the title song to the 1981 animated cult film] and I thought the 'I Can't Drive 55' video was hysterical," he said. "He's got a great voice, but he's not cool. He tries, but he just doesn't have the charisma. When he sings, he trying to get you to like him. When Dave sings, he doesn't care if you like him or not—he's gonna have a great time no matter what. Without Dave, Van Halen lacked attitude. It lacked balls. The music lacked danger."

Schaffer equated the music Van Halen did with Hagar as sounding "like something I'd hear in my dentist's office. Sammy's era was soft, watered-down hard rock for people who normally couldn't take anything heavier than Bob Seger." He believes the argument isn't really about one singer versus another, but on whose side of the Dave versus Eddie fight someone falls.

"If you like Sammy-era VH, that meant you thought Dave was a clown and that Eddie was the true genius of the band. If you were on Dave's side, that meant you understood that what made the original Van Halen work was the friction between those two musicians."

"THE OBVIOUS CHOICE"

Growing up in Northern California, David Perrine was already well aware of Sammy Hagar, both in Montrose and as a solo artist, when the singer joined Van Halen in 1985, putting him up there with Freddie Mercury and Bad Company's Paul Rodgers in terms of vocal abilities. Though he had been a fan of the Roth era—he was twelve years old when the debut came out—and calls the first six albums "lightning in a bottle," the frontman's antics began to wear on him.

"By the time he put out [*Crazy from the Heat*] and *Dave TV* [the singer's 1986 video and interview collection], it confirmed what I thought: Dave was all about Dave," Perrine said. "It also became evident to me that he saw himself as the star of the band and the one indispensable member. I have no doubt that Dave just assumed Mike, Al, and Eddie could not succeed or achieve any level of success without him."

Immediately after Hagar was announced as the new lead singer for the band, Perrine was excited about the possibilities of that voice and Eddie's guitar. "He just seemed the obvious choice . . . one of the smartest decisions the band has ever made.

"Sammy is a pro," he added. "I've never seen Sammy half-ass a concert or not give his best vocal performance possible. [He] strikes me as far more genuine and totally lacking the arrogance or the narcissism Dave appears to have in abundance. Watching the *5150* tour, it was really evident to me that the tension in that band was gone and those four musicians were generally enjoying playing together."

Perrine is of the belief that Sammy fans are far more accepting of the Dave era, though the former can take as good as they get. The hatred toward the Hagar years is unbridled for some, and they aren't shy about letting others know.

"The passion for this band is unrivaled," he said. "The 'Dave or the Grave' group believe Eddie needs Dave for his best playing and the music lost its edge without Dave. It became personal. I've never seen anything like it. People get genuinely upset debating Sam versus Dave. I think it was a particularly hard pill to swallow when Dave took such a nosedive shortly after leaving Van Halen. Those millions of Dave fans became even more bitter, and they still direct it at Eddie and Alex. Has to be their fault, nobody else's."

"I GOT TIRED OF THE BICKERING"

Tracey Bates, who hails from Kansas and now lives in the Northeast, discovered Van Halen in 1978, when she was listening to Casey Kasem's *American Top 40* and heard "Runnin' with the Devil." But though she was taken with how different the music sounded than anything else out there, she wasn't about to invest in the band based on one song and wanted to hear more. Someone Bates was a big fan of around that time was Valerie Bertinelli, and when the *One Day at a Time* star began dating Eddie Van Halen, she really seized onto the band.

"I felt disappointed [when Roth left]—I felt like I just started to really get into their music," Bates said, adding that she was hoping the band would play the Live Aid benefit concert in 1985 and she'd get to see them there. "I was holding out . . . then I saw that Sammy was the lead singer."

The music Van Halen created with Hagar didn't grab Bates the way the records with Roth at the helm did. To her, it became too commercialized and more acceptable for radio and MTV. Hagar played it safe, and the songs were "easy to forget," whereas Roth took a risk. The *5150* album is when Van Halen lost her, but once the back-and-forth in the press heated up as the '80s wore on, she completely tuned out.

"One of the reasons I stopped following is that I got tired of the bickering," she said. "It seemed to be coming from the Van Halen side about David. I never heard David say anything against them. I feel Eddie, Alex, and Michael did not understand David. I don't think they appreciated David. I believe that David brought out the best of everyone one of them. He did the hard part, keeping the band together and [pushing them to] create their own sound. He showcased Eddie's ability as a guitar player. By the time Sammy was in Van Halen, it was already established that Eddie is an amazing guitar player. He did not have to work that hard to be noticed. I have [seen] on YouTube that Sammy tries to be more like David, when he moves onstage and sings—but he can't."

"OLDER, GOOFIER, AND MORE ECCENTRIC"

Van Halen were the first "favorite band" of New Jersey's Mark Levitt. Like many, he had heard the name before, but he really became a fan when the videos from *1984* started blowing up on MTV. He'd also noticed Sammy Hagar on the channel, and the "I Can't Drive 55" clip led him to dig further into the Red Rocker's back catalogue. Up until *Crazy from the Heat*, he was on board with Roth, but, as a hard-rock fan, he found himself completely turned off by the EP.

"I realized then this was not the kind of music I was looking for, and Dave was not the 'rocker' I thought he was," Levitt said. "So, when I heard Sammy was joining, I thought it was perfect. I was already really into his music and thought he'd be a great fit!"

For many of the old-school fans of the group, what really leaves a bad taste in their mouth is how "poppy" the Hagar material turned out to be. Levitt agrees that it might not be as raw and guitar-based as the earlier material, but, from *5150* on, the music was hardly soft rock.

"[Dave fans] often state, when Sammy joined it was all 'ballads and Foreigner-like light pop,' which is ridiculous," he said. "Did Foreigner ever have any songs like 'Good Enough,' 'Get Up,' 'Black and Blue,' 'Source of Infection,' 'A.F.U. (Naturally Wired),' 'Humans Being'? They may not have liked the keyboard-heavy ballads, which is understandable, but they often neglect to mention 'Dancing in the Street,' which couldn't have been any more pop, or 'I'll Wait,' or 'Jump.'"

Levitt felt the divide between fans had lessened over time, with many people automatically tipping toward the Roth era due to the reunion tours with him. That said, he noted a shift toward the Hagar period in the past two decades, as each singer has gotten up in age.

"I've noticed many fans that have started to appreciate Sammy, and, at the same time, Dave's 'cool factor' has decreased as he's become older, goofier, and more eccentric—compared to Sammy, who is just clearly a real musician," he said. "It was almost always the Dave fans bullying anyone who didn't agree he was best, but that has definitely tilted the other way more over the years."

"PURISTS LOVE DAVE"

The son of a touring gospel-musician father who didn't much like his musical tastes, Gene Ingram was a high school freshman in Tennessee when he first got to see Van Halen on their 1982 tour. Hearing the news that Roth had left a few years later left him "devastated."

"They were my favorite band, he was my favorite frontman," Ingram said. "My favorite music was coming to an end. The music that got me through junior high and high school was over. The stories, memories, girlfriends, racing cars, smoking pot, listening to loud music of my favorite band was all over. The soundtrack to my high school life was over, and it seemed to be unfixable."

While he liked *5150* on the whole, Ingram thought the success the reconfigured lineup had was due to Hagar bringing in his audience to combine with the "crippled" Van Halen fan base. "The music turned into love songs and feel-good songs, instead of the wild, subtle, lyrical style of David Lee Roth. You didn't know if Dave was talking about a car, a girl, or your mom."

Ingram figures there's such a split among audiences across the eras because people in general want you to choose. "It's always implied, if you like Sammy era then you are anti-Roth; if you like DLR then you are anti-Hagar. I think the industry made more of the feud than Sammy and Dave did. But they approached music from different directions with different results. Most people love Dave until he opens his mouth and starts with his twisted-up verbiage and they can't follow him, or they think he is just jacked up on cocaine. He is someone that makes you want to hear or see what is going to happen next. I think purists love Dave because he was there in the beginning to develop the true sound of Van Halen."

"NO, MOTHERFUCKER—EDDIE IS THE GUY"

Robert Hinkle got exposed to Van Halen for the first time aged eight, courtesy of an older brother who was into rock and roll and brought the band's eponymous debut into their home in Lexington, Kentucky, in 1978. Obsessed with the cover art on the record, he'd pester his sibling to let him come into his room to listen to it, and he was particularly taken with Eddie's guitar, which was unlike anything he'd ever heard before. Hinkle also liked Dave, but when the singer left the band in 1985, he found he was the only one among his friends who was ecstatic about Hagar coming into the fold.

"When Dave left the band, I was fifteen, and I was ready to move on from him, but not Van Halen," he said. "I loved Sammy's voice, loved that he played guitar, and I thought his stage performance was just unbridled energy. I could not stand Dave's live performance. He talked every other lyric and strolled around shaking his ass and yelping his signature screams as fills. It always seemed like a waste. By *Diver Down*, I could not stand his schtick. He became a caricature of himself. By *1984*, probably before, he thought he was the guy. I was always like, 'No, motherfucker—Eddie is the guy.'"

Hinkle speculated that many fans are into the original era of Van Halen because that's what they associate with the innovativeness of Eddie's guitar playing, so they simply default to that period. He was especially harsh on Roth diehards, calling them "weak-minded saps who aren't aware that they are being condescended to by a third-rate 'singer.'"

"I think Dave fans have a hard time admitting that Sammy Hagar replaced their hero and made Van Halen more commercially successful," he said. "They seethe at the reality that Van Halen with Sammy Hagar scored four straight No. 1 albums, won an American Music Award, MTV Awards, and a Grammy, without 'Cubic Zirconia' Roth at the helm."

"FROM RAW AND ENERGETIC TO WIMPY AND SAPPY"

Nothing on the *5150* LP grabbed nineteen-year-old Albert Rowuin. A few years earlier, he had gotten into Van Halen via a girl he liked in high school, and now the band as he knew it was ruined. When *Eat 'Em and Smile* came out, he "quickly realized Dave was light years better than Sammy in Van Hagar," especially with the musicians he'd put together for the record. When Roth left his former bandmates, Rowuin felt, he took with him the drive, the attitude, intelligence, humor, confidence, and fun of the group.

"Mostly I didn't like the lyrics and style of the Van Hagar songs," he said. "We went from raw and energetic songs like 'Ain't Talkin' 'Bout Love' to wimpy and sappy songs whining about 'Why Can't This Be Love.'"

Rowuin, of Los Angeles, dug his heels into his Roth fandom. He said the *Eat 'Em and Smile* tour changed his life, but he lost interest for a bit in the late '80s, before coming back around again in 1999. He latched onto the Atomic Punks—a tribute band who focused on early Van Halen—for his Dave-era fix, and eventually became their webmaster. Rowuin, who's met the singer several times, became a member and moderator on the Roth Army website, and he did the same with the David Lee Roth Mailing List. He considered the Roth and Hagar eras as "different bands with different fans," noting that age needs to be taken into account when analyzing the rift between them.

"I really wish Van Halen had a more generic name, like Mammoth, so the three remaining guys wouldn't be the automatic owner of the band name when Dave split," he said. "The new Van Halen with Sammy was different, a lot of elevator/grocery store music sharing little in common with their rocking roots. There seems to be fan resentment that Van Hagar got so much of the media attention and accolades, while a lot of Dave's solo stuff—some of which was great—was mostly ignored.

"I know plenty of fans who like all VH eras—sometimes because they're Ed fans—regardless of the current singer. I'd say, generally, their respective fans are of different ages, separated by at least a decade, with different musical preference. When a fan of only one era confronts a fan of another era, even though they have the same band name, they will be divided over their preferences, and they feel the need to put down the other 'side' to try to prove their point."

"ISN'T THE BAND CALLED *VAN HALEN*?"

A fan of Sammy Hagar since he was nine years old, Troy J. Maturin of Abbeville, Louisiana, was all for it when the singer joined Van Halen. Never a fan of Roth's over-the-top persona, nor the sideshow he brought to centerstage in favor of the music, Maturin suggested that those who prefer the original frontman enjoy having a clown as the focus.

"Oh, he does great interviews where he dances around the questions with these longwinded answers that somehow entertain but never deliver on the answer," he said. "He was always the center of attention in the videos. Isn't the band called 'Van Halen?' Not 'Roth.'"

Even though he came of age when Roth fronted the group and liked a lot of the songs, Maturin just didn't enjoy the "in-your-face attitude" the singer had. It felt less like a band and more an entertainer on a solitary endeavor, not someone committed to being part of a unit.

"Sammy is just on a whole different level than Dave. [He's] a guitar player that doesn't mind jamming with anyone. Dave doesn't like to share the spotlight. Two totally different frontmen; I prefer the one that rocks and has fun taking his job seriously."

"VAN HAGAR IS JUST HIGH-POWERED JOURNEY"

Living in the mountains of North Carolina as a preteen in the late '70s, Patrick J. White wasn't exposed to a lot of cutting-edge music like Van Halen on the radio. He was twelve years old in 1980 when he first heard "Beautiful Girls" at a friend's house, and he was hooked by the time he saw VH at the Hampton Coliseum in Virginia on Halloween night, 1982. The next time around, it was at the same venue on his birthday. He said he felt like Sean Penn's character in the movie *Fast Times at Ridgemont High*, Jeff Spicoli, who, according to the film's postscript, saves Brooke Shields from drowning and then "blows reward money hiring Van Halen to play his birthday party."

White—who subsequently moved to Newport News, Virginia, and credited Roth's confident lyrics in assisting him in beating a crippling speech impediment—sided with the singer completely when he left Van Halen. He snuck backstage at the second show on the *Skyscraper* tour in Hollywood, Florida, and told Roth he was a twenty-year-old kid chasing "some crazy rock and roll dream," then asked for advice. The singer said, "Whatever you do, pal ... don't *ever* stop chasing it!"

Evidently, White isn't someone who was going to speak glowingly of Van Halen without Roth, and he didn't like the new sound coming from the band. "Van Hagar is just a high-powered Journey," he said. "Whereas Dave continued on with an even more talented band and produced music with that Van Halen feel . . . fun, confident, kick-ass. The music [in Van Halen] went soft, for the most part. Without Dave, Van Halen was missing the flair, the charisma, the frontman, and the essence of the band. Although the music was good enough to stand on its own . . . Dave delivered the music and especially the live performance. Sometimes, *what* you say isn't as important as *how* you say it. Van Halen's music was the *what* . . . Dave was the *how*."

22

FIRE IN THE HOLE

When exactly it took place remains up for debate, but at some point over the summer of 1996, Gary Cherone was invited to come out and audition for Van Halen by Ray Danniels, the band's manager, who also handled the singer's Boston group, Extreme. Two days later, Eddie asked him to join. He was in fact staying in the guest cottage of the guitarist's home while the whole MTV Video Music Awards scenario was playing out, and by then he had already laid down a few songs with the band.

While he may have been the last candidate to be brought in—or the one decided upon—Cherone certainly wasn't the first. Much earlier in the year, Eddie and Alex had auditioned songstress Sass Jordan, a rising star coming off the hit albums *Racine* (1992) and *Rats* (1994) who was likely suggested by Danniels, a fellow Canadian. Though she spent three months in the studio with the brothers—no Michael Anthony—she was never categorically offered the lead singer spot.

"I think I would've remembered that," Jordan said, laughing. "It was the weirdest thing. I can't imagine anyone else being in that position that I was in, and not thinking something was up. It didn't even occur to me. I thought they just wanted somebody to sing on these songs for them, so they could get an idea of how the song was going. Honestly, it never entered my mind that they would want a female. It's so ridiculous to my mind."

Unlike Patty Smyth before her, Jordan was a blues-based singer with a raspy, attitude-filled voice. If the group were looking for a female with a rough edge, they were in the right place. Strangely, there wasn't much happening over the ninety or so days at 5150 Studios; Jordan said all they really did was hang out.

"They'd tell me stories, then they'd get in fights, they'd talk about this and that, and then they'd send me out for beer and cigarettes, and then I'd be given lectures on 'not to tell anybody what's going on.'"

"After a while, it was like, 'What the fuck am I doing here?' Like, 'We never do any music stuff, why am I still here?' Then it just suddenly like, 'Oh my god. No. Wait a minute. No,'" she said, recalling the moment the reality of the situation—that they might want her to join the band—hit her. "And then, course, being me, I just blurted it out, and they just were like, 'What? No. Umm—no. Whoa—look at the time! Look at the *time!*' That kind of thing. They just looked so guilty. I was like, 'For fuck's sake—am I right? I might be right.' All I could think of was the idea of having this legacy as the person who destroyed Van Halen."

Someone else the band expressed interest in was Sebastian Bach. The wailer was about to leave his own band, Skid Row, due to growing tensions in the ranks, but he never even made it to 5150.

"There was definitely a meeting I had in about 1996 with [Bach manager] Doc McGhee, where it was told to me that Ray Danniels and Van Halen were inquiring to me about being a lead singer, but that's as far as it went," he said. "There was this whole thing about Eddie and Alex couldn't have a lead singer in the band who smoked pot. And I go, 'You know what? That's pretty fucking funny, because you know where I learned to smoke pot? A fuckin' Van Halen fuckin' concert.' [*laughs*]

"You know what else? That was [around the time] that Bill Clinton . . . kept saying 'I didn't inhale, I didn't inhale.' I thought to myself, 'It's a pretty fucked-up world where you can smoke pot and be the president of the United States, but if you smoke pot, you can't be the lead singer of Van Halen.' [*laughs*] Somebody explain that to me."

Solo singer Billy Squier, whose own career as a rock artist had long flatlined, called up and offered his services but was quietly blown off. It was speculated that David Coverdale, of Whitesnake fame, was also in the mix, which wouldn't be too surprising given his time in Deep Purple when they were having a revolving door of vocalists, and he had just finished up a brief partnership with another guitar god in Jimmy Page. But he said he hadn't seen Eddie in a number of years and that the story was false.

One person who said he was told he had the job was the then unknown Mitch Malloy, a Midwest singer/songwriter who had relocated to Nashville and was working on his third solo effort. Apparently, the band saw one of his videos and thought he was the perfect combination of Roth and Hagar. He was whisked to the studio in the summer—he too stayed in Eddie's guest cottage—and by his account he got on well with the guitarist, Alex, and Michael, nailing songs from both eras of the group. Floating around on the internet is audio of a band rehearsal of "Panama" with Malloy singing, plus an original they did together called "It's the Right Time."

Malloy said that he was asked to join Van Halen after just three days. They started working on new music in the days leading up to the MTV awards, which Eddie told him about without mentioning Dave's involvement. He watched the show from his home in Nashville, and his jaw dropped.

"That moment that Roth walked out behind them, I knew it was over," he told *Rolling Stone*. "I am not going to be in Van Halen. I just knew somehow. And so that was it for me."

"I think that would've been a disaster, an absolute disaster," said Stryper's Michael Sweet about the possibility of a Malloy-fronted Van Halen. "Thank God they didn't do that. That just felt so weird and did not feel right at all. It's not a good fit."

One week after the VMAs, Malloy had his manager fax over a letter to the band, thanking them for the opportunity and telling them he was going to have to "respectfully pass" because of prior commitments and excitement about the next stage of his solo career. He said Eddie called him to apologize and later provided some financial assistance for an album the singer was recording. About the decision to go with Cherone, Malloy said he figured that would happen, as Cherone was the only other vocalist in the mix.

Danniels said it wasn't until he received the fax that he realized Malloy thought he had the gig, and he made it clear that once Cherone was officially announced, that was the guy they wanted. "As a pure singer, Gary is a natural talent," the manager told *Billboard*. "He has the swagger that Roth has, and he's a great lyricist. We're as confident as we can get."

THE "MORE THAN WORDS" GUY

Gary Francis Caine Cherone was born on July 26, 1961, and was raised in Malden, Massachusetts, a town just north of Boston. He was one of five boys in an Italian American family and the younger in a set of fraternal twins. Growing up in a vibrant rock and roll scene—one where Aerosmith were local heroes—he started singing in bands. He found local success with the hard rock outfit the Dream in the early '80s. The band had copyrighted the name and sold the rights to the producers of a television show. They changed their name to Extreme (ex-Dream) and used the money to finance the demos that eventually got them signed. Guitar marvel Nuno Bettencourt joined the ranks, and the group's long-gestating eponymous debut came out in 1989.

Extreme played a unique blend of funk, metal, and hard rock that showcased Bettencourt's sharp playing. But they would be best remembered for the 1991 single "More Than Words," from their sophomore album, *Pornograffiti*, which came out the year before. The acoustic ballad was atypical of the group's sound, but it was massively popular, hitting the top spot on *Billboard* and forever pigeonholing them as a one-hit wonder.

At the Freddie Mercury Tribute Concert for AIDS Awareness in 1992 in London, Cherone was one of the highlights—first when Extreme did a medley of Queen songs, and later when the curly maned singer came out and performed "Hammer to Fall" with the surviving members of the group and Black Sabbath guitarist Tony Iommi. The energetic display and vocal performance he put on at Wembley Stadium blew away the audience watching there and around the world on the televised simulcast. He was only outshone on the bill by George Michael, whose take on a trio of Queen songs—notably "Somebody to Love"—was untouchable.

When Extreme were preparing to break up in 1996, Danniels said he was angling to get Cherone in as frontman for Queen, since there was talk at the time—later denied—that they were in the market for a vocalist, and Michael had politely declined. That's when the manager decided to put him in front of Van Halen.

Watching the MTV awards and seeing the reception Van Halen received with Roth, though, Cherone knew he was in for a bumpy ride. "It didn't help my situation," he said, adding that Eddie kept calling to reassure him, almost protectively, that he was the main choice for the group and that wasn't going to change, no matter what.

"There was always a measure of dysfunction, because the Van Halen machine was so huge, and everybody was pulling at them at all times," Cherone said, while acknowledging, "Fans get their hopes back."

Whereas Hagar came into Van Halen on the heels of his hit "I Can't Drive 55," an up-tempo number that rocked right in the same neighborhood as his new outfit's body of work, people who weren't familiar with Extreme other than their 1991 mega-hit were wary of Cherone. It wasn't just fans, either.

"I'd go into a town and the DJ would say, 'Van Halen's comin' to town, they got the singer, the 'More Than Words' guy,'" he said. "There would be this expectation of, you know, 'Mr. More Than Words.' But, by the end of the show, they saw the passion, they saw the performance, and they saw the band as a fan, and for me that was the best part of it."

"As much as he wasn't the perfect fit for Van Halen, it was something [Danniels] kind of forced him upon us, and then Ed became really good friends with him," said Michael Anthony. "It was a really weird time for us—Al was going through a messy divorce, but Gary and I always got along great. On tour, he always wanted to do all those old Van Halen tunes that even Sammy didn't want to do. It was great, stuff like 'Feel Your Love Tonight' we hadn't done in twenty years."

NEWORLD

Letting the dust settle, Van Halen laid low in the wake of the Video Music Awards fiasco. They didn't rush or pressure writing and recording with Cherone, using *Best Of—Volume I* as a stopgap to keep the label off their backs for 1997. It proved a wise move, as both of their previous singers had things to get off their chests that year.

First up was Hagar, who in May released a new solo album, *Marching to Mars*, with a vicious lead single directed at Van Halen called "Little White Lie." The video for the song took a swipe at Eddie by having a monkey with a cigarette hanging out of his mouth strumming a guitar. The penultimate shot shows the backs of three individuals holding a press conference, meant to represent the Van Halen brothers and Roth, with the word "LIE" overlaid underneath.

Then there was a re-energized Diamond Dave, who in October doubled down on his return to the headlines with his long-in-the-works autobiography and a solo greatest hits collection, *The Best*, featuring one new song, "Don't Piss Me Off." Unfortunately, it was a losing bet. The LP barely squeaked into the *Billboard* 200 at No. 199 before it immediately dropped off the chart.

Crazy from the Heat did better, though it didn't make any national bestseller lists. Many critics dubbed it an incoherent and erratic slog. Those who expected a linear tale had obviously never heard Roth speak at any great length, and his literary endeavor—reportedly shaved down from twelve hundred pages to less than a third of that—was no different from sitting in a room with him as he bounced from topic to topic with reckless abandon. There were nuggets throughout, but they took some digging to get to, although readers who flipped right to the "Reunion Blues" chapter weren't left disappointed with the singer's candor over the 1996 incident that remains one of the most discussed blunders in music history.

Trying to recover from that, Van Halen forged ahead with singer number three at the mic in 1998, but it was hard for fans to muster up much enthusiasm. They still felt hoodwinked by the situation, no matter the real story. It certainly wasn't Gary Cherone's fault; he could've been Freddie Mercury reincarnated and it would've been a letdown because he wasn't David Lee Roth or even Sammy Hagar.

"Ray had managed Gary Cherone and he had him in the wings, poisoning Eddie, 'I got this guy, he'll do anything you want. He's a team player. He's a great singer and he's this and he's that,' and they all bought into the shit," Hagar said. "Why would you replace Sammy Hagar with Gary Cherone? Is he a better singer? I don't think so. Is he a bigger star? I don't think so. Is he more talented or a better performer? I don't think so. [*laughs*] Then why'd you do it? It was so that Eddie could have control. He wanted control at that stage. I love Gary, he's a nice guy. When I'm comparing him to me, I'm just being my old, confident self."

The first taste of fresh music with Cherone came at the end of February 1998, when the lead single, "Without You," hit radio. Catchy and full of instrumental spunk, it was a high-energy track with some expectedly swift guitar histrionics and propulsive bottom end. Vocally, the song sounds a lot like the singer from

Extreme fronting a different group, but not exactly Van Halen. Missing were the patented high harmonies from Michael Anthony, which for whatever reason are missing or buried in the mix.

THIRD TIME IS NOT THE CHARM

Cleverly titled—at least moderately so—*Van Halen III* premiered in radio markets serviced by the Album Network on March 12, 1998, landing in retail outlets five days later, on St. Patrick's Day. It entered the *Billboard* charts at No. 4 and never went any higher, plummeting to No. 26 the next week and dropping off completely three months later.

Mike Post, the Grammy-winning composer of the theme songs to *The A-Team* and *Law & Order* and co-writer of "Theme from *The Greatest American Hero* (Believe It or Not)," was an odd pick for producer. A golfing pal of Eddie's, he had never worked on anything remotely close to a hard rock album.

The cover of the record shows the early twentieth-century carnival performer Frank "Cannonball" Richards getting shot in the stomach with a cannonball, with the band's name and album title overlaid on the cannon. The booklet and liner notes have a circus theme too, which may or may not have been a wink and a nod to the internal happenings in the band. A limited-edition run of the CD version in a square metal picture tin was also made available, containing a pink guitar pick with the VH rings logo on it, a sticker, and eleven cards with pictures and lyrics that could be slotted together.

"Without You" was the best choice for the lead single, and while Cherone's lyrics making him sound like an overexuberant "Get out the vote" volunteer, there are also some really interesting elements throughout "Ballot or the Bullet." Hearing Eddie play slide is always a treat, and it contrasts to the heaviness of the track. The maturity and musical growth on "Josephina" is one of the few places on the record where leaving the upbeat and often joyous music of the past behind actually works. Eddie incorporates a very Jimmy Page–like acoustic rhythm guitar melody at one point, and Cherone delivers some of his best vocals on the record.

"Year to the Day" offered a stark reminder that no Van Halen composition should run longer than eight minutes. Or six, for that matter. It meanders aimlessly between light and heavy, with a languidly paced guitar solo that borders on feeling uninspired. By the time Cherone is shouting "365! 365!" at the conclusion, it feels like the song has gone on for that many days.

"Some of the stuff you look at, in retrospect, maybe the stuff we were writing after the tour was more suitable for the first record," the singer said. "Stuff like 'Once' and 'Josephina,' these things were out of the box for Van Halen. In retrospect, did we do things maybe a little outside the box that might've turned off Van Halen fans?"

The question was rhetorical, to say the least.

Then there's "How Many Say I." The album closer quickly became the most maligned composition Van Halen ever released. One could call the six-minutes-plus track "experimental," and maybe there is some artist out there who would find praise for doing it. But for this band, it was just too far out in left field. Sung by Eddie, whose gravelly vocals sound like a fusion of Tom Waits and Roger Waters, the plaintive piano piece was a shock. And lyrics about homeless people and starving children—the latter inspired by the types of commercials featuring Sally Struthers that would run on overnight television—were a far cry from the backyard party days and singing about dancing the night away.

"I will take full credit that it's my fault," Cherone admitted. "I said, 'Eddie, that's fucking great man, you should sing it! He's like, 'What?' I go, 'Sing it!' In retrospect, was that the right thing for me to do? Uh—no. I was inspired. It just sounded like [sings 'Nobody Home' by Pink Floyd]. I encouraged him. I always thought it was a good song. The presentation probably wasn't the right one. At that point we were very comfortable with each other. I suggested it, and he goes, 'Okay.' It moved me. I don't mind takin' a hit for it. It wasn't a Van Halen song."

Eddie went on in interviews about how he'd waited twenty years for Cherone, calling him his musical "soulmate" and long-lost brother. He knew before Van Halen III hit the shelves that it was going to be a tough pill to swallow, comparing it to Fair Warning and insisting it had to grow on people. But for all his talk about how Van Halen were finally a real band with Cherone in the fold, the album sure had the sense of being more of a solo venture for someone who had been told what to do and how to do it by lead singers and producers for the majority of his musical career.

Maybe it was about evolution, though. Eddie had been sober for a long stretch, and he was beginning to embrace spirituality and openly discuss his belief that a higher power was responsible for the musical ideas that came to him. Cherone has said over the years how proud he is that *III* is the only record on which the guitarist sings. He defended the album against those who claimed it was nothing more than an Eddie Van Halen solo effort with a different singer, and that it was, in fact, an expression of freedom.

"It was basically Eddie's baby," Cherone said. "The songs, if we nurtured them, I think there was a few gems on that record. It was rushed in a sense that we didn't write enough material for it. We really became a band after the tour. If I was to do it all over again, it woulda been great if I joined the band, went on tour and played some hits, maybe a new song or two—and then do a record. Then maybe, maybe there woulda been a better chance for an audience to embrace the third singer."

Some of the music on *Van Halen III* was archival or had been demoed elsewhere. "Josephina" was almost left off the album—it was a choice between that and "That's Why I Love You," which had the same music as the demo Mitch Malloy turned in as "It's the Right Time." A version of the LP went to Warner Bros. executives with "That's Why I Love You" included, and it subsequently leaked to the internet. Some of the music, according to Hagar, was derived from castoffs of his time in the group. He also noted that elements of long-whispered-about songs like "Numb to the Touch" and "The Wish" might have ended up on *III*, but he was more than happy to use them too.

"I ended up [using] my lyrics I had for ['The Wish'], I think it was on [his solo album] *Ten 13*," the singer said. "And there's another one called 'Come Closer,' and I used that same concept, lyrically, on *Chickenfoot III*, finally, because it was [one of] my favorite deals. But the Van Halen song was a whole different song, a whole different lyric, but I had the words, 'I want you to come closer,' that 'reaching out' kind of love song."

Chickenfoot's "Come Closer," which came out in 2011, shares some of its musical roots with *Van Halen III*'s "Once," a lengthy, atmospheric song the label came back to Eddie about, asking if he could retool and trim it for submission to adult contemporary radio. He replaced the electric guitars with acoustic and even brought in a female singer to do backing vocals, but nothing ever came of it.

REVISITING THE PAST

To mark the release of the record, the reconfigured Van Halen did a show at Billboard Live on March 12 in front of just a few hundred lucky fans. The Sunset Strip venue was on the site of the old Gazzarri's, which had been shuttered in 1993, shortly after its founder and namesake, Bill Gazzarri, passed away. It was a cool way to signify a new beginning by returning to the spot where it all started for the band. The big surprise to come out of the night was how far back they dug into the catalogue during an abridged live set.

Cherone was open to doing older material, especially Roth-era songs that would help get him into the good graces of skeptics and fans alike. "Dance the Night Away," "Romeo Delight," and "Mean Street" hadn't been played live since 1983, while "Feel Your Love Tonight" and "I'm the One" were dusted off for the first time since 1981 and 1978, respectively. Though he chose the set list, the singer did get turned down when he petitioned for "Jamie's Cryin'," "Hear About It Later," and "Hot for Teacher."

When word spread that all three periods of the group would be represented in the live setting, it did pique curiosity a bit about the upcoming concerts, but audiences in North America would have to wait. The tour for *Van Halen III* first went to New Zealand and Australia—a region the band had never played before. It was a way to expose them to a long-neglected base of fans while giving Gary a chance to gel with Eddie, Alex, and Michael in concert outside of the spotlight of the United States. Unfortunately for the singer, a deal had been struck with MTV that a gig in Sydney in April—just six shows into the trek—would be broadcast on the channel, and any growing pains would be played out for all to see.

The band hit a handful of traditionally strong markets back in the States—including Philadelphia, New York, Dallas, and Cleveland—before the run went back overseas, this time to Europe, for a mix of headlining and festival spots. The leg was cut short after a rehearsal in Hamburg, Germany, where a three-foot-by-three-foot piece of plaster fell from the ceiling and landed on Alex's arm, missing his head by inches. The drummer had already gone back to using a neck brace since the jaunt kicked off—his back and neck issues were bothering him again—but thankfully nothing was broken in the accident.

One of the unique aspects to the tour was the way the band engaged with longtime fans and media in a way they never had before. An intimate Q&A

and performance with Eddie and Gary took place at the Hard Rock Café in the singer's hometown of Boston. The group also went on *The Howard Stern Show* for the first time live on radio, an appearance that was later shown as a two-part episode on the E! channel. Curiously, they didn't give a musical performance, instead engaging in banter with the host.

Eddie's behavior was bizarre on *Stern*—he seemed to be unaware of the cameras or the program at hand, randomly coming in and out of the studio and wandering off to work on his guitar setup. Many suspected he was under the influence of something, but it was likely an increase of insecurity at being interviewed on a show that had castigated him for years while its host buddied up to both Roth and Hagar. There were uncomfortable moments, though Stern broke down the band's guard when asking humorous questions like, "What about the rumor that Gary signed his contract in disappearing ink?"

There was a lot of fan service on the tour. Members of the Van Halen Mailing List—an email-based communiqué that went out to devotees, who went back and forth over the latest goings on of the band—were welcomed to cattle-call meet-and-greets around the country. But, under the circumstances, the invites felt dirty, and in hindsight it was an obvious case of gladhanding to satisfy a very vocal and highly critical group of hardcore fans.

Despite Van Halen playing ball with all those who would determine whether the Cherone-led edition of the group worked out and going over the top to show appreciation to those who stuck with them through everything, bringing in a third lead singer was a failure. The record tanked, and while the tour to support it was a boon to the hyper-dedicated, it was a bust in most markets. There wasn't even a novelty factor to lead casual fans to check it out, and, for those who did, interest rapidly waned. And that's a shame, because Eddie was on fire, playing better than he had in years. Cherone said the guitarist was playing "like he had something to prove."

It is difficult to deny how good the *Van Halen III* shows were and how tight the band were by the end of the dates. Yet, for the most part, all people saw was Eddie's infatuation with Cherone as something akin to watching someone enter a new relationship with stars in their eyes, blind to everyone and everything else going on around them, not realizing it was doomed from the very start.

23

IT'S ABOUT TIME

The *Van Halen III* tour drew to a close in late 1998 with a series of shows in Japan. The idea was to head back into the studio early the next year. Often, after a short rest, a band can begin working on new music, keyed up on the positives of having played together for many months and feeling inspired. That might have been the case with Van Halen, but even with some promising demos coming out of 5150, the hill to climb was too steep, as any audience-curiosity factor with Gary Cherone fronting the group had dimmed significantly. Nobody was blown away by the union, and there wasn't deep interest in what might come next.

"For me, it's the fact that they didn't reconcile with Roth," Greg Renoff said. "It probably colored the Cherone thing, because eighteen months ago, I thought we had Van Halen back together . . . and now we got Gary? That's not really a shot at Gary, it's a whole different thing than you were expecting."

For Michael Anthony, the *Van Halen III* tour "was the most fun I've had, but unfortunately the chemistry wasn't there during the creative process and doing the albums. It was kind of a left turn, and by no means is Gary a slouch singer. I'm a big fan of Extreme, but for the second record, it was good musically, but the lyrics and the melody—there were certain things that he didn't see the way the rest of the band did."

On November 4, 1999, it was announced in a joint press release that Cherone had left the band. The singer said he was leaving to pursue "new musical ventures." Eddie called him a brother and said their personal and musical relationship would continue. Less publicized was the exit of Ray Danniels, who followed the frontman out the door to fully clean house and wash the bad taste of the misstep away. It was another episode in the ongoing soap opera of Van Halen, but for once there were no hurt feelings when a singer was shown the door.

Contextualizing the Cherone era isn't a difficult undertaking. Even he would agree that his time in the group was a footnote, and it's unfair to compare his tenure with Roth's or Hagar's. At the end of the day, he was a fan who grew up listening to Van Halen, and he took the opportunity to sing for them like anyone else would in that situation. He got to call up his friend Nuno Bettencourt and excitedly tell the guitarist he was choosing the set list for the '98 tour, and ask what they should play off *Fair Warning*, which was the favorite LP of the ex-Extreme bandmates. Performing with the group made him a better singer, and he never took it personally when fans criticized him. His first love was always Extreme, and that's where he'd eventually end up returning.

"When I got the call [to audition for Van Halen], I said, 'Yeah, I'm not gonna get this gig,'" Cherone said, looking back. "It really was all good. I mean, I got no complaints. I found myself in the band for three years, doing a record and doing a tour—then it ended."

Days after the split with Cherone was announced, Eddie finally went to get the hip surgery he had been putting off since the *Balance* tour in 1995. The guitarist was back to drinking, partially to combat the pain but mainly because he was an alcoholic, and using the hip excuse could only last so long. He emerged from the operation with a fresh titanium replacement and was finally feeling back to his old self physically. Sadly, that wouldn't last. Following a routine visit to the dentist in January 2000, Eddie visited a specialist at the UCLA Medical Center to have a biopsy done on his tongue. It was confirmed that he had cancer, and he had a small section of his tongue removed before going to Houston for additional treatments. That spring, the media picked up on the guitarist's visits to University of Texas MD Anderson Cancer Center; doctors denied he had the disease and said he was simply taking part in clinical trials to help find a cure.

Despite having been a smoker since he was a preteen, Eddie didn't think it was related to his diagnosis. Rather, he came up with the idea that his body was having a reaction to the new titanium hip, coupled with how, for years, he used to play with a metal pick that he would often store on his tongue in the studio—an area ripe with electromagnetic waves. The guitarist ended up going to a doctor in New York for an alternative treatment, one he'd later refer to as "not exactly legal in this country."

A SECRET REUNION

Trying to find another frontman would've been career suicide in the wake of Cherone's departure, though according to guitarist Zakk Wylde in his 2012 book *Bringing Metal to the Children: The Complete Berserker's Guide to World Tour Domination*, Eddie said they were seriously considering Chris Cornell. That never came to pass, and the ex-Soundgarden singer would link up with the core of Rage Against the Machine under the moniker Audioslave. Instead, around the time of Eddie's cancer diagnosis, Van Halen began working with David Lee Roth again, unbeknown to anyone outside their close-knit inner circle. If the reunion had a chance of coming to fruition, all parties involved wanted to avoid anything resembling the fiasco from 1996, so they chose to keep it completely under the radar . . . for the most part.

Never one to stay silent for too long, Roth wasn't shy about revealing he was back in Van Halen when he was out on the town in Los Angeles. *Rolling Stone* reported that the singer was running his mouth about his status at the microphone at the Hollywood strip club Crazy Girls. The same story said the group was preparing to tour under the banner "Van Halen with David Lee Roth."

"At that point, it was the only logical choice because, how many singers can a band like us have and still try to have a career without people thinking it's a joke?" said Anthony. "After Gary, to try to pull in another singer? That's way too much drama—our fans don't want that. At that point, I'd rather people remember us for how it was."

Dave had reason to be enthusiastic. Unlike the last time he worked with Eddie, Alex, and Michael in the studio, he was now in prime condition vocally. The singer had put out his most impressive collection of songs in over a decade on June 1998's independently released *DLR Band*. Buoyed by the jaw-dropping playing on half the tracks from his latest guitar discovery, John Lowery— rechristened "John 5" after he joined Marilyn Manson—it was a modern salvo of rock and roll that was nearly impossible to ignore, except that's exactly what critics, fans, and radio did.

Roth didn't tour the record, but he hit the road the next summer as an opener for the original Bad Company at amphitheaters and arenas in the States, then as headliner at scaled-down venues. Roth's sets were almost entirely made up of Van Halen songs, save for the solo hit "Yankee Rose" and a cover of "Tobacco Road."

The music the reconstituted Van Halen were working on was, according to anyone who has spoken about the sessions, some of the best they'd ever done. At the National Association of Music Merchants (NAMM) convention in early 2001, Michael Anthony said that a new album was on the horizon, and he expected to be touring come the fall. Eddie confirmed three songs had been completed. Then it dissolved, and, to date, nobody really knows why.

"Unfortunately, [Dave] had some big egos that came right back out of the closet, and it was realized why he had left in the first place," Anthony said. "The first time it's like, 'Let's try to do an album,' second time it's, 'Let's try to do a couple of songs,' third time it's, 'Let's see if we can get out there and tour and just get along and see if the chemistry is still there.' Each time, there were things that he did that just killed it. He's 24/7, believe me. When he's offstage, he's onstage. I guess that's okay if that's the way you are, but it's like, us three guys are your fellow bandmates, we're your brothers; you don't have to put on a show for us. Unfortunately, he's onstage all the time."

The bassist doubled down by saying they had enough for an entire album from the sessions, telling the Van Halen News Desk years later that the music had been demoed and was "shaping up to be really good." Posting an audio recording to his official website on April 19, 2001, Roth revealed that he had gone to 5150 Studios about a year prior and played with Van Halen a couple of times, then spent several months working on new music. The result was "some of the most amazing, phenomenal . . . the hands fell off the clock, ladies and gentlemen, and we wrote three astonishing tunes." The singer added he was "in the shape of my life" and "ready to go."

Exactly one week later, Eddie posted a note to the official Van Halen website revealing he was battling cancer, which effectively shut down any talk of a reunion. He apologized for waiting so long to address the rumors but said the fight with the disease "can be a very unique and private matter." Dave instantly relayed his shock and support in a statement, saying, "You can whip this, champ. See ya down the road."

A little over a year after that, in May 2002—during the period when Eddie and Valerie were separating and effectively ending their marriage—the guitarist declared himself cancer-free. At some point, he underwent a procedure where about one third of his tongue was removed, and he subsequently told Howard Stern he had beaten the disease without any chemotherapy.

Shortly after announcing he was battling cancer in April 2001, Eddie spoke to *Maximum Golf* and blamed the attorneys for screwing up a reunion of the classic Van Halen. Before they stuck their noses in, he said, "everything looked pretty positive about gettin' together. But before you know it, attorneys are involved. These cats had me so beat down and confused, it made the cancer seem like a tiny zit on my ass. Everything seemed to fall apart after these guys got involved. I mean, we used to do it on a handshake. At this point, I don't have a clue what's going on."

WE CAN WORK IT OUT

Realizing a tour with Van Halen wasn't going to happen with either one of them anytime soon, David Lee Roth and Sammy Hagar did the unthinkable and announced a co-headlining jaunt together in the summer of 2002, dubbed "Song for Song: The Undisputed Heavyweight Champs of Rock and Roll."

In April, at a press conference at Sky Bar in Los Angeles, the deep divide in personality between the two was made clear even in how the longtime rivals showed up for the event. Hagar's more subdued demeanor was reflected in his red pants and yellow Cabo Wabo–branded T-shirt; Roth was clad head-to-toe in black and in theatrical mode, as evidenced by his being joined by *Playboy* Playmates the Dahm triplets, as well as a little person dressed as Andy Warhol.

"This is gonna be one helluva summer," Roth told the assembled media. "Sam and I are like fraternity brothers that have been through the same shitty hazing. There's a rivalry between us, so the audience gets the absolute best out of both of us."

The initial schedule of twenty-one dates blossomed to twice that as audiences expressed interest in the spectacle of seeing a musical matchup and a wealth of hit songs by snapping up tickets. The set lists would be as different as their conflicting personalities, with Roth focusing primarily on Van Halen songs while Hagar split his show with time in the band and solo songs. He was joined by then-Van Halen bassist Michael Anthony on some dates, and they even brought Cherone onstage for a few songs when the tour hit Boston. A much-anticipated duet between Roth and Hagar never happened, though.

"Right at the start, he rejected my suggestion that we sing a few songs together and make it a friendly thing," Hagar says in his memoir. "He envisioned something more along the lines of *WWF Smackdown.*"

The pair traded barbs in the press, and, as the run went on, it got more bitter. Hagar was particularly venomous in one tirade relayed to Page Six in the *New York Post.* "His voice is not too good," he said of Roth. "You sit there and go, 'I just saw a guy who was half the singer and half the performer he used to be, who spray-paints his hair on before he goes onstage and still acts like he's in Van Halen in 1982!' . . . It's a joke to me, it's like Liberace or something."

Ultimately, the final two dates of the tour—in Buffalo and Syracuse—were canceled, a move that was initially attributed to Hagar falling ill. The scrapped dates came the day after the sole time that summer that the pair shared a stage. At the 2002 MTV Video Music Awards on August 29, Sammy and Dave finally united for a tense co-presentation of the award for Best Rock Video. The two engaged in some good-natured ribbing at first, but it quickly turned somewhat nasty, with Roth asking Hagar, "What is your favorite Linkin Park song, Sam?" and cackling when Hagar was forced to admit he didn't know any songs by the band.

THE RED RETURN

Early in 2004, it was confirmed that Van Halen were hitting the road. The dates were locked in, as were the venues. What wasn't reported with any level of certainty was who was singing. There was no press release, no fanfare whatsoever; finally, just an update was posted on the band's website with a new picture and the caption "Eddie, Alex, Mike & Sammy Hit the Road," followed by a list of dates that began in June. It was an incredibly bizarre way to announce the return of Hagar after eight years—even for this group.

One main reason for a lack of elaboration stemmed from the uncertainty around what the band would be promoting on the road. Hagar had spent some time hashing things out with Alex at the end of 2003, and the Red Rocker was all in for an album and tour, with the former to be recorded in a few months' time and released that summer.

Eddie was in no shape for that. The guitarist was far from sober, and he had taken to always carrying—and drinking straight from—$5 bottles of wine. In his book, Hagar writes of Eddie, "He looked like he hadn't bathed in a week. He certainly hadn't changed his clothes in at least that long."

They barely got three songs done, packaging them on a new greatest hits collection, *The Best of Both Worlds*. The two-disc set came out on July 20, 2004, debuting on the charts at No. 3 and dropping from there. The artwork was a riff on the color scheme of Eddie's guitar—red, white, and black—and the track listing haphazardly ping-ponged between the two main eras of the band. None of the Cherone songs were featured.

Lead single "It's About Time" dropped in June. It was a heavy but disjointed number that sounded like a commercial for the tour at best, with Hagar singing about making up for lost time and turning the clock back. The song didn't feature Michael Anthony, nor did the other new numbers, as Eddie decided he would play bass on them.

"Up for Breakfast," the second track to promote the compilation, has lyrics so bad, it honestly felt like Hagar was getting his revenge for 1996 and trolling the group. Never the strongest writer, especially when it came to writing about sex, the frontman was barely punching the clock by using cherries and bananas as metaphors for his genitals. To make it worse, the music wasn't that bad, with an opening that calls back to "Why Can't This Be Love" and a funky riff from Eddie.

The obligatory Hagar ballad "Learning to See" was the best of the trio of new songs, but for the first time with the singer, Van Halen were making forgettable music. It was a far cry from what they put together with Roth just a few years earlier—something their ex-frontman referenced a couple of years later, when discussing it on his radio show.

"The music is amazing," Roth said of material they recorded in 2000. "It sounds like it came off of the first album; red smokin' hot. This stuff will change your freakin' haircut. It's off the map. I think that's the reason Eddie didn't use it on the last failin' of Van Halen with Sammy Hagar. Not surprised. He couldn't have sung it."

END OF THE ROAD

"Disastrous" is the phrase most often used to describe the 2004 tour. Ticket sales were softer than expected in many markets, and reviews weren't always positive. Eddie looked like a mess most nights, and his playing was pretty bad on a lot of them as well. He spent an inordinate amount of time getting caught up in his guitar cable and untangling it. His solo segment, typically the set highpoint, was rough on many occasions; seeing him appearing bored with the whole thing, he delivered a piece that was experimental in nature and as such reactions wavered between "killing it" and "glad it's over."

At some shows, his son Wolfgang would join him, with the thirteen-year-old playing the "316" portion of the solo. It was a sweet moment when it occurred, and the look of unmitigated joy on Eddie's face was priceless.

It was easy to get a sense that the tour was about the money and not much else. Whereas on the outing with Cherone the band were all about making the diehards feel welcome, going out of their way to shake hands and invite fans backstage, this time it seemed as if the intent was to shake them down. Van Halen were offering a $375 "five-star package" that provided a single ticket in the first ten rows, viewing of soundcheck, a deli spread, and a gift bag with luxuries like a tour program and T-shirt. A $175 "four-star package" promised a ticket in the first twenty rows and "possible additional surprises." While they were not the first act to offer such extravagances, jumping on that bandwagon made the overt friendliness in 1998 seem that much more disingenuous to some.

The stage was set up in a "V" shape, with "Golden Ring" standing room on each side that fans could place a bid on via a Ticketmaster auction. A portion of those proceeds would benefit the 1736 Family Crisis Center, a nonprofit offering prevention and treatment services for women, children, and families in severe crisis. Hagar would jump into the section and party with fans; Eddie was content to walk the ring around them and then untangle his guitar cable.

Hagar and the guitarist weren't getting along at all—even before the tour began. Alex and Eddie were still holding onto a good degree of residual bitterness about what had happened with Cabo Wabo Cantina. Hagar had gotten into the tequila business after he left the band in 1996, and, thanks to that and the success of the bar and restaurant the Van Halens sold their shares in, he had experienced a massive financial windfall. The brothers long thought they'd been swindled—that Hagar had purposefully run the place into the ground so he could buy them out and then went about turning around the fortunes of the spot and making it one of the hottest destinations in Mexico.

"I know Sammy Hagar—he's not that smart," said Jon Taffer of *Bar Rescue*. "It didn't happen that way. They opened the place, it failed. They wanted out. Sammy bought them out. Then cruise ships started showing up; that's the side of the story I believe. And Sammy's not a bad guy—I'm not suggesting he is. Sammy Hagar did not wake up one morning and decide to fuck the Van Halen brothers."

Still, the grudge stood, and Hagar's success with Cabo Wabo Tequila rubbed salt in the wound. When the contracts were drawn up for the 2004 run, there were all sorts of clauses related to the brand. Hagar talks about what happened in his book, but to hear Taffer tell it is just as entertaining—if not more so—as he was working on a proposed franchise with the singer at the time.

"They move 140,000 cases [of tequila] a year in sales, and Sammy later sells it for, give or take, $80 million," Taffer said. "All this is going on while the band had broken up over—what I believe—Cabo Wabo. Sammy's got the tequila going, he's got the club going, he's making all this money, and he's perceived as the coolest guy in Van Halen, and the Van Halen brothers have none of this.

"Eight years later, the band gets back together with Sammy for a summer tour. At this time, I'm working with Sammy on a Cabo Wabo New Orleans. In the contract that Sammy signed to go on tour with Van Halen, it said specifically that he's not allowed to say Cabo Wabo, wear Cabo Wabo shirts, do anything with Cabo Wabo onstage whatsoever. He signs the contract.

"Next day, Sammy goes out and gets the biggest fucking Cabo Wabo tattoo on his arm he can possibly get. Every promo picture has Cabo Wabo in it. Halfway through a planned world tour, they were ready to frickin' kill each other, and they [didn't go overseas]."

Whether it was the lingering bad feelings of the past coming to the forefront again, or the state Eddie was in, there's no dispute that the tour didn't live up to expectations, even though fans were having a good time. They'd waited for one of the most popular versions of the band to come back, and while that did come to pass, no matter how strained things were, it was so much more tense behind the scenes than anyone knew.

"It was the Sam and Dave tour all over again, only it was Sam and Eddie," Hagar writes in his autobiography. "[Management] kept us apart as much as they could. We flew in different jets. We stayed at different hotels. We had our own limos. They had their bodyguards. Mike and I had ours. I stayed in my own dressing room on the other side of the hall. The only time I saw that guy was when we stepped out onstage."

Everything that had been bottled up came to a head on the final date of the trek in Tucson, Arizona, on November 19. Valerie was in attendance with her new boyfriend and her brother Pat, and for some unknown reason Eddie took a swing at the latter during the show as he was watching from the wings. News reports said the guitarist kept repeating, "That's it, it's over," during the show. He also smashed two of his Peavy Wolfgang instruments onstage—something he'd never done before—destroyed his dressing room, and looked out of sorts in general, which had become a running theme.

To Hagar, the conclusion in Tucson was disappointing on a few levels. He didn't like seeing his onetime close friend and bandmate in such a condition. It became a depressing inside joke between him and Michael Anthony that whenever Eddie came out onstage with his hair up in a samurai-style bun, the two would share a look and roll their eyes as it typically signaled trouble ahead. Frustratingly, this was also the first time Hagar felt truly comfortable in the role as frontman for the group and no longer worried about living up to any expectations or legacy that may have preceded him.

"That's when I stopped trying," he said. "I was 'Sammy Hagar in Van Halen' on that tour. And I thought it was great. If Eddie woulda been really clean and sober and stuff, it woulda been really great."

The singer disappeared immediately after the Tucson gig; Anthony stayed in town an extra day just so he didn't have to ride the same plane home to California with the guitarist. It was the last time either of them played in Van Halen.

24

BLOOD AND FIRE

Less than three weeks after the 2004 reunion tour ended, the music world was rocked by the death of guitarist "Dimebag" Darrell Abbott, who was gunned down by a crazed fan while performing at a small club in Columbus, Ohio, with his band Damageplan. The killing took place on December 8, the same day John Lennon was shot to death outside his New York City apartment by a mentally unstable fan in 1980.

Dimebag had come to prominence in the early '90s in the Texas groove-metal outfit Pantera, and he was recognized as a once-in-a-generation guitar player. Like his musical idol, Eddie—the man who made him want to pick up the instrument in the first place—he also had his brother on drums in the band. When Pantera broke up in the early 2000s, he and his sibling, Vinnie Paul, formed Damageplan and continued playing together. On the night of the murder, Dime's last words to Vinnie were "Van Halen."

"We were warming up on the side of the stage like we always did, and we were both really excited; we only had two shows left, and we were gonna be going home for Christmas and to begin work on the second record," Vinnie Paul recalled in a later interview. "Our code word to let it all hang out and have a good time was 'Van Halen,' man! And that's the last two words we ever said to each other. I said, 'Van Halen,' and he said, 'Van Halen,' and we high-fived each other and went on the deck to do our thing . . . and a minute-and-a-half later I'll never see him again."

Several weeks before he died, Dimebag got to meet Eddie for the first time when the guitarist invited the Abbott brothers to the Van Halen show in Lubbock, Texas. They formed an instant bond and planned to reconnect in the future, with Eddie promising to "stripe up" a guitar for him. Before the funeral, when Vinnie Paul and Dimebag's longtime girlfriend, Rita Haney, were trying to decide which guitar to put in the casket, Eddie called and asked if he could do anything.

"So, I asked him if he'd stripe up a guitar for Darrell," Haney told *Billboard*. "He said, 'One of the red, white, and black ones?' And I said, 'No—Darrell always said that the yellow and black was your toughest guitar!'"

Upon arriving at the funeral, Eddie shocked everyone by bringing the actual "Bumblebee" guitar pictured on the back cover and liner notes to *Van Halen II*, rusty strings and all. According to Haney, he said, "An original should have an original."

"I thought about ways to word this so many freakin' times, but every time it jacks me up a little bit," said Pantera singer Phil Anselmo. "It's like, if Dimebag only knew that when he was going to be laid to rest that his freakin' hero, Eddie Van Halen, was going to give him a guitar, put it in his freakin' coffin and lay him to rest with that thing. I think Dimebag would've said, 'Well, I have lived.' It's gotta be the ultimate honor, really. I think very highly of Eddie Van Halen for doing that. It's slightly morbid to think about, but the truth of it is, Dimebag would've been beside himself, in a good way."

At the public memorial, held at the Arlington Convention Center, Eddie was in bad shape. He'd been palling around with Ozzy Osbourne guitarist Zakk Wylde, and the two were drinking heavily together. The pair went up to the podium at the service and spoke, with Eddie playing a poor-quality voicemail Dimebag had left him after they met from his cell phone. Then he kept interrupting Wylde anytime a higher power was mentioned, saying, "There is no God or Jesus, only yes or no."

The blows kept coming for Eddie, and he slipped further and further into the abyss. His and Alex's mother, Eugenia, died in the summer of 2005 at the age of ninety. Later in the year, after a lengthy separation, Valerie filed for divorce. In early 2006, Eddie appeared on the red carpet at the 14th Annual Elton John AIDS Foundation Oscar Party with mad-scientist hair and his teeth stained black with some of them missing, drawing headlines and concerns about his well-being.

A TIME OF UNCERTAINTY

It didn't look like anything was going to be coming from Van Halen the band anytime soon, especially with Sammy Hagar out again, Gary Cherone a distant memory, and David Lee Roth readying for a career in radio. For a moment, they were linked with the television reality show *Rock Star*, which had found a new singer for INXS in its inaugural season. Once word leaked out about the group taking part, though, the immediate backlash led to them pulling out and issuing a denial.

The David Lee Roth Show debuted on stations in seven cities at the start of 2006 as a replacement for Howard Stern, who'd left for the greener pastures of satellite radio. Expectedly offbeat, Roth was never given a real chance to find his footing in the format, and the show was canceled in mid-April. While he was on the air, he didn't talk much about his former group with his revolving door of guests and co-hosts, but, when he did, it was often tinged with frustration. During one show, the topic of crystal meth use came up, and Roth alluded to the drug having played a role in his failure to reconvene properly with Van Halen, and a not-so-thinly-veiled insinuation that Eddie's recent behavior and look were a consequence of the drug.

"It ruined a big part of my musical career, and not because I was doing it," he said cryptically. "A lot of people think they're doing one thing that's glamorous and, next thing you know, all productivity ceases. Van Halen, as a rock band, inarguably in the last ten years we've been offered a million dollars per show? Add that up times three tours? Probably close to four hundred million dollars have gone into the toilet."

Fans hoping for new Van Halen music were dismayed when it was revealed in the summer of 2006 Eddie was contributing two instrumentals and videos to an adult film titled *Sacred Sin*. The guitarist referred to the director, Michael Ninn, as "like a Spielberg to me," and allowed parts of the movie to be filmed at his house.

At additional public appearances throughout the year, the guitarist seemed to give up on caring about how he was perceived, dressing in what only could be described as "bum chic." He took to wearing motorcycle boots held together with Gaffer tape at high-profile events, his unkempt toes sticking out of the ends. They were the same ones he was pictured wearing while sitting courtside at a Los Angeles Sparks game the previous summer with Carla Christofferson, a woman he was seeing then who later bought the team.

"To see Eddie, the downward spiral, that was tough, because I love Eddie, as a human being," Gary Cherone said. "He's a great guy. To see him struggle through that was tough."

Eddie called in to *The Howard Stern Show* in September 2006 and laid a lot out on the table in an off-the-cuff rant. He insulted Hagar and Michael Anthony, indicating that the latter was out as Van Halen's bass player, replaced by his now fifteen-year-old son, Wolfgang. "My son is in and Sobolewski [Anthony's birth name] can do whatever he wants," he said. Eddie wasn't happy that the two ex-members of the group were doing shows as "The Other Half," adding, "My brother is the other half of Van Halen."

WOLFGANG ASKS DAVE TO REJOIN VAN HALEN

At a certain point in mid-2006, Wolfgang began rehearsing Van Halen songs with the intention of joining the band that bore his surname. Some would point to the fact that it was his birthright to play in the group. Others would never understand it.

Back in the early '80s, Eddie was fond of saying on multiple occasions how he'd wished he and Alex had another brother and would ask his mother something along the lines of, "Where's our bass player?" Now, he was able to make it a reality, in a roundabout way, through his own bloodline.

"One thing led to another, and we all thought it was a big risk to take, but Wolf stepped up to the plate by being respectful of the parts that Mikey played," Alex told *Modern Drummer*. "He didn't trash them, and it was a very mature choice for him to play the parts as they were on the record, but with a little bit of movement. But the second thing I told him after 'Great job' was 'Stay the fuck off my drums!'"

In November, Janie Liszewski—Eddie's stuntwoman-turned-publicist girlfriend—officially confirmed that Wolfgang had joined the band. She said all three Van Halens were busy rehearsing for a summer 2007 tour, but there was no confirmation of who was going to be joining them on vocals.

According to Andrew Bennett, a filmmaker who had been hired by Eddie to document the goings on at 5150 Studios, Wolfgang one day offhandedly said at rehearsal, "Dad, you should call David Lee Roth and see if he wants to reunite, and we can go on tour." His father, busy working on his guitar, replied, "So, call him then."

Bennett would later get into a nasty legal fight with Eddie over nonpayment and the former's plan to release the footage he'd shot. He later self-published a photobook titled *Eruption in the Canyon: 212 Days and Nights with the Genius of Eddie Van Halen*. Its publication led to angry criticism by some hardcore fans who thought Bennett was trying to make money on a period roundly considered the lowest point in the guitarist's life. However, he was privy to numerous landmark moments in the history of the group, one of them being when Wolfgang phoned up David Lee Roth and asked him to rejoin Van Halen. The way Bennett tells it, the bass player wrote out his pitch, practiced it a few times, made the call . . . and got the singer's voicemail. He left the following message:

"Hi, Dave, this is Wolfgang Van Halen. I am the new bass player in Van Halen. We have been rehearsing lately, and we were wondering if you'd like to get the band back together and maybe go on tour. Call me, or you can call my dad."

Dave did return the call—to Eddie. The guitarist told him to call Wolfgang and hung up. A few days later, the singer showed up at 5150 and rehearsed with the band. It sounded good. Shortly thereafter, the tour fans had been waiting twenty-two years for would be served up, but not without the requisite round of drama.

A ROCKY ROAD TO REUNITING

It was announced in January 2007 that Van Halen—in their fourth year of eligibility—were going to be inducted into the Rock and Roll Hall of Fame. Eddie, Alex, Michael, Dave, and Sammy were all inducted, with Gary left out in the cold. The ceremony was set to take place in New York City in March, and no matter what misgivings people had about the Rock Hall itself, the standards it held—or didn't hold—in terms of what artists were inducted, this was the one everybody wanted to see.

"It's great recognition—it's not what I live for, but I'll tell you what, it's going to be very interesting when we do get in," Anthony said, before the inductees were revealed. "See who's going to show up for the performance; I bet Dave is the first one there, because of the press and the media and whatever, he'll be right on that. I would hope, personally, to see everyone just get along, even if it's just for that night. I would be willing to go along with [whatever] if it was legitimate and not something cheesy."

Hopes were high that for just one night, the band could be honored and perhaps perform a song or two, or simply be mature enough to remain cordial in the time leading up to the event. Instead, after looking so promising at the outset, it didn't take long for it all to devolve into the rock and roll circus that had dogged the band since Roth exited in 1985.

The reunion with Roth was reported in news outlets coast to coast at the tail end of January and was officially announced on February 2. Though the cities and dates would ostensibly come later, forty shows were planned for the summer.

"I am having a blast playing songs we wrote with Dave, and I can't wait to get on stage and get it on with and for the fans!" Eddie said in a statement. "I am very excited to get back to the core of what made Van Halen."

On February 16, two weeks after news of the tour broke, *Rolling Stone* ran the first picture with the retooled Van Halen. Dave looked smart in a striped blazer and jeans. Alex looked like he always did, stoic and in sunglasses. Eddie was smiling, also wearing sunglasses, a striped stocking hat and holding his iconic red, white, and black guitar. Wolfgang stood tall in a black button-down and jeans.

Four days later, the tour was "indefinitely postponed."

It had gone off the rails somehow during the photo shoot. Eddie was under the influence; Wolfgang came home furious and relayed to Valerie that he was going to tell his father he wasn't doing the tour. Alex had also made it clear he wouldn't be going on the road with his brother unless the guitarist was sober. Dave avoided getting involved, expressing to the *Los Angeles Times* a diplomatic, "Hope springs eternal."

Just days before the Rock and Roll Hall of Fame induction, it was revealed that Eddie had checked himself into rehab.

"I have always and will always feel a responsibility to give you my best," the guitarist said in a statement. "At the moment I do not feel that I can give you my best. That's why I have decided to enter a rehabilitation facility to work on myself, so that in the future I can deliver the 110% that I feel I owe you and want to give you."

The Hall of Fame ceremony scorecard, with four days until airtime, read like a hockey playoff stat sheet. Eddie was out. Alex was a healthy scratch—he wasn't going if his brother wasn't going to be there. Singers Dave and Sammy were confirmed, along with and former bassist Michael Anthony. Then, the producers of the event decided the three could accept their award and speak, but the supergroup Velvet Revolver—made up of ex-members of Guns N' Roses plus ex-Stone Temple Pilots singer Scott Weiland—would be taking their place onstage, performing a song from each era after inducting the group.

"I don't make speeches for a living; I sing and dance for my dinner," Roth told the *Los Angeles Times*, adding that the choice "rips my heart out" to skip the event. "It's just not an option for me to go and watch some other band—who are only performing because they have some new record coming out—do *our* music," he said. "I have nothing against Velvet Revolver—I'm not familiar with their music—but that was my three minutes and twenty-two seconds up there."

The Rock Hall spectacle at the Waldorf-Astoria was so typically Van Halen it wasn't even funny. Velvet Revolver gave an induction speech with cookie-cutter aplomb, and the two people who went up to accept the honor weren't even in the band anymore. Anthony shouted out to Eddie and wished him the best. Proving himself eternally classy, he also mentioned Cherone, saying he was a part of it, too. Hagar, wearing a beat-up *OU812* T-shirt under a blazer, delivered his speech, also paying homage to Eddie. Velvet Revolver then played "Ain't Talkin' 'Bout Love" and an unrecognizable snippet of "Runaround" in a heavily chastised performance.

"We were just sort of stuck in the middle of it," said drummer Matt Sorum. "We just tried to survive all of it, and we just went because we felt like, 'Well, they asked us!' When you hear a band try to cover Van Halen, you don't want to fuck it up—it's a bit sacrilege. You're only gonna be criticized, because you're never gonna get it perfect.

"It was a very weird kind of thing, because Scott Weiland didn't really know Van Halen—I don't think any of the other guys in my band . . . I mean, Slash was friends with Eddie, but it's not like he sat down and played Eddie Van Halen riffs. He was more playing Michael Schenker and Joe Perry, [as far as] the guys who set the tone for his style; all the classic blues guitar players were Slash's influences. And Duff McKagan came from punk rock, and I don't think he was ever really a Van Halen fan. I'd been watching the band since I was fourteen years old.

"It was just a weird time . . . David Lee Roth didn't want to come . . . it got so political behind the scenes. Eddie didn't come, and it was just Sammy and Michael, and we were like, 'Well, should we play one with Sammy?' By the time we got there, we were very underprepared, and [the performance] wasn't well received, from what I remember. [*laughs*] It wasn't a great version, and I can't blame that on anybody except for the fact that, like I just said, we weren't the right fit for covering a Van Halen song, I don't think."

"A WHOLE NEW BEGINNING"

Eddie's emergence into the national spotlight, post-rehab, was the personification of a man transformed. He was tanned, with blond highlights in his freshly cropped hair, his teeth were fixed up to a gleam, and the boots he was wearing had just the right amount of scuff. The effortless and impish smile had returned when he appeared on April 21 as an honorary race official for the Subway Fresh Fit 500, the eighth race of the 2007 NASCAR season, and to help debut a Fender Stratocaster guitar to go to the winner. He even took a few laps around the track with driver Kurt Busch, but he didn't bring him any luck, as Jeff Gordon won the contest.

Less than four months later, Eddie, Alex, Wolfgang, and David Lee Roth held a press conference at the Four Seasons in Los Angeles to announce the first twenty-five dates of the long-awaited reunion tour. The false starts over the years were forgotten, and it felt like a new day as the four members strode out to the platform stage to the strains of "Jump," all smiles and all wearing sunglasses.

"This is the press conference that you probably thought you would never see happen; certainly not while we were all young, skinny, and good-looking," began Roth, who took command from the outset. He joked about not being the newest guy in the band, referring to Wolfgang, and called it "part of the colorful Van Halen history."

The singer turned to Eddie and said, "I'd like to start off with this." He hugged the guitarist, who said into his microphone, "My new brother," then kissed Dave on the cheek. The media went crazy for it, and even Alex clapped happily.

"This is not a reunion; this is a new band," Roth enthused, as he delivered quotable after quotable at a rapid-fire pace. "This is a revision with hits you're so familiar with; it's as familiar as the roof of your own mouth. Usually, when a band comes back like us, it's rockers with walkers—and this is everything but. Meet us in the future, not the pasture.

"It feels completely natural, strangely enough, after this many summers," he added, in a rare moment of candor. "I myself am certainly more aware than ever of how valuable this band is to me and my history, how valuable [Van Halen] is to the neighborhood, to the communities that this music appeals to—and it's a lot of communities."

Roth said that this undertaking was not going to be like the Police, who had also reconvened that summer, but made it clear a tour was as far as it was going. "We really have reformed this team like a brother team that it never was before . . . and we think we got it right this time," he said, inviting—begging—the press to come judge the performances and judge them harshly. The group addressed everything thrown at them, from Anthony's absence—Roth called him "part of the band's history—there's a lot of great alumni who have been through this band"—to whether they'd play the *Best Of—Volume I* songs . . . which Eddie said they hadn't learned yet.

"Know this: we are a band, and we are going to continue," the guitarist said. "It's a whole new beginning."

Apparently, for someone in the Van Halen camp, a new beginning meant changing the past. Two days after the press conference, all traces of Michael Anthony were removed from the band's official website, with Wolfgang even Photoshopped into his place on the cover of their 1978 self-debut album. The cover of 1980's *Women and Children First*, which features a photo of the group, had been excised completely, replaced with text of the band's name and the album title.

Everything returned to its original artwork in short order, but it didn't sit well with fans, especially as there was no clarification for why it transpired to begin with, or even an acknowledgment that it happened. Did they really think three decades of history could be deleted with a few digital alterations?

Years later, Wolfgang addressed the move when he was asked about it on Twitter, saying, "Yeah, and that was some dumbass on the website that did that dumb Photoshop shit. Not a band decision. We were never cool with that. It was ridiculous. Which is why, when we found out about it, it was undone immediately."

Why there was no explanation given at the time was simple: Van Halen weren't talking. At all. Jovial and forthcoming as they were at the press conference, that was it. No interviews. No *Rolling Stone* cover story. No in-depth MTV or VH1 mini-documentary with behind-the-scenes footage. Aside from the occasional and unavoidable discussions between Eddie and guitar magazines, the only talking done would be by the music.

25

STAY FROSTY

Van Halen's first tour with David Lee Roth in twenty-three years kicked off in Charlotte, North Carolina, on September 27, 2007. An elongated stage shaped like an "S" saw the lower part, a ramp, reaching out into the audience and the upper part wrapping around the back of Alex's drumkit. The curtain dropped to reveal Dave at the top, furiously waving a red flag, indicating that while a white flag means surrender, this was the red hot opposite. He was dressed in a waist-length matador-style coat and black leather pants, while Eddie was shirtless in cargo capris and sneakers.

Crashing out of the gate with the Kinks classic "You Really Got Me," the band were out to aggressively reclaim the mighty status that had been misplaced over the past decade-plus. During the second song of the set, "I'm the One," they stopped on a dime and brought the house lights up. Roth took a bow and gave an individual thumbs up to each of his bandmates before saying, to rapturous applause, "Well it only took twenty years to get this fucking far, huh?"

The singer strutted from start to finish, a maniacal grin leading his every step. For the first few songs, he looked like he was literally going to leap out of his pants—that was the level of energy and elation he was carrying about being back in a live setting with Van Halen. The kicks weren't as high as they were two decades ago, but he might very well have been in the best shape of his life, looking lean, ripped, and tanned. His ever-present stage banter was in fine form, and the rest of the band followed suit musically, all at the top of their respective games.

There was genuine pleasure, swagger, and all those hits that blasted out of a Camaro Z28 in 1984 and now sounded just as fresh pumping out of a 2007 SUV. "Panama," "Hot for Teacher," and "Unchained" were the reliable crowd-pleasers, but deeper cuts like "Atomic Punk," "Little Dreamer," and "So This Is Love?" were given a fresh coat, too. The pace barely left time to take a breath; seeing guys in their fifties plugging away at pounding, fist-pumping anthems for two hours plus was a testament to training and devotion.

A driving force behind the band's energy was Wolfgang, who, for the most part, was a pleasant surprise to those missing Michael Anthony: he showed he was a more than formidable player in his own right and an adequate backing vocalist while still seeking out a definable stage presence. The former bassist had written a note on his website over the summer to fans attending the shows: "Wolfgang is a great kid, so don't judge him too harshly. I'm sure he'll do just fine!!"

It wasn't all seriousness—this was the premiere party band, after all, and Roth wasn't above absolute silliness. For the show closer, "Jump," he walked out on the winding ego ramp to retrieve a monstrous inflatable microphone, which he then climbed on like a horse and rode as confetti dropped from the ceiling. It was hard to imagine another person in the building being so happy. Taking back the reins of Van Halen was clearly the greatest thing that had ever happened in his career.

The dates rolled on, garnering positive reviews in near unanimity. Skeptics were won over, many of them going out of their way to praise Wolfgang. Roth became fond of saying, "In Van Halen, we're now three-quarters original," before pointing to himself, adding, "And one quarter inevitable. It's old school meets new school; sort of like watching *Dragnet* on your iPod."

Eddie hadn't played so well in years. Looking fit and trim, he brought familiar songs and solos to a new level. It was like the proverbial night and day since the last time Van Halen hit the road, with Hagar in 2004, when the guitarist sloppily wound his way through songs, making mistakes and reducing his solo to a disappointing near lowlight. His playing was fluid and looked effortless, and he flashed that patented smile at every turn.

But in early in 2008, as the tour continued, cracks began to reveal themselves in the armor that had seemed so solid. Eddie's playing was noticeably falling off in spots. Then, in late February, the postponement of gigs started—first a few shows and then twenty-five in total. Reports had the guitarist back in rehab or battling a mystery illness, but less than a month later, the shows picked up, strong as ever, and all the affected dates were made up.

The reunion tour was beyond successful, pulling in $93 million, which made it the highest-grossing run in the band's history.

PLOTTING AND PLANNING

Once the 2007–2008 tour ended, there wasn't much news on the Van Halen front—at least in terms of the band. Eddie and Janie Liszewski were married in late June 2009; Alex built up his sunglasses collection and became an ordained minister; Wolfgang went back to finish high school; Dave kept a low profile.

Meanwhile, Sammy Hagar started the supergroup Chickenfoot with Michael Anthony, drummer Chad Smith, and guitarist Joe Satriani. The singer also released his memoir, *Red: My Uncensored Life in Rock*, which dished all sorts of dirt on his time in the band—much of it filled with frustration at how things ended, surprising many who thought it effectively burned all bridges with Eddie.

"There were a lot of times where I said, 'I really shouldn't say this,'" the singer said. "But I felt that my fans, who've been with me all this time, deserved the real story; they need to hear why and understand why I am who I am and why I've become what I've become and how I did it and what I went through for it. I just figured at this stage of my life I'm just gonna tell the whole story. A lot of it had to do with Van Halen; there was always a controversy of who said what and 'He did this and he did that,' and I wanted to tell the truth about all that."

It was obvious that, even with Roth back in the fold, Van Halen weren't going to be back on the "album a year" cycle. It was more about enjoying life, taking their time, and avoiding any potential conflicts. But to outsiders and fans, the pace felt glacial.

The rumor mill was activated as 2010 went on, placing the band in the studio and possibly mining through old demos for inspiration. The picture became clearer toward the end of the year, with confirmation the group would be entering the studio in January 2011 with producer John Shanks, who had previously worked with the likes of Bon Jovi, Stevie Nicks, and Melissa Etheridge.

A new album appeared imminent, and five dates were confirmed for Australia, marking the first time the band with Roth would play the region. Neither happened in 2011. A release date for the record was never officially set for the calendar year, while the series of shows Down Under were out of the band's control, with the organizers of the multi-city Soundwave Revolution festival ultimately pulling the plug on the whole event.

Not known or made public at all at the time was the news that Eddie faced two more serious medical issues. Cancerous cells were found in his throat and removed; then more were found in his tongue, leading to him having another piece of it removed. The treatments were a success, allowing for the Van Halen machine to move forward.

The day after Christmas, everything heated up with the release of a black-and-white commercial featuring performance footage of the band on the Roxy Theatre stage while a ticker revealed a 2012 Van Halen tour was happening, with dates on sale January 10. The group had been rehearsing at the Sunset Strip club a few times a week for months in preparation of the run. A graphic with the VH logo and a train on it started making the rounds, alongside the numbers 2.7.12—the date a new record would drop. The first single, "Tattoo," was coming on January 10.

To build a buzz about the upcoming album and tour, select members of the media and friends of the band were invited to Café Wha? in the Greenwich Village neighborhood of New York City, where a once-in-a-lifetime show would take place on January 5. Times had changed from five years before, when the group could subsist on nostalgia and curiosity. With a new record to pimp, the stakes were raised considerably.

Dressed in tan Carhartt utility overalls, a neoprene hoodie, and a tweed newsboy cap, Roth followed the Van Halens in via the front door of the tiny club, down the steps, through the audience, and to the stage. They ripped through a vicious eleven-song set featuring the backyard classic-rock barbecue roll call of "Runnin' with the Devil," "Somebody Get Me a Doctor," and "Everybody Wants Some!!" Eddie, in a black V-neck, jeans, and New Balance sneakers, was his typical toothy-grinned self. Wolfgang brimmed with more confidence than he'd showed on the last tour, now comfortable in his place as the unlikely architect of the band's future.

The 220-capacity club pulsated when a new track premiered in "She's the Woman," a fast blues boogie retooled from the 1977 Warner Bros. demo that was never released officially but heavily bootlegged. Missing from this version was the original solo, which ended up in "Mean Street" from 1981's *Fair Warning*, so Eddie dropped a new, blistering fret barrage in its place.

Roth quipped about how the last time the band had played on a stage so low, they had to have the car home by midnight, before paying homage to his uncle Manny, the former owner of the club who was in attendance that night at ninety-two years old. That moment cut to the heart of the show, which the singer dubbed "one of the best ever"—agreement coming from the smile and never-ending nods of the sunglasses-clad Alex Van Halen, who reveled the most in DLR's tales from back in the day.

ADDING TO THE SIX-PACK

A Different Kind of Truth, the first full length studio effort with Roth in twenty-eight years, came out on February 7, 2012. Kept off the top spot on *Billboard* by Adele's *21*, the LP was a welcome addition to the revered "original six-pack" that made up the first era of the Van Halen catalogue. It was recorded largely at Henson Records Studios but mixed at 5150.

The cover artwork for the album, which was the group's sole release on Interscope Records, depicts a New York Central Hudson steam engine locomotive coming out of a circle of black and white, overlaid on a red background. It's the same train that appeared on the cover of the Commodores' 1975 record *Movin' On*, and it would later be used by former Styx frontman Dennis DeYoung for his 2020 solo work *26 East, Vol. 1*. The title, *A Different Kind of Truth*, and the traditional Van Halen logo from the second record are in the upper right-hand corner. Roth's handwritten lyrics and artwork are featured in the liner notes, which are best seen in a limited-edition double-LP package released on red vinyl.

Musically, it was the first comeback album in history by an iconic rock act that stood up against anything else on the shelves. There was a bit of a "meh" response to the first single, "Tattoo," which was a misfire in that it never should've been the initial track people heard and would have been better served as a deeper cut. Overall, though, Eddie put forth a scorching determination, and Roth was intent on doling out head-spinning linguistic gymnastics. The banshee scream may have been tempered by age, but the attitude wasn't.

Immediately, a faction of hardcore fans began to criticize the fact that so many of the songs were built on the foundation—or entire structure—of demos from the band's past. Critics latched onto this and used it as fodder for negative reviews, of which there were very few, turning it into evidence the group had nothing new left in the tank. Not only was the assessment lazy, it was also unfair. Contemporaries like Aerosmith and AC/DC had been doing the same thing for years, with the difference being that *their* demos had never made it out in bootleg form to the degree Van Halen's had.

In truth, seven of the thirteen songs on *A Different Kind of Truth* are known to have drawn heavily on previous material. Almost all of the lyrics were fresh, though, save for some of the choruses. "She's the Woman" had been part of the Gene Simmons demos in 1976, as had "Outta Space," "Big River," and "Beats Workin'," which were formerly known as "Let's Get Rockin'," "Big Trouble," and "Put Out the Lights," respectively. "Bullethead" was a song the band had played live in 1977. The single, "Tattoo," was based on "Down in Flames," a live track from 1978. "Blood and Fire" had previously taken the form of an instrumental Eddie did for Cameron Crowe's 1984 film *The Wild Life*, before being resurrected and demoed as a song Gary Cherone wrote lyrics to when working on the aborted follow-up to *Van Halen III*.

Some of the remaining six tracks weren't totally original either. "As Is" and "Honeybabysweetiedoll" use pieces of older material. And probably some of the others did too, though Roth noted that "Stay Frosty," a close blood relative of "Ice Cream Man," was all new.

The most obnoxious element was the way that, as the information snowballed, the narrative quickly shifted from "Van Halen looked to past demos for new material" to "Van Halen's new album is all re-recorded demos." While that's not the case, what if it were? Many fans were saying in the leadup to the release how much they hoped it would sound like classic Van Halen. What's more "classic Van Halen" that finding motivation in compositions from the exact same era that those untouchable first handful of albums came from?

"I love the record—they made a Van Halen record," said Cherone. "For me, as a Van Halen fan, I think it's the best thing since *Fair Warning*. It's for Van Halen fans. It's not for radio, it's not for what the single is, because that's all bullshit. This is the record everyone's been waiting for since *Fair Warning*. The king just took back his crown."

A DIFFERENT KIND OF TOUR

To support the new record, Van Halen embarked on a jaunt that launched in Louisville in February. The band had grown tighter since the reunion tour ended in 2008 and gotten more adventurous live, all thanks to Wolfgang's curation of the set list. New songs like "Tattoo," "She's the Woman," "China Town," and "The Trouble with Never" were played, while some deep, deep cuts were rotated in and out each night. "Women in Love," "Outta Love Again," "Girl Gone Bad," "Hear About It Later," "And the Cradle Will Rock . . .," "The Full Bug," "Bottoms Up," and "Hang 'Em High" equally astonished and thrilled longtime fans when they were pulled out.

Production-wise, everything was completely stripped-down. Gone was the rarely used "S" walkway. Roth didn't dress like a matador, and he didn't end the show by riding a giant inflatable microphone. He began the tour with a ridiculous-looking headset but ditched it a few dates in for the more familiar handheld microphone. He also incorporated a dance floor smack dab in the middle of the stage where he slid about and shimmied for much of the evenings, occasionally doing a jumping spin kick.

The rapport between the singer and Eddie seemed as strong as ever, with no hint of the animosity that had caused so much friction in the past. Dave donned what he called an "adventure hat" as Alex drummed out the jungle beat that begins "Everybody Wants Some!!," then ran over to Wolfgang to sing him the lyric about taking a mobile light and looking for a moonbeam, punctuating it with, "I wrote the words and I still don't know what that means!"

Not everybody was a fan. "He's gotten sillier," said Hagar of Roth. "This new stuff, I'm just watching some of the YouTube things, and I saw the video and I'm just goin', 'Geez . . . okay, I dunno.'

"I guess whenever you're young and you are one thing, in your twenties, it's the hottest time of your career. You're physically strong, you got it all together, you want it bad, and you become something that works, and it helps you get to where you want to be—and that's all good. But when you're fifty, sixty years old and you still try to be that person, it's impossible. So, you gotta find a new schtick. Roth's kinda found a new schtick, but, unfortunately, he dove in farther—in my opinion—to the stuff I didn't like about him to begin with. The idea, I think, of getting older in this business is you have to stop pretending and expose yourself to who you really are and what you believe in and completely expose what you are in your heart and soul. To still have a schtick and an act when you're sixty years old can start looking really goofy [*laughs*], and that's silly."

"They're a nostalgia band," former manager Noel Monk said. "I saw a little bit of what they did, and it was pathetic. Don't get up there and embarrass yourself. Leave the fans, the ones that saw the '78 to '85 shows, with an image of a brilliant band—which they were. Don't embarrass yourself and get up there and be a shadow of what you were. The fans will say, 'Oh, it was really great!' Well, lemme see the show in '82 . . . or the '84 show. Then you'll see a show."

Hagar and Monk's takes notwithstanding, the audience ate it up—so much so that another two North American legs were added in the summer, as well as fall shows in Japan. Shortly after the dates were announced, though, all of them were postponed and subsequently canceled. A report came out indicating that the band weren't getting along, which led to Roth putting out a video titled "Public Relations" to dispel any such nonsense, claiming it was a scheduling conflict and that the concerts would be made up.

Any plans to reschedule the shows were dashed when, in August 2012, Eddie required emergency surgery after a severe bout of diverticulitis, a digestive disease in which pouches in the inside lining of the intestine, usually in the colon, become inflamed or infected. He popped some stitches after the surgery and spent three weeks in the hospital. The estimated recovery time at home afterward was three to six months.

The shows in North America were a wash, but in the spring of 2013, Van Halen finally made it to Australia, where they headlined the Stone Music Festival, followed by four shows in Japan. They circled back to the States for two appearances in July, at the Rock USA Festival in Wisconsin and as part of the week-and-a-half-long California Mid-State Fair in Paso Robles.

JAPANESE INFLUENCE

When the 2012 tour went down the drain, David Lee Roth moved to Japan. He was not vacationing; he had relocated to the country. While he was there, he further immersed himself in *kenjutsu*—Japanese swordsmanship—along with learning *sumi-e*, a kind of black ink painting, and the local language.

Roth also began the arduous process of getting what he called a "Japanese Tuxedo"—a traditional Japanese tattoo that covered his entire back, upper arms, and chest, with a band of virgin skin running down the middle. He said it took three hundred hours over two-and-a-half years, rounding the cost to around $300 an hour.

The Far East influence extended to Van Halen, who released their first official concert recording featuring Roth, *Tokyo Dome Live in Concert*, on March 31, 2015. The two-album set peaked at No. 20 on the *Billboard* 200 the week it came out. The cover of the LP features French artist Cassandre's famed 1935 painting of the SS *Normandie*, with added text indicating that it's a Van Halen live album.

The recording was taken from the band's *Different Kind of Truth* tour show at the Tokyo Dome on June 21, 2013, and listeners were struck at the warts-and-all representation—notably with the vocals. Unlike the last Van Halen concert release, 1993's heavily overdubbed *Live: Right Here, Right Now*, *Tokyo Dome Live in Concert* was largely untouched. Eddie told *Guitar World* it was "completely live" and that they had let Dave pick which show to put out.

"There are mistakes," the guitarist said. "After it was mixed, I listened to a few parts and went, 'Okay, I fucked that up.' [*laughs*] But that's how it sounded that night, so we just left it. It's like a photograph of that evening, and we didn't Photoshop it. We did nothing. When you fix parts or mistakes, it's not a real live experience anymore."

Releasing a live album wasn't the original idea. Roth had hinted at a secret project the band were working on in the spring of 2014, likely referring to one of two endeavors that fell through at 5150 Studios. One of them involved the Warner Bros. 1977 demos and the other a live album from the early days.

"What I originally wanted to do was remix the original twenty-five song demos," Eddie told the *Washington Times*. "That would have been really cool. But the tapes are lost. They are gone. So that was out the window. Then we started digging through bootlegs from the club days. We tried our best to make those sound good, but ultimately it wasn't good enough to put out. The quality of the recording was so bad that we tried to enhance them and make them better. Once we made them better, you lost that fly-on-the-wall aspect of it. It just didn't jive. So, we decided, 'How about a live record?'"

To coincide with the release date of the album, the band booked their first ever live appearance with Roth at the helm on U.S. television, on the late-night program *Jimmy Kimmel Live!* And, like so many momentous opportunities over the years with Van Halen, it would turn into a disaster of comical proportions.

Hollywood Boulevard was shut down for the performance on March 30, which would be broadcast over two nights. A full stage was erected in the middle of the street. An eight-song set—including Eddie's solo—was planned in front of some six thousand people. While spinning his microphone stand at a breakneck pace as the opening chords to "Panama" rang out, Dave slipped in his usual precision, cracking himself across the nose and drawing blood instantly. He waited until the song's breakdown to seek assistance.

Eddie, Alex, and Wolfgang continued to jam for the crowd while medics tended to the singer. He reappeared, already looking zany with a Canadian tuxedo—a denim jacket and pants—over his Japanese one, and now with the kind of Band-Aid found in the average viewer's medicine cabinet stuck across the bridge of his nose. Wolfgang and Eddie could barely contain their laughter at the sheer absurdity of the moment.

A tour to promote *Tokyo Dome Live in Concert*—shorter in length than the previous two—kicked off over the 2015 Fourth of July weekend and ran through October. A few weeks before it, *Billboard* published an interview with Eddie in which he made some unflattering comments about Roth, Cherone, and Anthony. Hagar was so incensed by the guitarist saying he had to show the group's ex-bassist how to play his parts and diminishing his backing vocals that he recorded a reaction video and posted it on YouTube. "Michael Anthony is a bad motherfucker," the singer said. "Fuck you Eddie Van Halen for saying that about Mikey. You're a liar."

The ensuing firestorm did little to dampen enthusiasm for the tour. Eddie was now being likened to Obi-Wan Kenobi, his short gray hair and goatee giving him a passing resemblance to the *Star Wars* character. He certainly commanded the guitar like a wise Jedi master, and fans and critics praised his playing on the trek as some of the best in his career.

As on the previous tour, the band thrilled fans by going deeper than ever into the catalogue for some bold choices, courtesy of Wolfgang's delightful prodding. In addition to digging up "In a Simple Rhyme" for the first time since the club days, they busted out "Dirty Movies" and "Drop Dead Legs" from *Fair Warning* and *1984*, respectively, for the first time *ever*. And the *Van Halen II* deep cut "Light Up the Sky," which they had not played live since 1980, audaciously began each show.

Eight years into the reunion with Roth, with a creative spark courtesy of Wolfgang's involvement, there was obviously more left in the tank for Van Halen. They weren't afraid to take risks, and they let their honesty hang out in print, on record, and in concert, having finally reached the point where all the feuding and fighting of years past felt like inconsequential drops of rain pinging off the steel roofing covering the amphitheaters where they were playing to full houses. They were the band for the summertime, and in the end that was all that mattered.

At the final date of the tour, about halfway through the second of two nights at the Hollywood Bowl, there was a musical breakdown during "Dance the Night Away," allowing Roth to riff on whatever came to mind. He made a joke about the quarrel between Jon Bon Jovi and his estranged guitarist, Richie Sambora, the relationship comparisons obvious to his own situation, and said the difference in Van Halen was they decided to apologize every couple of years and come share the good news. Then he got serious and made his way over to Eddie.

"I said it earlier—just so you know that I mean it, Ed—the high points of my life have been onstage working with you . . . you too, Al," the singer said, turning back to the drummer. He whispered something briefly in Eddie's ear, and the guitarist kissed him on the side of the head and pulled him in for a half-hug and hair-ruffle.

Roth then pointed to Wolfgang and proclaimed, "Welcome to the family, homeboy!"

EPILOGUE
THE AFTERSHOCK

The roaring horns signaling the launch of Van Halen on "Runnin' with the Devil" all those years before fell silent on October 6, 2020. Wolfgang broke the heartbreaking news via a statement on social media.

"I can't believe I'm having to write this, but my father, Edward Lodewijk Van Halen, has lost his long and arduous battle with cancer this morning. He was the best father I could ever ask for. Every moment I've shared with him on and off stage was a gift. My heart is broken and I don't think I'll ever fully recover from this loss. I love you so much, Pop."

Tributes poured in from around the world. Fans, friends, musicians, and everyone in between expressed their sadness, stories, and feelings of emptiness at the guitarist's passing. All current and former bandmembers paid homage.

David Lee Roth posted pictures to his social media of himself and Eddie from their recent tours with the caption, "What a long great trip it's been." Likewise, Michael Anthony shared pictures of the two from the '80s on Instagram and wrote, "No words . . . heartbroken, my love to the family."

"Heartbroken and speechless," said Sammy Hagar, who posted a shot of the pair from 2004. "My love to the family." Gary Cherone chimed in and said, "Whether you were blessed to have known him or not, he was a kind and gentle soul . . . his impact on ALL our lives was immeasurable! His music, eternal! My deepest sympathies to the Van Halen family . . . Love you Ed."

Perhaps none were as poignant as a simple message from the guitarist's brother, who sent the Van Halen News Desk a black-and-white picture of the two of them as children: Alex standing behind his younger sibling, who is sitting on a rocking horse, smiling, holding a drumstick in each hand. "Hey Ed. Love you. See you on the other side. Your brother, Al."

A month after Eddie's passing, Wolfgang released the first taste of his solo material: "Distance," a gorgeous and aching piece he'd written while his father was going through various health issues. The video for the track compiled home video footage that demonstrated the rich and deep bond the two shared, both musically and emotionally. It was also a powerful reminder of their love for one another, and an indication as to why a father would want to have his son play alongside him in Van Halen, any and all criticisms be damned.

The guitarist had been sick for some time, having been diagnosed with stage-four lung cancer in 2017 and given six weeks to live. He went to Germany for some sort of treatment that helped him beat back the disease, then got into a motorcycle accident, after which doctors found a brain tumor. Speaking to Howard Stern, Wolfgang said, "As time went on . . . shit just kept on stacking up and stacking up. It just . . . it never let up."

Fans were handed a bittersweet blow as Wolfgang addressed rumors of a classic Van Halen reunion that turned out to be even wilder than the speculation. Preparations had been made for what he and his father dubbed "the kitchen-sink tour," featuring not only the original lineup but participation from Hagar—who had secretly made up with Eddie in recent months—and Cherone.

As the months wore on, the void of Eddie's passing was fully realized. Despite suggestions from misguided fans who wanted to see either Wolfgang or another musician replace him, it was clear Van Halen could never continue without the guitarist—he was the heart and soul of the group. Thoughts then moved toward the musical imprint left by the band. What was the legacy of Van Halen, and where did they rank in the pantheon of United States hard rock bands?

"They have to be in the conversation of best American rock group ever," said *Van Halen Rising* author Greg Renoff. "I'm not willing to crown them as that because it would just sound ludicrous if the man who wrote about Van Halen would crown them the best."

"There's only one Van Halen, and they were really, really good," Tony Iommi said. "They were innovators at what they did."

"I think they're the greatest American rock band—period," said Stryper's

Michael Sweet. "By a landslide. They blow Aerosmith out of the water—there's literally no comparison. My top three would be: Van Halen, Van Halen, and Van Halen."

"They're at the top of the heap," added Alice in Chains singer William DuVall. "Especially when you talk about American bands. They're right at the top of the heap. Hard rock, guitar-based, nobody did it better than Edward. We're talking about the guy who redefined the approach to guitar, in our lifetime—he's the guy that did that. He was always in a state of joy. That's significant, I think. They also kind of carved their own lane in terms of being all about fun and joy—they're gonna always stand out in that regard. Even Roth, any dark lyric he wrote, it was always with a wink and a smile."

"Top five, definitely," said Nina Blackwood. "I would put Van Halen right up there. There are excellent musicians and then there are geniuses. Eddie was, indeed, a musical genius."

"I think they're top five, top three, top two . . . it's an explosive legacy," said Phil Anselmo. "It's cemented. They kicked every ass that was in front of them. They played all the gigs. They wrote all the badass records and kept innovating with all those frickin' records. The guy was a beast on his instrument, he always had that smile on his face, which is a pleasant thing, and what's there not to like about Eddie Van Halen? He didn't really talk the talk, but he sure as hell walked the walk. And he did it with that smile on his face. Everybody watched and enjoyed the whole ride."

"One of the greatest American rock bands that ever existed," said Ratt's Stephen Pearcy. "Ed's up there with the best of them, Hendrix . . . they'll go down in history as one of the premier American rock bands. And it can never happen again."

ACKNOWLEDGMENTS

The number of friends, family, and acquaintances who said this is the book I was destined to write was encouraging, but none of it would've happened without Edward and Alex Van Halen, Michael Anthony, David Lee Roth, Sammy Hagar, and Gary Cherone. And Wolfgang Van Halen deserves special recognition, as without him there would not have been such a triumphant exclamation point to the band's career, which saw his father at the happiest and most dialed-in live, jubilant to have the opportunity to share the stage with his son from 2007 through 2015.

There were a number of musicians, industry people, fellow writers, and those intimately familiar with the history of rock and roll who were interviewed over the past year and beyond to talk about Van Halen for this book, and for that, I am extremely grateful. Among them were Kristi Adair, Eric Alper, Philip H. Anselmo, Michael Anthony, Sebastian Bach, Jason Becker and the Becker Family, Nina Blackwood, Adam Carolla, Gary Cherone, Liz Ciavarella-Brenner, William DuVall, Bruce Gowers, Sammy Hagar, Tony Iommi, Sass Jordan, Liz Kennedy, Brian Mayes, Noel Monk, Stephen Pearcy, Greg Renoff, Matt Sorum, Michael Sweet, Jon Taffer, and Jane Wiedlin. Note that every quotation contained within the main text, unless otherwise noted, is from an interview conducted by the author.

At Backbeat Books, thanks to John Cerullo for helping to greenlight this project after he probably got very tired of my endless pestering about it. And to Tom Seabrook, who could run a clinic on how to be an outstanding editor. Also, thanks to Barbara Claire and Carol Flannery for their guidance, and to my agent, Robert Lecker.

Shout out to those editors I continue to work with on a regular basis. Michael O'Connor Marotta at *Vanyaland*, who has dubiously indulged my love of Van Halen as far back as the *Boston Phoenix* (R.I.P.), trusting me to give *A Different Kind of Truth* four stars. Thanks to *Ultimate Classic Rock*'s Matthew Wilkening, who continues to let me drill down into the depths of the band's history and do things like write seven hundred words about a Van Halen B-side that initially came out only in Japan. Also, thanks to Vince Carey and Donald Botch at MediaNews Group, notably for being patient when I was way behind on deadline because of being wrapped up in this book.

Additional gratitude to the photographers, artists, and their representatives who were so kind with licensing their work, including Ralph Hulett, Colleen Bracken, Ebet Roberts, Rick Gould, Eddie Malluk, Helen Stickler, Derek at Photofest, Rick Pinchera, Erin Kelly at Rentokil, and Charles Hannah at Norman Seeff Productions.

Van Halen has some of the most devoted—and opinionated—fans around, and I appreciate all those who were kind enough to be interviewed for this book to express their thoughts. They will tell you exactly why, when it comes to the different singers in the group, this can't be love. And thanks to the ones who tirelessly put their dedicated fandom of the band on display at the Van Halen News Desk, especially Jeff Hausman, who's been flying the flag since the days of *The Inside*; Brett Norton at VH Links; and all those who run the various forums, websites, and Facebook groups.

David Lee Roth might not be talkin' 'bout it, but much love to all the friends and family who really, truly understand this passion I have for Van Halen—and music in general—and are always there to patiently lend support and champion me along the way. Pat Higgins, if it weren't for you, I'd still have discovered VH, but showing me just how cool it was to be a fan will leave me forever indebted. Enough can't be said about the hours Jack Strong spent helping me flesh out topics and the intricacies of such a convoluted band history. Jeff Strong, we've spent more hours discussing this group than anything else, which is why myself, you, and your cousin will always be one of three, TFB. Phil Boucher, who successfully took DLR's "I say" and made it into his own catchphrase. R. Drass, who still thinks Dave sings "I have a new sweater" in "Ain't Talkin' 'Bout Love." Thanks to my parents, Cindy and Jack

Bowman, for all that you continue to do and the faith you've shown in me. Phoebe Goodwin for direction and understanding. Richard Michael Lucas, all those who let me go on endlessly about Van Halen but still remain close: Uncle Bones, John Barton, Michael Tabor, Sean Ciancarelli, Cowboy, Doug Sherman and Sligo Pub in Somerville, Dan Miller, Michael D. Wady, Ricky Newcomb, Monica Concepcion, Rosy Hosking, Robert Majovski, and the Icelandic Crüe: Richard Baxter, Simon Roche, and Jakob Bekker-Hansen.

Chip, this one's for you.

SELECTED BIBLIOGRAPHY

BOOKS

Bennett, Andrew. *Eruption in the Canyon: 212 Days & Nights with the Genius of Eddie Van Halen.* Andrew Bennett, 2020.

Benson, Joe. *Uncle Joe's Record Guide: Hard Rock Volume 1.* J Benson Unltd, 2015.

Chilvers, C. J. *The Van Halen Encyclopedia.* Oak Lawn: Malpractice Pub., 2001.

Christie, Ian. *Everybody Wants Some: The Van Halen Saga.* Hoboken: John Wiley & Sons, 2007.

Dodds, Kevin. *Edward Van Halen: A Definitive Biography.* Bloomington: iUniverse, 2011.

Hagar, Sammy, and Selvin, Joel. *Red: My Uncensored Life in Rock.* New York: HarperCollins, 2011.

Matthews, Gordon. *Everything You Want to Know About Van Halen.* New York: Ballantine Books, 1984.

Prato, Greg. *MTV Ruled the World: The Early Years of Music Video.* Greg Prato, 2011.

Renoff, Greg. *Van Halen Rising: How a Southern California Backyard Party Band Saved Heavy Metal.* Toronto: ECW Press, 2015.

Roth, David Lee. *Crazy from the Heat.* New York: Hyperion, 1997.

Marks, Craig, and Tannenbaum, Rob. *I Want My MTV: The Uncensored Story of the Music Video Revolution.* New York: Dutton, 2011.

Monk, Noel, and Layden, Joe. *Runnin' with the Devil: A Backstage Pass to the Wild Times, Loud Rock, and the Down and Dirty Truth Behind the Making of Van Halen.* New York: Dey St. Books, 2017.

Templeman, Ted, and Renoff, Greg. *Ted Templeman: A Platinum Producer's Life in Music.* Toronto: ECW Press, 2020.

MAGAZINES AND NEWSPAPERS

Appleford, Steve. "KISS's Gene Simmons Remembers a 21-Year-Old Eddie Van Halen: 'You Couldn't Believe Your Ears.'" *Los Angeles Times*, October 7, 2020.

Balinsky, Marc. "Friendly Competition Between Roth 'n' Hagar." CNN.com, August 2, 2002.

Beaujour, Tom and DiBenedetto, Greg. "Eddie Van Halen Regains His 'Balance.'" *Guitar World*, February 1995.

Boucher, Geoff. "Van Halen Road Plans Have Taken a Rocky Turn." *Los Angeles Times*, February 23, 2007.

Boucher, Geoff. "David Lee Roth Muted." *Los Angeles Times*, March 9, 2007.

Brodsky, Rachel. "Patty Smyth on Turning Down Van Halen, Getting Patti Smith's Mail, and Releasing Her First New Music In 28 Years." *Stereogum*, July 23, 2020.

Bryant, John. "Old-Fashioned Rock and Roll a Tough Act for Willie to Follow." *Austin American-Statesman*, July 2, 1978.

Cohen, Scott. "Heavy Metal Meltdown—Van Halen Takes on Black Sabbath." *Circus*, October 10, 1978.

Colothan, Scott. "Sammy Hagar:

'David Lee Roth Won't Acknowledge Van Halen Was More Successful with Me.'" *Planet Rock*, July 5, 2019.

Corgan, Billy. "Billy Corgan Interviews Eddie Van Halen." *Guitar World*, April 1996.

Crisafulli, Chris. "Ain't Talkin' 'Bout Love." *Los Angeles Times*, October 20, 1996.

Del Barrio, Ron and Meisler, Andy. "18 with . . . Eddie Van Halen." *Maximum Golf*, August 2001.

Elliott, Paul. "Van Halen: 'On 5150, Dave Lee Roth Was the Enemy of All Enemies.'" *Classic Rock*, January 29, 2014.

Epstein, Dan. "'Dimebag' Darrell's Longtime Partner Rita Haney: 'He'd Actually Be Surprised at How Many People He Touched.'" *Billboard*, December 8, 2014.

Everly, Dave. "Sammy Hagar Interview: Diamond Dave, the Van Halens, and a Long Life in Rock." *Classic Rock*, October 9, 2019.

Fricke, David. "Van Halen Without David Lee Roth: Can This Be Love?" *Rolling Stone*, July 3, 1986.

Garcia, Rene (prod.). *Van Halen Unleashed*, 1986. MTV.

Gett, Steve. "Van Halen Denies Doing Dirty Deeds." *Billboard*, July 19, 1986.

Giles, Jeff. "How Michael McDonald Ended Up Co-writing Van Halen's 'I'll Wait.'" *Ultimate Classic Rock*, March 2, 2014.

Ginsberg, Merle. "*Psychedelic Furs Sitting Pretty;* David Roth Stands Up for Himself," *Palm Beach Post*, March 7, 1986.

Gill, Chris. "Tony Iommi and Eddie Van Halen Discuss Their Careers, Friendship, and the Past Three Decades of Our Favorite Instrument." *Guitar World 30th Anniversary*, 2010.

Gill, Chris. "Eddie Van Halen Discusses 'Tokyo Dome Live in Concert,' Van Halen's First Official Live Record with David Lee Roth." *Guitar World*, April 23, 2015.

Greene, Andy. "Steve Perry Looks Back on Touring with Van Halen and the Eddie Collaboration That Might Have Been." *Rolling Stone*, October 19, 2020.

Harrington, Richard. "Rock's Misbehavin' Man." *Washington Post*, July 28, 1981.

Hiatt, Brian. "Did Van Halen Have a Fourth Singer? Mitch Malloy Tells His Story." *Rolling Stone*, February 10, 2019.

Kemp, Loring. "Elliot Gilbert on His Work with the Cars, Tom Waits, Van Halen, and the Motels." *Cover Our Tracks*, January 9, 2017.

Krenis, Karen. "Shhhh! David Lee Roth Is Not a Jerk." *Public Opinion*, August 8, 1991.

LeBlanc, Larry. "Danniels' Grace Under Pressure." *Billboard*, October 26, 1996.

McClure, Steve. "Van Halen's New Album Art Out of 'Balance' in Japan." *Billboard*, February 25, 1995.

Miller, Debby. "Van Halen's Split Personality: How a Geek and a Physique Created Thud Rock's Most Successful Oddsemble." *Rolling Stone*, June 21, 1984.

Milward, John. "*For Unlawful Carnal Knowledge*: Review." *Rolling Stone*, August 22, 1991.

Obrecht, Jas. "Playback: 'Diver Down' by Eddie Van Halen." *Guitar Player*, December 1982.

Pond, Steve. "Van Halen Feel the Burn." *Rolling Stone*, July 14, 1988.

Quan, Denise. "Eddie Van Halen Deconstructs His Collaboration on 'Beat It.'" CNN.com, November 30, 2012.

Rensin, David. "20 Questions: David Lee Roth." *Playboy*, August 1987.

Robinson, Lisa. "A Shocking Interview with David Lee Roth." *Rock Video Magazine*, July 1984.

Rosen, Steve. "The Life and Times of Van Halen." *Guitar World*, July 1985.

Rowland, Mark. "Slash 'N' Eddie." *Musician Magazine*, March 1995.

Scapelliti, Christopher. "Vinnie Paul Recalls His Last Words to Dimebag Darrell Before He Was Murdered." *Guitar World*, December 9, 2016.

Simmons, Sylvie. "Halen High Water: Sylvie Simmons Fathoms Out 'Diver Down with David Lee Roth.'" *Sounds*, June 26, 1982.

Smith, Giles. "The Man, the Band, and the Widdly Bits: He Drinks, He Smokes, He Does Bad Things in Hotel Rooms. And He Doesn't See What's So Funny About Spinal Tap. Giles Smith Meets Eddie Van Halen." *Independent*, April 14, 1993.

Stemkovsky, Ilya. "'Give Me Some Emotion!': The 2020 Interview." *Modern Drummer Legends*, 2020.

Uhelszki, Jaan. "Diamond Dave May Be Back in Van Halen." *Rolling Stone*, January 28, 2000.

Warlaw, Matt. "Mick Jones Recounts 'Crazy S--t' He Went Through with Van Halen.' *Ultimate Classic Rock*, May 26, 2013.

Wardlaw, Matt. "When Sammy Hagar First Met Eddie Van Halen." *Ultimate Classic Rock*, September 23, 2015.

Wild, David. "Eddie Van Halen: Balancing Act—The Rolling Stone Interview." *Rolling Stone*, April 6, 1995.

—— "177 Arrested at Coliseum Concert." *Cincinnati Enquirer*, April 25, 1980.

—— "Eddie Van Halen Goes Deep on the Playing and Tone Secrets Behind 10 Iconic Van Halen Tracks." *Guitar World*, December 1996.

—— "Interview: Rick Derringer (Solo, Johnny Winter, Edgar Winter, Ringo Starr)." *Hit Channel*, April 22, 2020.

—— "Interview with Michael Anthony, David Lee Roth, and Alex Van Halen." *Rockline*. February 20, 1984. Radio.

—— "No More Solos for Sammy." *New York Daily News*, February 23, 1994.

MOVIES AND PODCASTS

Dibildox, Eduardo Eguia (dir.). *The Van Halen Story: The Early Years.* 2003; North Hollywood, CA: Passport Video, 2003. DVD.

Maron, Marc. "Episode 1034: David Lee Roth." *WTF with Marc Maron*, July 8, 2019.

INDEX

A&M Records, 30

Abbott, "Dimebag" Darrell, 208–9

AC/DC, 79, 95, 135–6, 222

Accept, 95

Adele, 137

Aerosmith, 43, 52, 53, 73, 93, 157, 170, 190, 222, 230

Affe mit Schädel (artwork), 144

"A.F.U. (Naturally Wired)," 181

"Aftershock," 159

"Ain't Talkin' 'Bout Love," 39, 87, 129, 130, 134, 176, 184, 214

Alabama, 119

Algorri, Mark, 22–3

Alice Cooper, 16

Alice in Chains, 47, 134, 154

Alive! (album), 42

Alpine Haus, 16

ALS, 153, 175–6

Amazon rainforest, 81–2

American Prayer, An (album), 27

Amigo Studios, *see* Warner Bros. Recording Studios

"Amsterdam," 160, 161

"And the Cradle Will Rock . . .," 57

Anderson, "Big Ed," 81

"Angel Eyes," 22

Angel, 41–2

Angelus, Pete, 97, 98, 110, 126, 166

*Animal (F**k Like a Beast)* (album), 100

Anselmo, Philip H., 56, 73–4, 134–5, 209, 230

Anthony, Michael, 8, 10, 23–4, 40, 49, 50, 58, 70, 76, 80, 87, 88, 98, 104–5, 116, 124, 128, 142, 170, 191, 193, 198, 201, 203, 204, 207, 211, 213, 216, 218, 219, 226, 228

Apple, 82, 86

Armstrong, Louis, 73

"As Is," 222

"Atomic Punk," 39, 218

Atomic Punks, the, 184

Aucoin, Bill, 27, 28

Audioslave, 200

"Babe Don't Leave Me Alone," 28

"Baby I'm Easy," *see* "I'm Easy"

Bach, Sebastian, 188

Back in Black (album), 135

Back to the Future (film), 106

"Backdoor Shuffle, The," *see* "Can't Get This Stuff No More"

"Bad Motor Scooter," 113

Baker, Ginger, 16

Balance (album and tour), 139, 157–9, 160–1, 162, 170, 199

Ballard Jr., Clint, 49

Ballard, Glen, 169

"Ballet or the Bullet," 193

Barrett, Syd, 135

Bates, Tracey, 180–1

Beach Boys, the, 18, 106, 166

"Beat It," 84, 85, 106

Beatles, the, 15, 18, 113, 138, 139, 144, 176

"Beats Workin'," 222; *see also* "Put Out the Lights"

"Beautiful Girls," 49, 185

Beavis and Butt-Head (TV show), 159

Beck, 172

Becker, Jason, 153, 175–6

"Beer Drinkers & Hellraisers," 81

"Believe Me," 22

Bennett, Andrew, 211–12

Berle, Marshall, 30, 40, 41, 45

Berle, Milton, 30

Berry, Chuck, 19

Bertinelli, Valerie, 63–4, 65, 66, 70, 95, 106, 108, 110, 142, 149, 151, 180, 202, 207, 209, 213

"Best of Both Worlds," 123, 130

Best of Both Worlds, The
   (album), 204
Best Of—Volume I (album),
   170–1, 174–5, 177, 191, 216
Best, The (album), 192
Bettencourt, Nuno, 190, 199
"Between Us Two," 163
Beverly Hills 90210 (TV show),
   145
Bewitched (TV show), 171
Bhang, Dave, 40–1, 50
"Big Bad Bill (Is Sweet
   William Now)," 78
Big Bopper, 123
"Big Fat Money," 159–60
"Big River," 222; *see also* "Big
   Trouble" (Van Halen song)
"Big Trouble," 28, 77, 222
   (Van Halen song)
"Big Trouble" (Roth song), 125
Billboard charts, 48, 50, 57,
   70, 76, 79, 84, 93, 95, 97,
   108, 114, 122, 125, 137,
   139, 141, 142, 143, 145,
   146, 150, 158, 174, 190,
   192, 193, 221, 225
Billboard Live, 196
Bingenheimer, Rodney, 26, 29
Bissonette, Gregg, 124, 126,
   145
Bissonette, Matt, 145
"Black and Blue," 144, 146,
   181
Black Crowes, the, 8, 166
Black Oak Arkansas, 19
Black Sabbath, 16, 21, 30, 43,
   44–5, 113, 135, 190
Blackmore, Ritchie, 37
Blackwood, Nina, 97, 100,
   134, 230
Blair, Linda, 27
Blue Angels, the, 126

Blues Bustin' Mambo
   Slammers, the, 166, 167
Bon Jovi, 157, 161, 220
Bon Jovi, Jon, 101, 227
Bonham, John, 148
Boston (band), 53
"Bottoms Up," 49, 223
Bowie, David, 85, 88
Boyz, the, 26, 27
"Bring on the Girls," 31, 49;
   see also "Beautiful Girls"
*Bringing Metal to the Children:
   The Complete Berserker's
   Guide to World Tour
   Domination* (book), 200
Brown, James, 21, 167
Brown, Mick, 26
Bruce, Jack, 16
Bruce, Lenny, 18
Buckcherry, 8
Buell, Bebe, 26
"Bullethead," 222
"Bumblebee" guitar, 50, 209

Cabo Wabo Cantina and brand,
   148–9, 158, 202, 205–6
Cabo Wabo Rock Radio
   Festival, 155
"Cabo Wabo," 148
Cactus, 11
Café Wha?, 17–18, 220–1
Cal Jam II, 61
CaliFFornia World Music
   Festival, 52
"California Girls," 106, 107,
   166
California Mid-State Fair, 224
"Can't Get This Stuff No
   More," 170, 174–5
"Can't Stop Lovin' You," 159,
   161
Canned Heat, 37

Capitol Records, 113–14, 117
Carolla, Adam, 134
Cars, the, 35, 56
Carvey, Dana, 142
Casablanca Records, 41–2
Cash, Johnny, 119
"Cathedral," 77, 88
"Champagne Supernova," 171
"Chantilly Lace," 123
Chapman, Mark David, 65
Chartmasters, 139
Cheap Trick, 56
Cherokee Studios, 23
Cherone, Gary, 9, 133–4, 172,
   173–4, 175, 177, 187, 189,
   190–1, 192, 193, 194, 195,
   196, 197, 198–9, 200, 203,
   204, 205, 210, 211, 214,
   222, 223, 226, 228, 229
Chickenfoot III (album), 195
Chickenfoot, 195, 219
"China Town," 223
"Christine Sixteen," 33, 34
Christofferson, Carla, 210
Cinderella, 148
Circus (magazine), 107
Clapton, Eric, 16, 25, 148
Clash, the, 40, 55, 86–7
Clinton, Bill, 188
Cobain, Kurt, 156, 159
"Coconut Grove," 106
Collins, Phil, 135
"Come Closer," 195
Commodores, the, 221
Continental Club, the, 16
Corgan, Billy, 67
Cornell, Chris, 200
Coverdale, David, 135, 188
Crazy from the Heat (book), 19,
   57, 70, 81, 169, 179, 192
Crazy from the Heat (EP),
   106–7, 118, 126, 166, 181

Crazy from the Heat (film project), 109, 110, 124

Cream, 16

Criss, Peter, 135

"Crossing Over," 160, 161

Crowe, Cameron, 106, 222

Crystal Pepsi, *see* Pepsi

Cult, the, 25

Culture Club, 95

Cure, the, 55

"Daddy, Brother, Love, Little Boy (The Electric Drill Song)," 151

Damageplan, 208

"Dance the Night Away," 49, 71, 178, 196, 227

"Dancing in the Street," 75–6, 77, 181

Dandy, Jim, *see* Mangrum, Jeff

Danforth, John C., 99–100

Danniels, Ray, 158, 163–4, 168, 187, 188, 189, 190, 191, 199

Darwin Ape (artwork), 144

Dave Clark Five, the, 15

David Lee Roth Show, The (radio show), 210

Day of Rock 'n' Roll, 53

de Bont, Jan, 163

Deep Purple, 37, 135, 188

Def Leppard, 95, 100

Denver, John, 119

Depeche Mode, 9

Derringer, Rick, 37

Destroyer (album), 28, 138

Detroit Rock City (soundtrack album), 174

DeYoung, Dennis, 221

Different Kind of Truth, A (album), 28, 31, 137, 221–2

Dio, 95

Dio, Ronnie James, 46, 135

"Dirty Movies," 227

"Distance," 229

Diver Down (album), 77–9, 93, 105, 183

DLR Band (album), 175, 178, 200

"D.O.A.," 49

Dokken, 26, 146

"Don't Piss Me Off," 192

"Don't Tell Me (What Love Can Do)," 159

"Donut City," 106

Doobie Brothers, the, 30, 91

Doors, the, 27, 55

"Down in Flames," 222

"Dreams," 126, 130, 152

"Drop Dead Legs," 227

"Drop Down," 163

Duran Duran, 62

DuVall, William, 47, 71–3, 124, 134, 230

Dylan, Bob, 17, 27, 65

"Easy Street," 106

Eat 'Em and Smile (album and tour), 125–6, 127, 130, 131, 144, 165, 183, 184

Edgar Winter Group, 106, 113

Electric Lady Studios, 27, 29

Electro-Harmonix Mini-Synthesizer, 67

Elton John AIDS Foundation, 209

"Eruption," 11–12, 36–7, 38, 42

Eruption in the Canyon: 212 Days and Nights with the Genius of Eddie Van Halen (book), 212

Etheridge, Melissa, 220

Everett, Betty, 49

"Every Breath You Take," 159

"Everybody Wants Some!!," 57, 65, 93, 130, 167, 220, 223

Everything You Want to Know About . . . Van Halen (book), 104

Exile on Main St. (album), 148

Exorcist, The (film), 27

Extreme, 158, 173, 187, 190, 191, 198, 199

Fabulous Picasso Brothers, the, 110, 126, 166

Fair Warning (album), 66–9, 70, 73–4, 93, 194, 199, 221, 223, 227

Fairbairn, Bruce, 157, 158, 159

Farm Aid, 119, 129

Fast Times at Ridgemont High (film), 106, 185

"Feel Your Love Tonight," 191, 196

"Feels So Good," 146

Fields, Billy, 126

"Finish What Ya Started," 146

"Fire," 176

5150 (album and tour), 42, 122–4, 127, 128, 129–30, 136, 137, 140, 142, 143, 145, 149, 152, 177, 178, 180, 181, 182, 183

5150 Studios, 83, 90, 92, 116, 122, 148, 150, 152, 158, 159, 168–9, 174, 177, 178, 188, 201, 211–12, 221, 225

Fleetwood Mac, 43

Flex-Able (album), 124

Flick of the Switch (album), 135

"Fools," 57

Footlose (soundtrack album), 137

INDEX

For Unlawful Carnal Knowledge
(album and tour), 138,
149–52, 154–6, 157, 167
Ford, Lita, 26
*4th Annual New Year's Eve
Rock 'n' Roll Ball* (TV
special), 103, 107
Fox, Jackie, 26
Fox, Michael J., 106
"Frankenstrat" guitar, 50–1, 98
Freddie Mercury Tribute
Concert, 190
Frehley, Ace, 33, 135
"Full Bug, The," 223

Gabriel, Peter, 135
Gallagher, Liam, 171
Gazzarri, Bill, 22, 26, 196
Gazzarri's, 20, 22, 25–6, 196
Geffen Records, 114, 117, 141,
156, 157
Geffen, David, 117
Gene Simmons (album), 34
"Gene Simmons demos," 27–8,
49, 77, 222
Gene Simmons Vault (box set),
33, 34
Genesis (early Van Halen
brothers band), 16, 18
Genesis (UK band), 16, 37,
135
"Get Up," 181
Gilbert, Elliot, 40–1
Gilbert, Paul, 151
Gillan, Ian, 135
Gilmour, Dave, 135
Ginsberg, Allen, 18
"Give to Live," 142
Go-Go's, the, 118–19
Goats Head Soup (album), 27
Godfather, The (film), 154
"Goin' Crazy!," 126

"Good Enough," 116, 123,
181
Good Morning America (TV
show), 141
"Good Times Bad Times," 176
"Goodbye to You," 110
Goodman, Mark, 86
Gore, Tipper, 99, 100
"Got Love for Sale," 33, 34
Grand Funk Railroad, 21
Gretzky, Wayne, 99
Guns N' Roses, 25, 149, 154,
214

Hackett, Steve, 37
Hagar, Betsy, 146–7, 159
Hagar, Bobby, 113
Hagar, Gladys, 113
Hagar, Kari, 152, 159, 162
Hagar, Sammy, 32, 33, 45,
112–16, 117, 118, 119–20,
121–3, 127–8, 129–30,
131, 133–4, 136, 138,
139, 141–2, 144, 146–7,
149–50, 152, 153, 155, 156,
157, 158, 159, 160, 162–4,
166, 167, 168, 175, 177–8,
179–80, 181, 182–5, 191,
192, 202–4, 205–7, 210,
211, 212, 214, 219, 223–4,
226, 228, 229
"Hammer to Fall," 190
"Hands and Knees," 142
Haney, Rita, 209
"Hang 'Em High," 77, 223
"Happy Trails," 76, 77
"Hard to Handle," 167
Hartman, Phil, 99, 142
Harvey, Carlos, 87–8
Hawkins, Paula, 100
"Hear About It Later," 67, 70,
196, 223

Heart, 43, 53
"Heartbreak Hotel," 81
"Heartbreaker," 11
Heavy Metal (soundtrack
album), 178
Hendrix, Jimi, 17, 25, 30, 41,
56, 175, 230
Hendry, Susan, 70
Hide Your Sheep! tour, 79–80,
81
Highway to Hell (album), 135
Hinkle, Robert, 183
Hit Parader (magazine), 107
"Honeybabysweetiedoll," 222
"Hot for Teacher," 93, 98–100,
126, 175, 196, 218
House of Lords, 148
"House of Pain," 28, 77, 93
"How Many Say I," 194
Howard Stern Show, The (radio
show), 166, 173, 197, 211;
see also Stern, Howard
Hughes, Glenn, 135
"Humans Being," 163, 174,
181

"I Can't Drive 55," 112,
114–15, 119, 121, 129, 179,
181, 191
I Never Said Goodbye (album),
141–2
I Want My MTV (book), 86,
152
"I Want You (She's So
Heavy)," 176
"Ice Cream Man," 42, 130,
222
"I'll Fall in Love Again," 114
"I'll Wait," 91, 92, 123, 181
"I'm Easy," 125–6
"I'm So Glad," 87
"I'm the One," 31, 196, 217

"In a Simple Rhyme," 23, 57, 227
"In the Midnight Hour," 93
In Through the Out Door (album), 56
Ingram, Gene, 182
"Inside," 129
"Intruder," 76, 77
INXS, 210
Iommi, Tony, 21, 43, 46, 190, 229
"It's About Time," 204
"It's the Right Time," 189
"I've Got the Fire," 113

Jackson, LaToya, 102
Jackson, Michael, 83–4, 85, 95, 96, 136–7
Jackson, Victoria, 142
Jacksons, the, 95
Jagged Little Pill (album), 169
James Brown, 21, 167
"Jamie's Cryin'," 42, 196
Jefferis, Kurt, 101–2
Jimmy Eat World, 8
Jimmy Kimmel Live! (TV show), 226
John 5, 200–1
Johns, Andy, 148, 149–50, 151
Johnson, Brian, 135
Johnson, Danny, 37
Jones, Janet, 99
Jones, Mick (Clash guitarist), 86
Jones, Mick (Foreigner guitarist), 122
Jones, Quincy, 83, 85, 102
Joplin, Janis, 114
Jordan, Sass, 187–8
"Josephina," 193, 194, 195
Journey, 42, 111, 185
Joy Division, 55

Judas Priest, 85
"Jump," 7, 90–1, 92, 97, 98, 104, 123, 129–30, 167, 178, 181, 215, 218
"Just A Gigolo / I Ain't Got Nobody," 106, 107–8
"Just Like Paradise," 145, 167
Just Push Play (album), 93

Kasem, Casey, 180
Kaufman, Vaughn, 94
Kessel, Barney, 37
Kingdom Come, 146
Kinks, the, 30, 42, 75, 78, 129, 154, 217
KISS, 26, 27, 28, 33, 34, 42, 56, 58, 61, 62, 134–5, 138–9
"Know Your Rights," 86
Kurelek, William, 68–9

"L.A. Is My Lady," 102
La Mirada Country Club, 16
"Ladies' Nite in Buffalo?," 125
Landee, Donn, 32, 36, 66, 83, 90, 92, 122, 143, 149
Las Vegas residency by Roth, 166–7, 178
Late Night with David Letterman (TV show), 107, 141
Le Transperceneige (graphic novel), 10
Lean Into It (album), 151
"Learning to See," 204
Led Zeppelin, 11, 19, 56, 73, 148
Leffler, Ed, 148, 156, 157, 160, 165, 168, 175
Leiren, Rudy, 45, 51
Lennon, John, 55, 65, 208
Leo, Kid, 60
"Let Me Swim," 11

"Let's Get Rockin'," 28, 222; *see also* "Outta Space"
Levitt, Mark, 181–2
Liberace, 203
Life (magazine), 79–80
"Light Up the Sky," 51, 59–60, 227
Linkin Park, 203
Liszewski, Janie, 211, 219
Little Ain't Enough, A (album), 153–4
"Little Dreamer," 81, 218
Little Feat, 30
"Little Guitars," 77
Little Mountain Sound Studios, 158
"Little White Lie," 191
"Little Wing," 176
Live Aid, 180
Live Without a Net (album), 42, 130, 142
Live: Right Here, Right Now (album), 154–5, 168, 225
"Living in America," 167
Lloyd's of London, 65–6
Loder, Kurt, 172
Lost Weekend (film), 101
"Lost Weekend with Van Halen" (MTV contest), 101–2
Lou Brutus Experience, the, 176
Love Gun (album), 34
"Love Walks In," 123, 130
Lovin' Spoonful, the, 106
Lowery, John, *see* John 5
Lukather, Steve, 176
Lynch, George, 26

M&M's, 61–3, 66
Madonna, 139
Malloy, Mitch, 189, 195

Mammoth, 16, 19, 20–1, 24, 184
"Man in the Box," 154
Mancini, Ray "Boom Boom," 150
Mandel, Harvey, 37
Mangrum, Jeff, 19, 20
Manilow, Barry, 121
Marching to Mars (album), 191
Marilyn Manson, 200
Marriott, Steve, 135
Mars (company), 61–2
Martha and the Vandellas, 75
Martin, Dean, 102
Maturin, Todd, 184–5
May, Brian, 106
Maze, The (painting), 68–9
McDonald, Michael, 91–2
McGhee, Doc, 188
McKagan, Duff, 214
MCMLXXXIV (album), see 1984 (album)
"Me Wise Magic," 8, 170, 173, 174–5
"Mean Street," 31, 72, 196, 221
Mellencamp, John Cougar, 101, 119
Mercury Records, 30
Mercury, Freddie, 179, 192
Metallica, 136, 146
Miller, Dennis, 142, 171
"Mine All Mine," 144
Minimoog synthesizer, 77–8
Miranda, Mario, 22–3
Missing Persons, 102
Monk, Noel E., 41, 53, 58, 62, 65–6, 70, 77, 79, 82, 84, 85, 89, 104, 105, 109, 132, 133–4, 224
Monsters of Rock tours, 95, 136, 146–7

Montrose, 30, 32, 113, 115, 129, 150, 179
Montrose, Ronnie, 42, 113
Moore, Gary, 95
"More Than Words," 190, 191
Morissette, Alanis, 169
Morrison, Jim, 27, 55
Morrison, Van, 30
Mötley Crüe, 85, 95, 101, 115, 156
Movin' On (album), 221
Mr. Big, 151, 176
MTV (Music Television), 8, 42, 71, 75, 76, 84, 95, 96–8, 101–2, 126, 137, 141, 149, 181, 216
MTV Video Music Awards, 9, 118, 121, 152, 154, 170–2, 187, 189, 203
Müller, Lillian, 99
"My Name Is Bocephus," 142

Naha, Margo, 93–4
NASCAR, 215
National Association of Music Merchants (NAMM), 201
National Association of Record Manufacturers (NARM), 96–7
National Coalition on Television Violence, 99
National Museum of American History, 15, 38
Nealon, Kevin, 142
Neil, Vince, 156
Nelson, Willie, 119
Neon Christ, 72
Never Say Die! (album), 44
Newton, Helmut, 57–9
Newton, Wayne, 166
Nguyen, Viet and Duc, 160–1
Nicks, Stevie, 220

Nielsen SoundScan, 139, 150
1980 Invasion tour, 59–60, 71–3, 104
1984 (album and tour), 28, 91–4, 103, 105, 109, 122, 136–7, 146, 174, 181, 183, 227
Nineteen Eighty-Four (book), 93
Ninn, Michael, 210
Nirvana, 22, 154, 156, 159
No Problems tour, 81, 82
"Nobody's Home," 194
Nugent, Ted, 43
"Numb to the Touch," 195
Nursery Cryme (album), 16

Oakland Coliseum footage, 70–1, 75, 96
Oasis, 171
Obi-Wan Kenobi (Star Wars character), 226–7
Off the Wall (album), 83
"Oh Sherrie," 111
"Oh, Pretty Woman," see "Pretty Woman"
Olympic Games, 102
"On Fire," 28, 130
"Once," 194, 195
One Day at a Time (TV show), 63, 180
"One Foot Out the Door," 67
"One I Love, The," 159
Open Fire (album), 42
Orwell, George, 93
Osbourne, Ozzy, 43, 46, 85, 88, 95, 135, 209
Ostin, Mo, 30, 32, 152
Other Half, the, 211
OU812 (album and tour), 143–4, 145, 146–7, 150, 152, 214

"Outta Love Again," 134, 223
"Outta Space," 222, 223
Over the Edge (film), 56
Over the Top (film), 141

Page, Jimmy, 11, 25, 56, 189, 193
"Panama," 93, 97, 98, 104, 118, 129–30, 167, 189, 218, 226
Pantera, 56, 134, 208
Paper Money (album), 113
Paranoid (album), 21
Parents Music Resource Center (PRMC), 99
Parker, Ed, 18
Pasadena City College, 23
Pasadena High School, 18, 24
Pearcy, Stephen, 34–5, 37, 44, 108, 230
Pearl Jam, 154
Penn, Sean, 185
Pepsi, 136–7, 152–3, 161
Permanent Vacation (album), 157
Perrine, David, 179–80
Perry, Joe, 214
Perry, Steve, 111
Pickett, Wilson, 93
"Piece of My Heart," 114
Pink Floyd, 135, 194
"Pink Houses," 101
Planet Waves (album), 27
Poison, 115, 149
Police, the, 159, 216
Polydor, 41
Pornograffiti (album), 190
Post, Mike, 193
"Poundcake," 151, 154
Powerage (album), 135
Presley, Elvis, 81, 138
"Pretty Woman," 76, 96, 130

Prima, Louis, 106, 111
Private Life, 149
Private Parts (film), 168, 175
"Private Parts," 175
Pump (album), 157
"Push Comes to Shove," 67
"Put Out the Lights," 28, 222
Pyromania (album), 100

Queen, 139, 190
Quiet Riot, 85
Quinn, Martha, 97, 103

Racine (album), 187
Radecki, Thomas, 99
Ramo, Francisco, 144
Ramones, 56
"Rat Salad," 21
Rat Salade, 21
Rats (album), 187
Ratt, 35, 44
Ratt, Mickey, 34–5
Recording Industry Association of America (RIAA), 48, 137–9
Red Ball Jet, 19–20, 22
Red Hot Chili Peppers, 154
Red: My Uncensored Life in Rock (book), 114, 155, 219
Redding, Otis, 167
R.E.M., 159
Renoff, Greg, 35–6, 57, 117, 132, 197, 229
"Respect the Wind," 163
Rheinhold, Hugo, 144
Richards, Frank "Cannonball," 193
Rickles, Don, 167
"Right Now," 152, 153
Riverfront Coliseum, 59
Rochette, Marc, 10
"Rock and Roll," 119, 129

Rock and Roll Hall of Fame, 18, 212–14
Rock and Roll Over (album), 27, 28, 33
"Rock Candy," 113
Rock Star (TV show), 210
Rock USA Festival, 224
Rodin, Auguste, 144
Rodney on the ROQ (radio show), 29
"Rolling in the Deep," 137, 221
Rolling Stone (magazine), 108, 110, 128, 131, 151, 213, 216
Rolling Stones, the, 18, 27, 52, 74, 79, 113, 148
"Romeo Delight," 57, 87, 196
Roth Army (website), 184
Roth, David Lee, 7, 15, 16–21, 22, 24, 27, 31, 32, 36, 39–40, 43, 57–8, 59–60, 62, 65–6, 67, 72, 75, 79–80, 82, 86, 87, 88, 91, 92, 96, 97, 99, 100–1, 103, 104, 106–7, 108, 109–10, 112, 118–19, 121–2, 124–6, 127, 128, 130, 131–2, 134, 136, 138, 142–3, 145–6, 153–4, 164, 165–7, 168, 169–70, 171, 173–4, 175, 177–8, 180, 182, 183–4, 185, 189, 192, 198, 200–1, 202–4, 210, 211–2, 214, 215–16, 217, 218, 221, 222, 223, 225, 227, 228
Roth, Manny, 17–18, 221
Roth, Nathan, 16, 17, 18, 20, 40
Roth, Sybil, 16, 18
Rowuin, Albert, 183–4
Roy Rogers and Dale Evans Show, The (TV show), 76

Ruffin, David, 115
"Runnin' with the Devil,"
 10–11, 28, 29, 31, 171, 174,
 180, 228
Runnin' with the Devil (book),
 62
Rupert, Donna, 99

Sacred Sin (film), 210
Sambora, Richie, 227
Santana, 21, 111
Satriani, Joe, 219
Saturday Night Live (TV show),
 99, 142
Savage Garden, 62
Savoy Brown, 43
Scandal, 110
Schaffer, Matthew, 178–9
Schenker, Michael, 214
Scorpions, 85, 146
Scott, Bon, 135
Seduction of Gina, The (TV
 film), 106
Seeff, Norman, 54, 58
Senate Subcommittee on
 Children, Family, Drugs, and
 Alcoholism, 100
"Seventh Seal, The," 159
Sex Pistols, 55
Shanks, John, 220
"She's the Woman," 25, 28, 31,
 221, 222, 223
Sheehan, Billy, 104, 124, 125,
 145, 151, 165, 176
Shields, Brooke, 185
"Show Your Love," 31; *see also*
 "I'm the One"
"Shyboy," 125
Simmons, Gene, 26–8, 29,
 33–4, 36, 138
"Simple Rhyme," *see* "In a
 Simple Rhyme"

Sinatra, Frank, 102, 126
"Sinner's Swing," 67
Skid Row, 188
Skyscraper (album), 145, 185
Slash, 214
Slippery When Wet (album),
 157
Small Faces, the, 135
Smashing Pumpkins, 67
Smear, Pat, 156
Smeck, Roy, 37
Smith, Chad, 219
Smith, G. E., 142
Smyth, Patty, 110, 187
Snake, 23–4
"So This Is Love?," 70, 218
Sobolewski, Michael Anthony,
 see Anthony, Michael
"Somebody Get Me a Doctor,"
 28, 31, 49, 87, 220
"Somebody to Love," 190
Song for Song: The
 Undisputed Heavyweight
 Champs of Rock and Roll
 tour, 202–3
Sonrisa Salvaje (album), 125
Sorum, Matt, 25, 214
"Source of Infection," 181
"Spanish Fly," 49
Squier, Billy, 188
SRO Management, 158
SS Ryndam (boat), 14
Staley, Layne, 134
Stallone, Sylvester, 141
Standing Hampton (album), 114
Stanley, Paul, 26, 28
Star Fleet Project (EP), 106
Starwood, the, 26, 30, 32
"Stay Frosty," 222
Stern, Howard, 71, 168, 175,
 197, 210, 229
Stewart, Rod, 135

"Stompin' 8H," 142
Stone, Mark, 16, 22–3
Stone Music Festival, 53, 224
Street Talk (album), 111
Strummer, Joe, 86–7
Struthers, Sally, 194
Stryper, 46
"Summer Nights," 116, 123,
 130
"Summertime Blues," 81
"Sunday Afternoon in the
 Park," 67
Sunset Marquis, 33
Sunset Sound, 31, 35, 49, 55,
 66, 77, 90, 92
Supernatural (album), 111
Sweet, Michael, 46, 133, 189,
 229–30
Sweet, Robert, 46
Swingers (film), 167
synthesizers, use of, 67, 77,
 90–1, 123–4, 145, 165

Taffer, Jon, 134, 206
"Take Your Whiskey Home,"
 23, 25, 57
Talas, 104, 124
Tangier, 148
tapping (guitar technique), 11,
 36–8, 49, 84, 151
"Tattoo," 220, 221–2, 223
*Ted Templeman: A Producer's
 Life in Music* (book), 32
Templeman, Ted, 12, 30–2, 36,
 40, 41, 42, 49, 55, 67, 76, 77,
 83, 90–1, 92, 107, 113, 114,
 117, 118, 122, 149–50
Temptations, the, 115
Ten 13 (album), 195
Ten Years After, 19
Texxas World Music Festival,
 43, 52–3

"That's Life," 126

"That's Why I Love You," 195

"There's Only One Way to Rock," 114, 119, 129, 130

Thinker, The (artwork), 144

"Three Lock Box," 119

Three Lock Box (album), 114, 115

"316," 151, 205

Thriller (album), 94, 95, 136–7

"Thriller," 96, 97

Tidwell, Floyd, 88

Tiger Beat (magazine), 105

"Tight," 175

TNN (the Nashville Network), 119–20

"Tobacco Road," 201

Tokyo Dome Live in Concert (album), 225, 226

Ton Wijkamp Quintet, the, 14

Tonight Show with Jay Leno, The (TV show), 166

Top Gun (film), 126

Torpey, Pat, 176

Tour of the World, 94–5

Travis, Dennis, 16

Triumph, 85

Troggs, the, 120

"Trouble with Never, The," 223

Trunk, Eddie, 32

Tucker, Tanya, 119

"Tunnel of Love," 33, 34

Turner, Ike and Tina, 58

26 East, Vol. 1 (album), 221

Twister (film), 163

U2, 139, 154

UCLA Medical Center, 199

Unboxed (album), 157

"Unchained," 67, 70, 71, 93, 130, 167, 218

University of Texas MD Anderson Cancer Center, 199

Unuson Corp., 85

"Up for Breakfast," 204

US Festival, 82, 83, 85, 86–9, 90, 96, 106

Vai, Steve, 124, 125, 126, 145, 165

Valente, Rick, 123

van Beers, Eugénie, see van Halen, Eugenia

Van Halen, Alex, 7, 13–16, 18, 22, 23, 24, 28, 33, 40, 54, 58, 67, 69, 75, 76, 80, 93, 98, 104, 109, 128, 141, 146, 148, 155, 158, 162, 163, 169, 170, 172, 187, 196, 204, 211, 213, 215, 219, 228–9

Van Halen, Eddie, 7, 9, 11–12, 13–16, 21, 24, 25, 27, 28, 33, 36–8, 41–2, 43–4, 46, 48, 49, 50–1, 56, 63–4, 65, 66–7, 69, 70, 72, 73–4, 76, 77, 80, 83–4, 87, 90, 92, 95, 98, 102, 104, 106, 108, 109–11, 112, 115, 119–20, 121, 124, 127, 128, 131, 140–1, 142, 143, 146, 149, 151, 152, 156, 157–8, 160, 162, 163, 168–9, 170, 171–2, 173, 175, 176, 179, 180, 181, 183, 187, 189, 191, 192, 193, 194–5, 197, 198–9, 200, 201–2, 204, 205, 207, 209, 210–11, 212, 213–14, 215, 218–19, 220, 222, 224, 226, 227, 228–9, 230

van Halen, Eugenia, 13, 14, 15, 209

van Halen, Jan, 13–14, 16, 69, 78, 140, 143, 146

Van Halen, Wolfgang, 23, 151, 205, 211–12, 213, 215, 216, 218, 219, 220–1, 223, 226, 227, 228, 229

Van Halen (album), 10–11, 28, 36, 40–2, 48, 49

Van Halen II (album), 28, 49–1, 55, 57, 209, 222

Van Halen III (album and tour), 193–5, 196–7, 198

Van Halen Rising (book), 18, 30, 35, 36

Van Halen Unleashed (documentary), 33

Velvet Revolver, 214

Velvet Underground, the, 17

Victory Tour, 95

Video Hits—Volume I (home video), 174

Vigon, Jay, 94

Village Recorder Studios, 27, 33

Viva Van Halen Saturday (TV special), 149

VOA (album), 32, 114–15, 116, 150

"Voodoo Queen," 31; see also "Mean Street"

Vox AC30 (amp), 34–5

Waits, Tom, 194

Waldo (character), 99, 100

Walker, Dave, 43

Walmart, 62

Ward, Bill, 46

Warhol, Andy, 202

Warner Bros. demos, 31, 33, 49, 76, 77, 221, 225

Warner Bros. Recording Studios, 77

Warner Bros. Records, 30, 31–2, 33, 35, 40, 41–2, 53, 70, 75, 91, 92, 113, 117, 122, 126, 131, 145, 149, 155, 167, 168, 170, 195

Warrant, 149

"Warrior, The," 110

W.A.S.P., 100

Waters, Roger, 194

Weiland, Scott, 214

Western Exterminator Company, 94

Westlake Recording Studios, 84

"When It's Love," 145–6

"Where Have All The Good Times Gone!," 78

Whisky a Go Go, 30, 34–5, 155

White Lion, 149

White, Patrick J., 185–6

Whitesnake, 188

Who, the, 52, 59–60

"Why Can't This Be Love," 122, 123, 130, 146, 184, 204

Wiedlin, Jane, 119

Wild Life, The (film), 106, 222

"Wild Thing," 120

Williams Jr., Hank, 142

"Winner Takes It All," 141

Winnick, Tom, 101

Winter, Edgar, 167; *see also* Edgar Winter Group

"Wipe Out," 176

"Wish, The," 195

With the Beatles (album), 144

"Without You," 192, 193

Wolfgang guitars, 174, 207

"Woman in Love," 28

Women and Children First (album), 7, 23, 57–9, 63, 66, 205, 216

World Invasion tour, *see* 1980 Invasion tour

World Vacation tour, 51–3

Wozniak, Steve "Woz," 82, 85–6

Wylde, Zakk, 200, 209

Y&T, 95

"Yankee Rose," 125, 126, 168, 201

"Year to the Day," 193–4

"You Really Got Me," 30, 37, 40, 42, 46, 56, 75, 129, 130, 155, 217

"You're No Good," 49, 72

"Young and Wild," 78

Young, Neil, 119

Your Filthy Little Mouth (album), 166

"Your Love Is Driving Me Crazy," 114

Zampolli, Claudio, 112, 114, 142

Zappa, Frank, 58 124

"Zero," *see* "Gene Simmons demos"

ABOUT THE AUTHOR

Michael Christopher is a journalist and music historian. He is the author of *Depeche Mode FAQ: All That's Left to Know About the World's Finest Synth-Pop Band*. A senior writer for the online music magazine *Vanyaland*, where he was a founding member and later managing editor, he contributes regularly to *Ultimate Classic Rock*, *Loudwire*, and *LA Weekly*, and appears regularly on television, radio, and podcasts as an expert on a variety of music-related topics. He also has a syndicated music and lifestyle column for a series of newspapers in the Philadelphia metro region and beyond under the MediaNews Group banner. His work has appeared in the *Boston Phoenix*, *Boston Magazine*, *Rockpile*, *Ronda*, *Screen Rant*, and *Diffuser*. He lives in Boston, building a respectable vinyl collection.